पुरातत्त्व
PURĀTATTVA

Bulletin of the Indian Archaeological Society

No. 10 1978-79

Editor
K. N. Dikshit

D.K. Printworld (P) Ltd.
New Delhi

Cataloging in Publication Data — DK
[Courtesy : D.K. Agencies (P) Ltd. <docinfo@dkagencies.com>]

Purātattva : bulletin of the Indian Archaeological
Society, no. 10, 1978-79 / editor, K.N. Dikshit.
p. cm.
Includes bibliographical references.
ISBN 8124602867

1. Archaeology — India — Periodicals. 2. India
— Antiquities — Periodicals. 3. India — Civilization
— Periodicals. I. Dikshit, K.N. II. Indian
Archaeological Society.

First Published in 1981
First Reprinted in 2005
ISBN 81-246-0286-7
Price for volume 10 (1978-79): Rs. 800 US $ 40

Reprint authorised by
Indian Archaeological Society
New Delhi - 110 016

The Editors are not responsible for the opinions expressed by the Contributors.

Purātattva is published annually.

Manuscripts (whether in the form of articles or notes or book reviews) offered for publication should be sent to the Editor, Purātattva, Indian Archaeological Society, B-17, Qutab Institutional Area, New Delhi - 110 016.

Published and printed by:
D.K. Printworld (P) Ltd.
'Srikunj,' F-52, Bali Nagar
New Delhi – 110015
Phone : (011) 2545 3975, 2546 6019 Fax : (011) 2546 5926
E-mail : dkprintworld@vsnl.net
www. dkprintworld.com

PURATATTVA

NUMBER 10, 1978–79

CONTENTS

PURATATTVA

NUMBER 10 1978-79

Editorial

The Indian Archaeological Society is happy to publish the tenth issue of *Puratattva* with a grant from the Indian Council of Historical Research and its own limited financial resources. The first issue of this Journal was published in 1968 and thereafter efforts were made to publish it regularly fulfilling the needs of Indian archaeologists and other fellow workers. The present issue contains the latest data analysing different aspects of archaeology in India as well as of the neighbouring countries. However, it was not possible to publish all the material due to financial constraints, although an effort will be made to incorporate it in the future issues of this Bulletin.

Grateful thanks are due to all learned contributors who have supplied the unpublished material in the midst of their heavy preoccupations for inclusion in the present number. It would not have been possible to bring out this number without the various kinds of help and suggestions from Dr. S. P. Gupta and Dr. Dilip K. Chakrabarti, and young colleagues Sarvashri A. K. Sinha, Pramod Kumar Trivedi and S. Jamal Hasan of the Society. Thanks are also due to M/S Amrit Printing Works for their whole-hearted cooperation with us.

OBITUARY

SHRI AMALANANDA GHOSH

The Indian Archaeological Society mourns the untimely death on August 25th, 1981 of Shri Amalananda Ghosh (born 10th March, 1910) an archaeologist of international repute, who was the Director General of the Archaeological Survey of India from 1953 to 1968, the longest period after Sir John Marshall. Shri Ghosh was associated with various international societies both in India and abroad, particularly the Royal Society of Antiquaries, London of which he was an Honorary Fellow. He was the Vice-President of the Royal India, Pakistan and Ceylon Societies, London; a Fellow of the Royal Society of Antiquaries, London; the German Archaeological Institute, Berlin-Dahlem; a member of the Permanent Council of the International Congress of Prehistoric and Protohistoric Sciences, the International Committee for the Study of Megaliths, the International Committee on Monuments, Artistic and Historical Sites and Archaeological Excavations, UNESCO, the International Committee of Museums, UNESCO; and several other learned societies. In India itself, he had been president of various Conferences and Seminars, including. those of Indian Archaeological Society, Numismatic Society of India, All India Oriental Conference, Indian History Congress, and International Conferences on Asian Archaeology. He was also honoured by the Asiatic Society of Bengal in 1978.

As Director General, he was responsible for introducing a new annual publication viz, *Indian Archaeology-A Review* from 1953-54 which incorporates within itself the survey of all important archaeological researches of sites/monuments and activities including maintenance of monuments. Before this, there was no such publication which contained all these information.

The credit of the creation of two Temple Survey branches, Prehistory branch, School of Archaeology and the expansion of Arabic and Persian branches of Epigraphy also goes to him. For his scholarly attainments and organizational capacity, he was awarded the *Padma Shri* by the Government of India in January, 1962.

He was one of those scholars who combined in themselves the traditional knowledge of Epigraphy, Numismatics and Sanskrit literature with modern methods of Scientific archaeology. His explorations of the Ghaggar Valley in 1951 extended the horizon of the Indus civilization eastwards into the present day boundary of India; as a result number of Harappan sites along the dry beds of Sarasvati and Drishadvati were discovered.

By his death, a great void in Indian archaeological scholarship is created.

I. A. S.

Shri Amalanand Ghosh (10.3.1910 — 25.8.1981)

Sringaverapura: A Key-site for the Protohistory and early History of the Central Ganga Valley

B. B. LAL AND K. N. DIKSHIT

IIAS, Simla, ASI, New Delhi

INTRODUCTION

Falling in Allahabad district, U.P., which for all practical purposes may be regarded as the central part of the Ganga valley, Sringaverapura is 36 km. north-west of the district headquarters, a little off the Allahabad-Unnao State highway. It is approachable through village Bhagwatipur (near Mansoorabad) by covering a distance of about 3 km. from the highway. The ancient site, sprawling roughly north-south along the left bank of the Ganga, lies in the revenue limits of Singrur, a small village occupying a sizable portion of the site. Seven different parts of the mound, named SVP-1 to SVP-7, were selected for excavation. However, the highest portion of the mound (SVP-1), rising to about 10 m. above the natural soil, and a low-lying area (SVP-4) immediately to the north-east of the former, were taken up for large-scale operations. The excavations, begun in December 1977 and continued for three field-seasons were carried out under the joint auspices of the Indian Institute of Advanced Study, Simla, and the Archaeological Survey of India, New Delhi. The work constituted a part of the National Project, 'Archaeology of the Ramayana Sites'.

THE SEQUENCE OF CULTURES

A combined cross-section of the mound provided a sequence of cultures starting from about the end of the second millennium B.C. up to the early mediaeval times. In brief, the culture-contents of the various periods are as follows:

Period I (c. 1050-1000 B C.) :

Right on the natural soil and imperceptibly merging with it was a 30-60 cm. thick deposit of yellowish clay (labelled layer 19E), which yielded a red ware industry.

The ware falls into two broad categories : one made of well-levigated clay, nicely potted and well fired; and the other having a coarser texture, somewhat indifferently potted and insufficiently fired. There is an occasional use of slip in both the varieties. A few sherds with raised horizontal bands and shallow incised designs, such as wavy comb-like pattern, parallel lines, etc., were also found. The types include : jars with prominently out-turned rim, bowls with featureless or everted rim, shallow basins with horizontally splayed-out rim, vases with disc-base, and platters. Some of the fragments are suggestive of types like the dish-on-stand (?) and bowl or basin with tubular or short channel. There are also a few specimens of lid, with either a central depression made by fingers, or a curved knob. While it remains to be seen as to how far this ware compares with the Ochre Colour Ware, it seems clear that it has no typological connection with the red ware reported from Kakoria in this region. Remnants of burnt earth with reed-impression, suggestive of wattle-and-daub hutments, were also noticed. Not

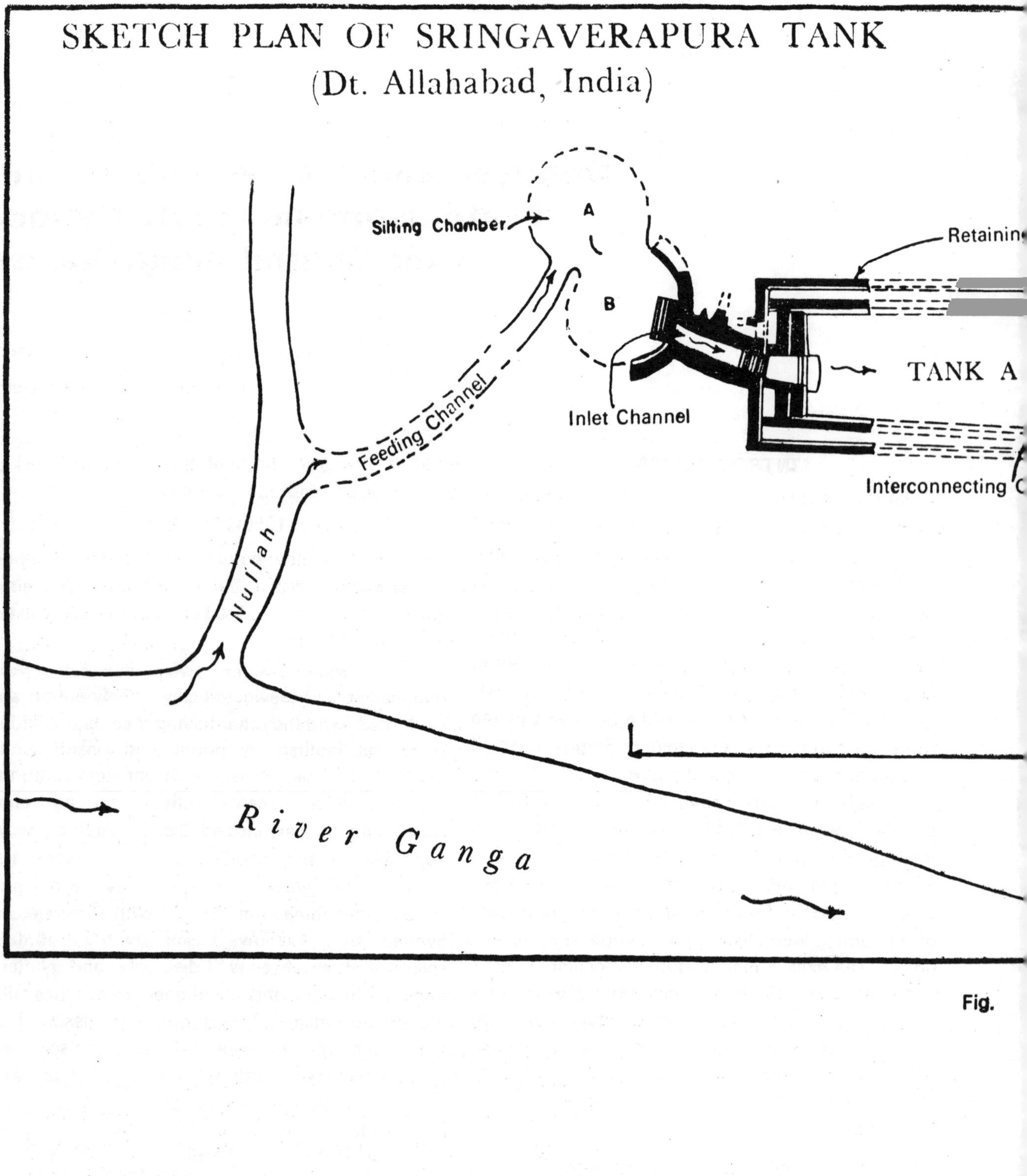
SKETCH PLAN OF SRINGAVERAPURA TANK
(Dt. Allahabad, India)
A
Silting Chamber
B
Retainin
TANK A
Inlet Channel
Feeding Channel
Interconnecting C
Nullah
River Ganga

Fig.

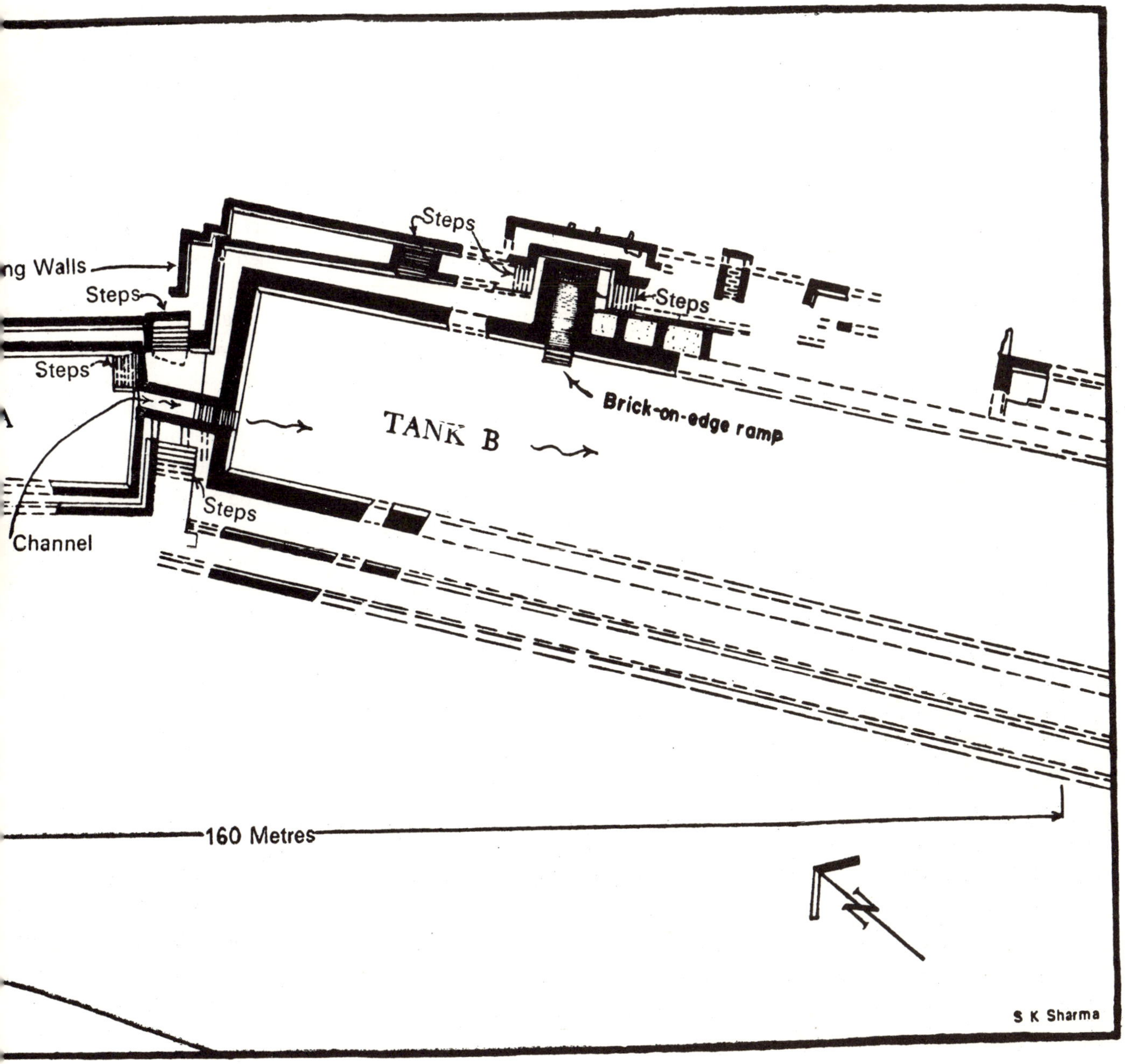
Steps
ng Walls
Steps
Steps
Steps
Brick-on-edge ramp
TANK B
Steps
Channel
160 Metres
N
S K Sharma

1

many antiquities were recovered from this period. These, however, comprised pottery-discs, with or without a central perforation, and a small fragment of a flake of carnelian.

Above layer 19E is layer 19 which is darker in colour than the former, though composition-wise it is also clayey like 19E. On the other hand the next higher layer 18, consists of black earth, somewhat loose. Thus, lithologically, layer 19 goes more with 19E than with 18. However, layer 19 has given red ware sherds of layer 19E type, accounting for only 21% of the total, whereas it has yielded the black-slipped, black-and-red and associated red wares to the tune of 79%. These latter are characteristically different from the pottery of layer 19E, but constitute the principal ceramic industry from layer 18 upwards. It may also be added that in layers 18 and 17 the typical pottery of layer 19E type gets reduced respectively to 0.68% and 0.09% of the total. Such a situation militates against a real temporal overlap between the two cultures. However, since the evidence is very meagre and confined to a small area, it would not be proper to pronounce a final judgement on the issue. In case there was a time-gap, as seems more likely, the thermoluminiscence and ^{14}C dates (cf. below,) indicate that it may have been of about fifty years or so.

Period II (c. 950-700 B.C.)

Period II comprises layers 19 to 14, accounting for a thickness of 1.40 m. This period is characterized by black-slipped, black-and-red, burnished grey and associated red wares. It is possible to further sub-divide this Period into IIA (layer 19 and 18) and IIB (layers 17 to 14), the former being characterized by the occurrence of coarse black-and red ware and burnished grey ware which tend to peter out in IIB Here it would be of importance to add that a few sherds of the Painted Grey Ware (PGW) have also been found from layer 17 upwards. Such a situation would suggest a stage of contact between the PGW culture and the Black-Slipped Ware Culture in this area early in the eighth century B. C. Amongst the antiquities of Period II as a whole mention may be made of points and a barbed arrow-head of bone, a bone pendant and beads made variously of terracotta, jasper, etc., and one of gold as well. The presence of clay lumps with reed-impression indicates that during this period also the houses were made of wattle-daub.

Period III (c. 700-200 B.C.)

Without any break of occupation from the previous one, Period III is characterized by the use of the Northern Black Polished Ware (NBPW). Having an average thickness of 2.80 m., it is divisible into three Sub-periods, A, B and C. In Sub-period IIIA the NBPW occurred in great abundance, and in a variety of shades: golden, silvery, indigo, steel grey and, of course, black. The black-slipped ware also continued in this Sub-period. A few sherds of the Painted Grey Ware were also found. Specific mention may, however, be made of a sherd which had a fine grey ware fabric, was painted on the interior with black lines, and had the typical NBPW finish on the exterior over which a row of sigmas was further painted in black pigment. Such a sherd clearly shows the close physical inter-relationship between the Painted Grey Ware and the Northern Black Polished Ware. In Sub-period IIIB, the miniature bowl, Ahichchhatra type 10a, and carinated *handi* made their appearance, whereas in Sub-period IIIC the quality as well as the quantity of the NBPW were on the wane, and coarse grey ware became preponderant. It may also be added that no burnt brick-structures were met with in Sub-period IIIA, and their presence in IIIB was also not very clear. However, burnt-brick structures were duly noted in Sub-period IIIC. The end of this period was marked by a burnt layer running all around the section.

The important antiquities of this period as a whole included: three copper vessels (one of them spouted), a long-handled laddle, dishes and bowls; terracotta female figurines and balls; beads of semi-precious stones, gold and terracotta; cylindrical weights of agate and chalcedony; bone points; copper and iron objects; and punch-marked coins of silver as well as copper.

Period IV (c. 200 B.C.-A.D. 200)

Having an occupational thickness of about 2.75m., this Period is divisible into two Sub-periods·

The notable characteristic of this period as a whole is its red ware industry, there being no NBPW nor even the grey ware. Bowls with incurved rim and dishes with flat base and vertical rim are the notable features of the red ware pottery of Sub-period IVA. In IVB bowls with vertically sharpened rim, sprinklers, vases with long vertical neck, ink-pot type lids dominate the scene. Burnt-brick structures ascribable to different phases were also noticed. In this context, particular mention may be made of a structural complex in SVP-1, which consisted of several rooms with successive brick-floorings, a drain and a soakage pit. The last-named was dug down to a depth of about 4 metres without reaching its bottom. It was lined with bricks, the number of courses being over 90.

Amongst the antiquities of Sub-period IVA particular mention may be made of a coin of the Lanky Bull type and of coins of the rulers of Ayodhya, besides Sunga terracottas. The antiquities of Sub-period IVB comprised seals and sealings, one of them reading *Dhankasa*, and another *Gosalakasa* in characters of the 1st century B.C.-A.D., and coins of Wima Kadphises.

Ascribable to Sub-period IVB was a massive burnt-brick tank consisting of two units, with an elaborate inlet and interconnecting system, excavated in the natural soil in the low-lying area (SVP-4) to the north of SVP-1. The sides of the tank were retained in a terraced fashion by three successive burnt-brick walls with battered back against the natural soil. Besides being the largest tank ever revealed through an excavation in the country, it is unique in a number of other ways.

The tank was fed through a channel cut into the natural soil. It lay immediately outside the northern end of the tank and received the water of the Ganga through a *nullah* when the river was in spate. Through this feeding channel, the Ganga water first got into two successive silting chambers, the exact outlines of which yet remain to be determined. However, it was noted that their bottom was much deeper than that of the tank proper. As a result, all the mud settled down in these chambers and clean water entered the tank. At the point of entry there was an arc-shaped structure made of kiln-burnt bricks. About the middle of this arc, there was a 1.60 m. wide inlet channel lined with kiln-burnt bricks through which the water entered the tank, cascading over a flight of steps. The walls of the channel were strengthened by cross walls at the back. Also, the bottom of the channel and a part of the floor of the tank at the point of the fall of the incoming water were paved with unusually large bricks, measuring 64×48×12 cm. Otherwise, the average size of the bricks used in the tank was: length 42-43 cm., width 27.5-28.5 cm. and thickness 6-7 cm.

The first unit of the tank from the intake side (called here Tank A) has a length of 34 m., width of about 13 m., and a depth of over 4 m. The full length of the second tank (Tank B) has not been ascertained so far. However, the available length so far is about 120 m, the width and depth being 26 m. and 7 m. respectively. The two tanks were interconnected with a channel which measured about 5.30 m. in length and 1 35 m. in width. Staircases have been provided at a number of places in Tank B. Of these, special interest attaches to a set of two staircases descending from two opposite directions to a common level from which a brick-on-edge ramp leads down to the bed of the tank.

From the bed of tank B terracotta figurines of Hariti holding a child in the left lap were found, which appear to have been ceremoneously immersed in it. This would indicate that the tank was used for religious purposes as well, besides, of course serving the prime need of water-supply to the people.

Period V (A.D. 300-600)

The distinguishing feature of the pottery of this period was a bright red slip. As to the shapes while variants of the ink-pot type lids and sprinklers continued, bowls with footed base and jars with drooping rim were the new forms. Moulded pots also appeared. Amongst the antiquities, particular mention may be made of terracotta figurines stylistically ascribable to the Gupta times.

Period VI (c. A.D. 600-1300)

It is marked by the post-Gupta stage, from about the sixth-seventh century A.D. A noteworthy find of this period was that of thirteen silver coins of the Gahadvala king Govinda Chandra, which lay in a small pot along with some jewellery, including a gold ring.

Period VII (A.D. 17th—18th Century)

To the last occupation, found in the excavation, belonged a large house-complex. In a few instances the walls had been robbed but the plaster was still standing, which gave the outlines.

THE BASIS OF DATING

The thermoluminescence dating technique, applied by A.K. Singhvi of the Physical Research Laboratory, Ahmedabad, to the potsherds from Sringaverapura has yielded some useful information. For the earliest Period, represented by a single layer, 19E, three TL dates are available, as follows: 3015±280 B.P.; 2855±270 B.P.; and 2900±380 B.P. Since on the one hand, the margin of error in these dates is quite wide and, on the other the deposit of Period I is very thin (being only 30-60 cm.), it would be desirable to place this period within a narrow range of time, the beginning of which may not be earlier than the earliest of these dates. Thus, period I may be assigned to c. 1050-1000 B.C.

As for Sub-period IIA, there is a ^{14}C date of 2855±200 B.P. i.e. 905±200 B.C., for layer 19 which, on MASCA correction comes to 960±1010 B.C. For the next higher layer, viz. 18, there are two dates; a TL date of 2743±300 B.P. and a ^{14}C date of 2700±130 B.P. While the former comes to 793 B.C., the later, on MASCA correction, is 820-840 B.C, Thus Sub-period IIA may be placed between 950-800 B.C. For the earliest layer of Sub-period IIB, viz. layer 17, there are three TL dates: 2769±400 B.P.; 2690±280 B.P.; and 2660 ±280 B.P,. which give the values respectively as 819, 740 and 710 B C. Since there is some more deposit above layer 17, the end of Sub-period IIB may be dated around 700 B.C., or somewhat later.

There is no break of occupation between Periods II and III. Hence the beginning of Period III, characterized by the first appearance of the NBPW may also be placed around the first quarter of the seventh century B.C. In layers which post-dated the NBPW were found successively a coin of the Lanky Bull type, and a Sunga terracotta. Therefore there is very good reason to suppose that the NBPW come to an end towards the close of the third century B.C.

The subsequent periods are very well dated on the basis of coins, terracottas, etc. and the same are therefore, not being discussed here in detail.

SIGNIFICANCE OF THE RESULTS

One of the major contributions of the excavation at Sringaverapura is the identification in the mid-Ganga valley of a red ware industry which, for all one can say at the moment, is associable not with any thing eastern but probably with the Ochre Colour Ware (OCW) of the western Ganga valley. This would suggest the penetration of the OCW Culture much further to the east than was hitherto known, for example from Saipai in Etawah District. Though the method of thermoluminiscence dating is still in its infancy, the available dates for the Sringaverapura specimens suggest that the OCW continued in the mid-Ganga valley up to the end of the second millennium B.C. This agrees fairly well with the TL dates for the OCW Culture in the western region, for example for sites like Atranji-Khera, Jhinjhana, Nasirpur, etc., which indicate a time-range around 1500 B.C. At Sringaverapura one thus meets the fag-end of the OCW Culture. However, since at this site there seems to be a break of occupation after the OCW Culture, one does not yet know if and in what manner this culture contributed to the subsequent cultures of the region.

The culture of Period II, characterized by burnished grey, black-and-red and black-slipped wares. is evidently a *continuum* of the one dominating western Bihar (e.g. in the chalcolithic levels of Chirand) and parts of eastern Uttar Pradesh (for example that found at Kakoria). Sringaverapura Period II, datable to *circa* 950-700 B.C. represents perhaps the last stage of this culture.

Another significant discovery at Sringaverapura is the occurrence of a few sherds of the Painted Grey Ware as early as layer 17, which, as discussed above, is ascribable to c. 8th century B.C. The occurrence of these PGW sherds in a limited quantity at Sringaverapura shows a contact with that culture around the beginning of the 8th century B.C.

A no less noteworthy point is about the first appearance of the Northern Black Polished Ware at the site, marking the beginning of Period III. Since there is no break of occupation between Periods II and III, the appearance of the NBPW over here will have to be placed around the beginning of the 7th century B.C. In these early NBPW levels also there occur a few sherds of the Painted Grey Ware, showing that it was around this time that the PGW was coming to an end and the NBPW was emerging.

With the excavations at Sringaverapura it is now possible to sub-divide the NBPW Period into three Sub-periods, viz. IIIA, IIIB and IIIC, the characteristic features of which have already been discussed in the foregoing pages. It is Sub-period IIIA that constitutes the lowest common denominator at the sites associated with the Ramayana story, viz. Ayodhya, Sringaverapura, Bharadvaja Asrama, etc. This would place the story early in the seventh century B.C.

The first century B.C.-A.D. tank, mentioned in some detail in the foregoing pages is, of course, the most notable contribution of Sringaverapura to the early historical archaeology of the country. It is a monumental structure throwing much valuable light on the skill and foresight of Indian hydraulic engineers some two thousand years ago.

The Development of Eastern Bactria in Pre-classical Times

J. C. GARDIN
C.N.R.S., Paris

A recent article by B. Lyonnet (1981) has thrown new light on the ancient history of Bactria, in the north-east of Afghanistan, long before this province came to be known for the wealth of its cities and the prosperity of its land, in classical times. Following an archaeological survey carried out in the eastern part of Bactria, south of the Amu Darya (fig. 1), a detailed study of the hundreds of thousands potsherds collected in that area was undertaken by B. Lyonnet and myself in order to refine the tentative chronology which we had first devised for a preliminary presentation of our data (Gardin & Lyonnet 1978-79). One of the first results of this study - which is still under way was the identification of a small assemblage of Chalcolithic sherds found in the Taluqan area, showing analogies with the pottery of a number of sites scattered between the Hilmend valley and the Indus basin. The interpretation of these analogies is not yet totally clear. The first hypothesis which comes to mind is that of an expansion of the Chalcolithic cutures from Baluchistan and Indus valley towards the North, across the Hindukush, as early as the beginning of the 3rd millennium B.C., in connection with the development of the lapis lazuli trade between Badakhshan and the Near East (Elam, Mesopotamia) during that period (fig. 1). Another possibility, however is the indigenous development of a Central Asian Chalcolithic Civilisation north of the Hindukush, grown out of the well-established neolithic cultures of Tadjikistan and North-eastern Afghanistan, which could have spread southward and interacted with contemporary settlements between the Hilmend valley and the Indus basin, a number of recent finds in Tadjikistan tend to give some support to this alternative interpretation (discussion and references in Lyonnet 1981, 3).

The purpose of the present paper is to reconsider the early development of Eastern Bactria in the light of this new evidence, without having to choose at this stage between the two interpretations. Our starting point is the *existence* of settled communities in the Taluqan plain as early as the first half of the 3rd millennium B.C. rather than any particular theory on the *origin* of the settlers. I shall concentrate on two questions: (a) what kind of relationship, if any, can we establish between the growth of the Taluqan area in the Chalcolithic period and the development of the Shortughai plain in the Bronze age less than a hundred kilometers to the north (Francfort & Pottier, 1978) ? (b) More generally, is it not time to stress the progress of Eastern Bactria prior to the Achaemenian and Hellenistic periods, long regarded as periods of sudden prosperity following a protracted Dark age ?

From Taluqan to Shortughai : discontinuity or growth ?

Let us first recall the overall view of the Shortughai settlement which has gradually evolved following its discovery in 1975 (Lyonnet 1977) and the excavations conducted by H. P. Francfort from 1976 to 1979 (Francfort 1981). Large quantities of Harappan or Harappa-like materials have been found in the earliest occupation level, and interpreted as the product of activities by newcomers of Indian origin during the last quarter of the 3rd millennium B.C. : mud-brick architecture, wheel-made pottery, bead making, metallurgy, and of course agriculture, exten-

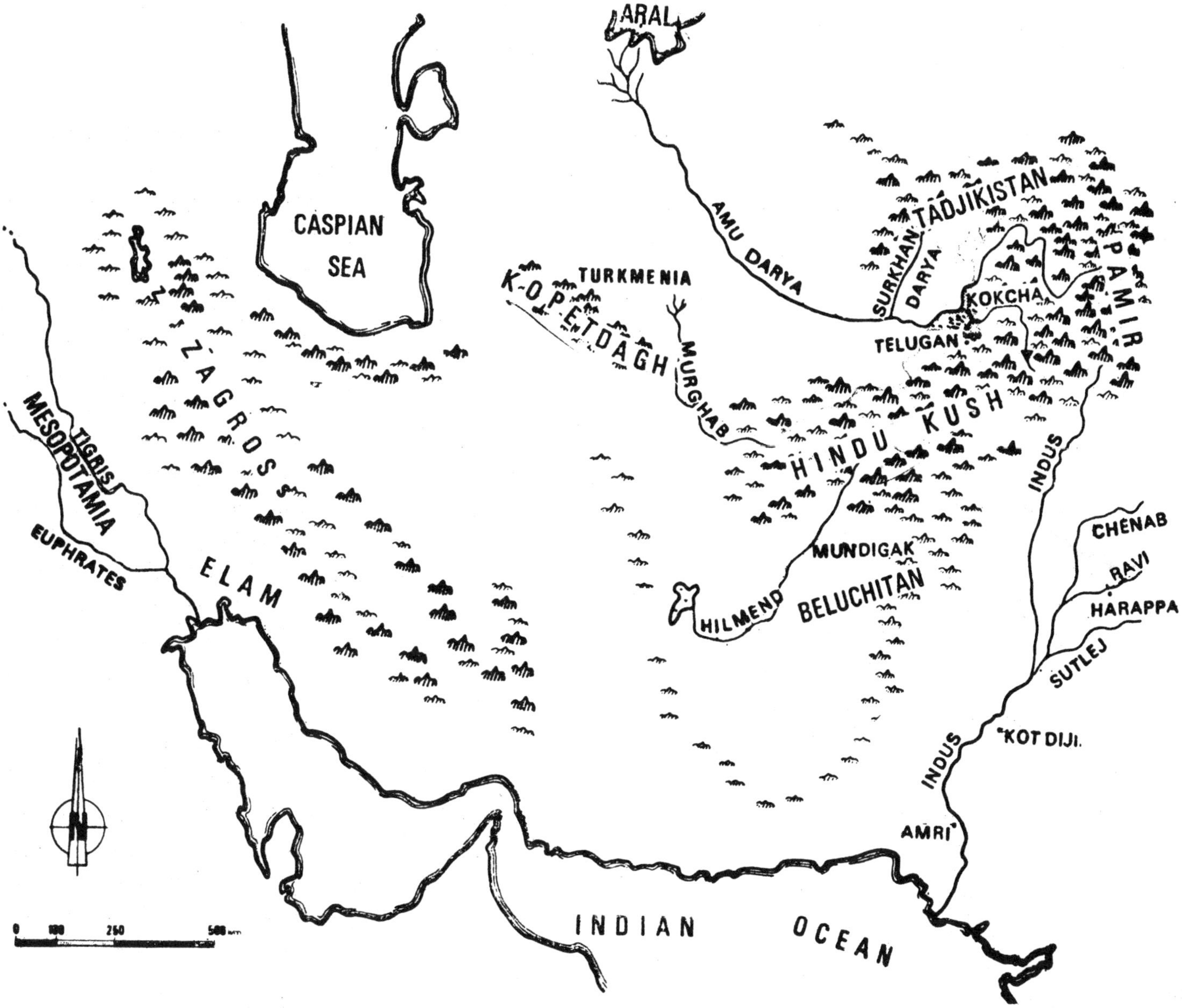

Fig. 1

Fig. 1. The situation of Taluqan (top right) at the foot of the high hills leading eastward to the Hindukush and Pamir mountains; the triangle on the upper course of the Kokcha marks the approximate location of the lapis lazuli mines in Badakhshan. The hatched area around Taluqan indicates the region covered by the Eastern Bactrian Survey (1974-78); the range of its relations with other parts of Asia in the 3rd millenium is illustrated by the scope of this map, from the Indus to the Tigris.

sively developed in the surrounding plain thanks to an irrigation canal drawn from the Kokcha (fig. 2). The later, post-Harappan levels provide evidence of a local evolution related to similar developments further to the west in Bactria (especially in the Surkhandarya valley), until the site is abandoned around 1600 B.C., as new peoples from the north seem to appear on the southern shores of the Amu Darya (Francfort 1981).

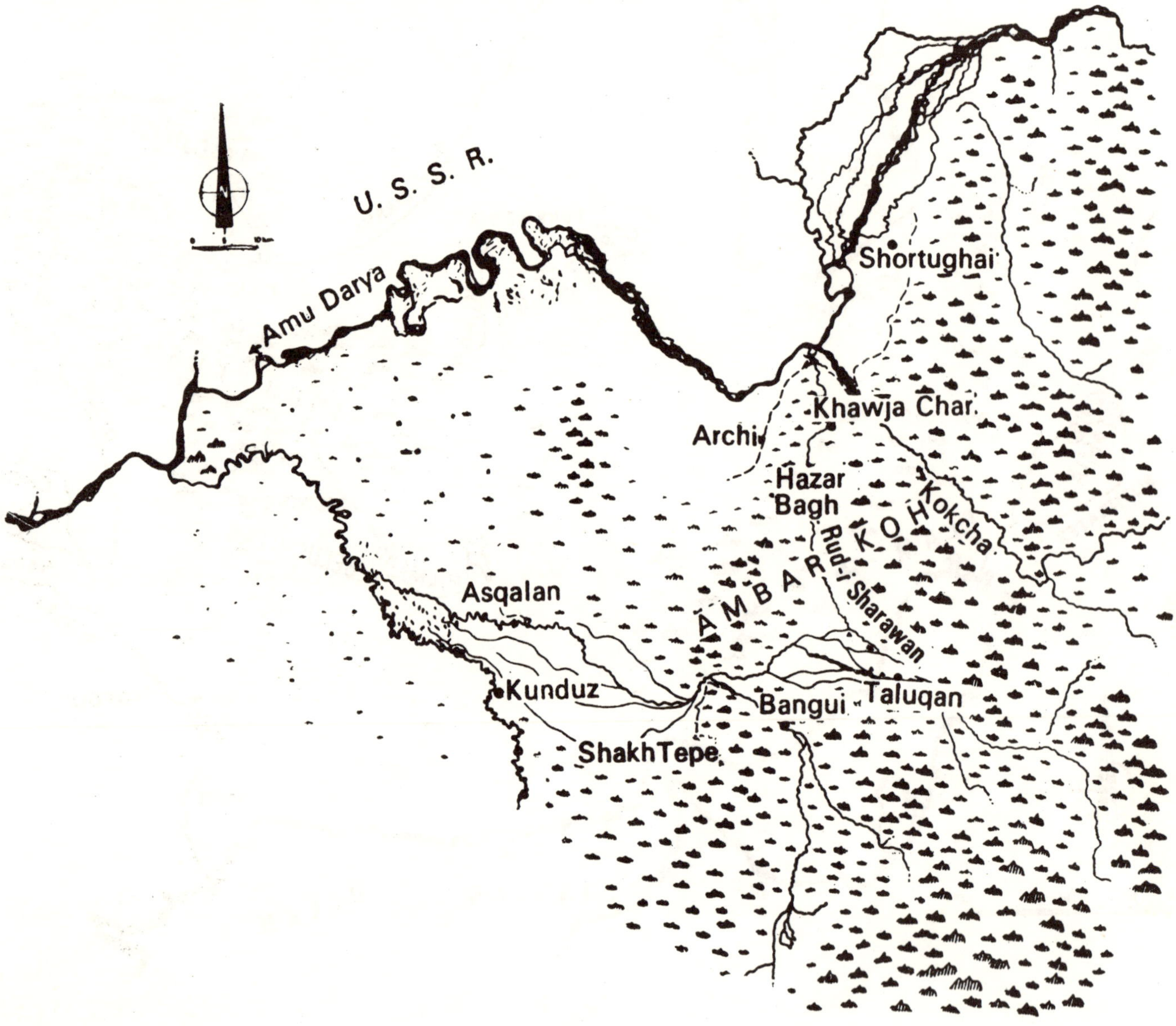

Fig. 2

Fig. 2. The major irrigation systems in Eastern Bactria before the Hellenistic conquest. The earliest one was Taluqan in the Chalcolithic period (first half of the 3rd millennium); then Shortughai (end of 3rd millennium), Archi, Kunduz (first half of the 2nd millennium) with the later addition of the terraces overlooking the Kundus plain to the North (Asqalan) and to the South (Shakh Tepe), finally, the Rud-i-Shahrawan project, undertaken in the first half of the 1st millennium, but completed only under the Greeks with the digging of secondary canals in the Khwaja Ghar and Hazar Bagh areas (not indicated in this map).

With the recent discovery of an older settlement in the Taluqan area, several centuries before the Shortughai phase, we may have to qualify the concept of the so-called Harappan "colonization" of Eastern Bactria. Not that doubts should be raised as to the Harappan origin of crafts and craftsmen in the early Shortughai period, irrefutable as ever; but we now have stronger reasons to believe that the surrounding regions and perhaps the Shortughai plain itself were already inhabited long before that period, even though we have found no Chalcolithic remains other than in the Taluqan area. The argument runs as follows. Our Chalcolithic sherds, in the Taluqan area, have been found on natural ridges which emerge here and there from the plain, formed in geological times by the meanders of the Taluqan river. These ridges show little evidence of occupation, except in the form of large modern cemeteries or isolated monuments of relatively recent date. It is therefore largely by chance that we discovered a few patches of sherds on some of those ridges. No such discoveries were made in the low-lying fields, extensively irrigated and cultivated, which surround these barren ridges; but we have no reason to believe that Chalcolithic settlements were only found on the latter. The more probable inference is that most of them have disappeared under the plough, the past millennia, as indeed we were able to observe for many sites of later times (Gardin & Lyonnet 1978-79: 107-8). Our scanty distribution of sites for the Chalcolithic period has therefore little historical meaning, except as a token of the strength of post-depositional factors in the loess-covered plains of Bactria (Gardin 1980 : 490—1).

It follows that we are not in a position to assert that the Taluqan plain was the only part of Eastern Bactria occupied during the first half of the 3rd millennium B.C. In fact, the more likely picture is that of a progressive expansion of chalcolithic settlements throughout the region, possibly reaching the Shortughai plain itself before it became the seat of the so-called Harappan colonization. If this reconstruction is correct - which will only be decided on the strength of further surveys or excavations our colonization concept will have to be replaced by a more subtle one, giving due regard to the indogenous development on the Bactrian plains prior to the Harappan influx. We would then come to a more satisfactory explanation of the Harappan phase itself, at Shortughai, seen as a consequence of the growing prosperity of Eastern Bactria in *pre*-Harappan times. This was the period when the trade between Badakhshan and the Near East was most flourishing, for lapis lazuli and probably other precious goods (Lyonnet 1981, notes 33-35) : we may assume that groups of people were attracted from the regions south of the Hindukush to the Eastern Bactrian plains, throughout the 3rd millennium, in the hope of taking a share, even if indirectly, in the benefits of that trade. Both the Taluqan and the Shortughai settlements probably grew as a result of this polar position of the Eastern Bactrian plains in connection with the exploitation of mineral resources from Badakhshan : these plains were the nearest wide and flat areas where agriculture could be developed on a large scale, at the foot of the high hills leading to Badakhshan.

This last statement may seem over-emphatic : having discovered no more than a dozen chalcolithic and early bronze age sites in the two areas, all of minor size to say the least, how can we speak of large-scale agriculture? Our answer will be based on the study of another category of archaeological evidence which is in many respects more resistant to post - depositional factors than sites, namely irrigation systems, to which we shall now turn.

THE DEVELOPMENT OF EASTERN BACTRIANS IN THE BRONZE AND IRON AGES

The vital role of irrigation in the development of Central Asia has been stressed many times Even through archaeologists still disagree on the matter of climatic changes in this part of the world during the past five or ten thousand years, the general opinion is that the progress of agriculture in the plains which extend North of the Hindukush and Kopet Dagh ranges would not have been possible, after the Neolithic period without resorting to irrigation techniques of some kind, as necessary then as they are today in the same areas. Our survey of Eastern Bactria provided ample confirmations of this view : traces of ancient irrigation systems have been found everywhere, many of them in areas that were once inhabited and fertile, judging from the density of mounds and ditches that can still be detected on the surface. The sherds collected in those areas usually constitute a sufficient basis determining periods of activity ; by combining the evidence from different areas, we can follow the growth or decline of irrigated surfaces from any given period to the next, or their shift from one region to another in the course of time-a far safer indicator of demographic and economic development than the size and quantity of sites, for well-known reasons (Gardin 1980 : 492-7).

Prior to the discovery of chalcolithic settlements near Taluqan, however, our picture of the progress of irrigation techniques in Eastern Bactria was biassed in one respect : the earliest irrigation system, in the Shortughai plain (ca. 2200 B.C.) was so sophisticated that we tended to regard it as the product of foreign craftsmanship brought full-blown from the Indus valley by Harappan settlers (Gardin & Lyonnet 1973-79 : 131). This hypothesis remains plausible ; but another one now emerges, according to which the Shortughai irrigation system, complex as it is, could be regarded as skilled version of the Taluqan system, developed a few centuries earlier some fifty miles to the south, across the Ambar Kuh (fig. 2).

Let us first summarize the major features of each system. The Shortughai plain is locked between two rivers (the Amu Darya and Kokcha) and a range of foothills to the East ; owing to the accumulation of alluvial deposit from the Kokcha, it slopes gently toward the North, and can only be irrigated by a canal drawn from that river rather than from the Amu Darya (Gentelle 1978). However, the Kokcha runs about 30 meters lower than the level of the terrace above ; in order to bring water to the top, a long canal has to be dug on the stiff slope of the terrace from a distant point upstream-a technique which has been practised throughout Central Asia for centuries, but which requires a high degree of topographical expertise, as demonstrated by a recent unsuccesful project in the same area. Indeed, the design of such a complex system at the end of the 3rd millennium first seemed improbable to many archaeologists. Soundings were therefore dug at Shortughai on two or three spots along the supposed course of the Bronze Age canal, reconstructed through a careful topographical study of the whole plain ; they revealed a number of superimposed ditches, the earliest of each contained sherds of the Harappan period, exclusively. (Francfort 1981).

The Taluqan system in the Chalcolithic period was certainly quite different. The larger plain on the right bank, of the river where Chalcolithic sites have been found, was probably crossed then as now by a number of streams derived from the main course of the river, as shown on fig. 2. Several of them have cut deep ravines in the loess-covered plain : they are in fact natural arms of the Taluqan river, formed long before the Chalcolithic period, but which could readily be used here and there as source of artificial channels, as they are today. Yet there was a danger that the whole system might collapse if the natural arms dried up as a result of changes in the course of the Taluqan river. This is the case at present : the major stream which waters the Taluqan plain is still called a river (*Rud*-i Shahrawan), but it has in fact become a canal, the head of which has to be continually upkept as an *artificial* derivation of the Taluqan river.

It is impossible to say when this transition from a natural to an artificial irrigation system began: but we can draw inferences from our ecological data without answering this question. The main point is that the Taluqan plain is ideally suited to the development of irrigated agriculture, for the topographical and hydrological reasons just discussed. No large-scale investments are needed, neither physically nor conceptually: the derivation of channels from any of the several arms of the river toward the low-lying plain requires no big labour force nor any special topographical skill. The difference between the Taluqan and the Shortughai irrigation systems is in this respect enormous; but the early existence of the former, in the first half of the 3rd millennium, now helps to understand the growth of the latter, a few centuries later. What I mean here is that the kind of knowledge accumulated by Taluqan settlers as they extended their control of water channels towards the foothills—the more likely process of land expansion in this case—would eventually give them the capacity to undertake more sophisticated irrigation projects, such as the one just described at Shortuguhai. The reference to Harappan expertise is in this case unnecessary.

The later progress of irrigation systems in Eastern Bactria confirms the high degree of skill reached by local masters in meeting the most difficult topographical challenges. We have shown elsewhere that after the decay of the Shortughai settlements towards the middle of the 2nd millennium B.C., the Kunduz area further South eventually became the main focus of development (fig. 2): the large citadel today known as the Bala Hissar was probably built during that period, while additional irrigation systems came into existence on the high terraces overlooking the Kunduz-Khanabad plain, both to the North (Asqalan) and to the South Shakh Tepe) (Gardin & Lyonnet 1978-79 : 134-6). The Shakh Tepe project, in particular, is quite remarkable: it consists of canal dug across the hills which separate the Kunduz plain from the Bangui river, some 30 kilometers to the East, in order to bring water from that distant river to the Shakh Tepe plateau.

This amazing development of irrigation went on during the Iron Age, down to Hellenistic times. Indeed, the most ambitious project of all, in Eastern Bactria, probably took shape early in the 1st millennium B.C., when the *Rud*-i Shahrawan was extended from the Taluqan plain to the Amu Darya, some 50 kilometers to the North across the Ambar Kuh highlands (fig. 2). The goal was to bring water to hitherto barren areas in the foothills which overlook the Amu Darya and the plain of Archi. According to our surface finds, the digging of the *Rud*-i Shahrawan itself took place during the Achaemenian period or even earlier, while the secondary foothill systems were only completed under the Greeks, around the 3rd century B.C. (Gardin 1980 : 498-500). The fact that these systems were soon abandoned, early in the Kushan period (Gardin & Lyonnet 1978-79 : 140), suggests that their upkeep raised difficulties, as would be expected in such an unpropitious milieu; they nevertheless indicate a propensity to irrigate more and more land against all kinds of economical and technical odds- a movement which we can now trace back to the Bronze Age instead of rooting it traditionally in the "classical" period of Bactria, whether Persian or Greek.

BIBLIOGRAPHY

Francfort, H. P. 1981 "Shortughai: an Indus valley settlement on the river Oxus", *Archaeology* (in print)

Francfort, H. P. & Pottier, M. H. 1978 Sondage preliminaire sur l'etablissement protohistorique harappeen et post-harappeen de Shortughai (Afghanistan du Nord-Est)", *Arts Asiatiques,* tome XXXIV, pp. 29–86

Gardin, J. C. 1980 "L'archeologie du paysage bactrien", *Comptes Rendus de l'Academic des Inscriptions et Belles-Lettres.*

Gardin, J. -C. & Lyonnet, B. 1978-79 "La prospection archeologique de la Bactriane Orientale (1974-1978): premiers resultats", *Mesopotamia,* tome XIII-XIV, pp 99-154

Gentelle, P. *Etude geographique de la plaine d'Ai Khanoum et de son irrigation depuis les temps antiques,* Editions du C.N.R.S., Paris.

Lyonnet, B. 1977 "Decouverte de sites de l'age du bronze dans le Nord-Est de l'Afghanistan: leurs rapports avec la civilisation de l'Indus", *Annali dell'Istituto Orientale di Napoli,* vol. 37, pp. 19-35.

1981 "Etablissements chalcolithiques dans le Nord–Est de l'Afghanistan : leurs rapports avec les civilisations du bassin de l'Indus", Paleorient (in print).

Explorations along the Sahibi River in District Gurgaon

C. MARGABANDHU AND R. P. SHARMA
Archaeological Survey of India, New Delhi

The present paper covers the exploration by the authors in the catchment area of the river Sahibi in Gurgaon district. Here it is pertinent to point out that in Haryana, administrative boundaries are changing due to the emergence of new districts. Presently Faridabad is a separate district and, tehsil Rewari which was originally a part of Gurgaon, is in Mahendragarh district.

The original boundaries of the district, prior tothe integration of the princely State of Pataudi, are taken up for the present study. It is bounded in the north-east by the river Yamuna which separates from the districts of Buland-Shahr and Aligarh of Uttar Pradesh; in the south by the districts Mathura of Uttar Pradesh and Bharatpur of Rajasthan; in the South West by the district Alwar of Rajasthan; in the West and north-West by the Mahendragarh and Rohtak districts of Haryana and in the north by the Union Territory of Delhi. This area falls between lat. 27° 39′ N and 28° 31′ N and long. 76° 18′ E 77° 34′ and forms the south-estern corner of the Haryana State.

The topography of the district presents considerable variety. Two rocky outcrops represent the continuation of the Aravalli chain, cut through the flat plain from south to north. They are bare. The western range divides the northern plains into two natural divisions. Eastward the valley in-between the two ridges is wide and open throughout. Below the escarpment of the eastern ridge an alluvial level extends unbroken upto the river Yamuna. At the foot of the uplands lie a series of unuulating hollows, which turn into swamps during the rains. The area to the west of the western range comprises sandy plains and low-lying land dotted with sand dunes and mounds Numerous torrents of monsoon currents from the hills discharge into the river Sahibi, and lead to natural formations of basins and lakes. The Aravalli outliers comprise slate and quartzites of the Delhi system. The slate is in fissile clay state and is quarried near Rewari.

The flora is mainly of north-eastern Rajputana variety, though several desert forms are found in the south-west. The Yamuna basin and the north-eastern corner of the districts belong botanically to the upper Gangetic plains.

The entire drainage of the district is controlled by Yamuna and Sahibi. Sahibi is a powerful stream that rises from a point near Shahpur nearly 14 km. south of Kot-Qasim in district Jaipur. A few kilometers north of Bahror the combined streams of Sahibi and Sota-nala enter the alluvial tract of Gurgaon district. In these lower reaches the river flows for about 70 km. receiving waters of Indori-nala near Pataudi and Badshahi-nala, further north. Beyond a few kilometres north of Pataudi, the course of the river is not well-defined. It extends in two directions i.e. north-west and north. The latter course joins Yamuna *via* Najafgarh lake and Drain no. 6, While the former links it with Jhajjar depression and Drain no. 8. which in turn also joins Yamuna. Actually Sahibi is a tributary of Yamuna, merging with it on its right bank near Delhi. This expanse is a vast alluvial tract in the form of a depression which streches from Najafgarh in Delhi at the south-west, to near Rohtak in the north and Sonepat in the north-east forming a triangular depression. It is believed that this relict landscape evolved as a result of dichotamic pattern of distributaries initially and then its subsequent dessication. This suggests that the creation of this depression is subsequent to the creation of distributaries. It may however as well be attributed to the age of river which in old age flattens near its mouth. Actually Sahibi is passing through its old age.

The early history of the district is less known. Tradition maintains that Gurgaon was a village and Palwal (than known as *Apelava)* was a town-ship during the Mahabharatra period. Earlier, the country to the south and south-west of Indraprastha was ruled by the Matsyas (*Rgveda* V11.18.16). The Kurus were settled at Indraprastha during the later vedic times. It seems that northern Gurgaon was under the Matsyas. The region formed part of the Mauryan empire and later the Kuru Kingdom of Yaudheya-ganas followed by Indo-Scythians, Kushanas and then the Guptas. A few centuries later it came under the rule of Yadu-Vamsi Rajputs, who ruled upto A.D. 1296. In the southern part they were succeeded by Nikumbhas and Khanzadas. It is believed that Chauhans ruled in Rewari. Raja Karampal, son of Chhatrapal, the nephew of Prithviraj founded Buddhi Rewari in the year A D. 1000. Sohna changed hands, from Bahadur Singh Ghasera to the Khanzadas. During the time of Akbar, Rewari and Suhar or Pahari were *Sarkars* whereas Bahora, Taoru, Rewari, Sohna, Lohna, Kohana and Hodal were *Dāsturs.* After the Mughals, Bilochs, Marathas Jats and the English ruled over the district.

The exploration of Sahibi-*nala* was undertaken with a view:

(a) to trace the migrational pattern of the late-Harappa culture along Sahibi

(b) to bring to light the cultural milieu of the late Harappans,

(c) and to trace the archaeological sequence of cultures of this area.

The exploration started from Kot-Qasim in south, covered a distance of 90 kms. along the river-bed traversing 10 km. on either sides of the river and terminated at Siwari in north.

A brief description of the antiquities and the villages where they were found is given below :

1. *Jatauli* :--It is located on the Pataudi-Haileymandi road across the railway line. The mound is situated one km. west of Jatuali village. It is 2 metres high with habitation. The pottery from the mound is late medieval.

2. *Jataula* :—It is about 3 km. towards north-east of Jatauli. To the east of the village is a 2 metre high mound in east-west orientation, one side of the mound is nearly 500 m. This is also a late medieval mound.

There is another mound, east-west in orientation to the west of the village, but of insignificant height. Some doorjambs and pillars of a buried medieval temple were found scattered on this mound of early historical period.

3. *Bhasonda* :—The village is situated around 3 kms to north of the village Jataula. It has a 5 metre high mound lying east-west. The habitational deposit as revealed from section is 4 m. The ceramics comprise of Red Ware contemporary to that of N.B.P. and Kushan red ware. The popular types are different varieties of vase. Coarse greyware was also found in small quantities.

4. *Mahchan-ka-Khera* :—It is 3 kms. from Machana on Machana-Farrukhabad road. The mound on the roadside is of insignificant (1 m.) height. It has yielded coarse greyware and obliquely cut Kushan bowls.

5. *Garhi Harsaru* :—It is situated 19 kms. north-east of Pataudi on Farrukhabad Road. The mound is partly occupied by the village and partly open. It has yielded typical 'Rang Mahal' and early Rajput pottery.

6. *Jori Sampka* :— It Is around 10 kms. from Pataudi on Gurgaon road. It is an imposing 10 m. high mound in north-south orientation, to the west of the village. The mound measures 300 m x 100 m. The ceramics recovered from the site

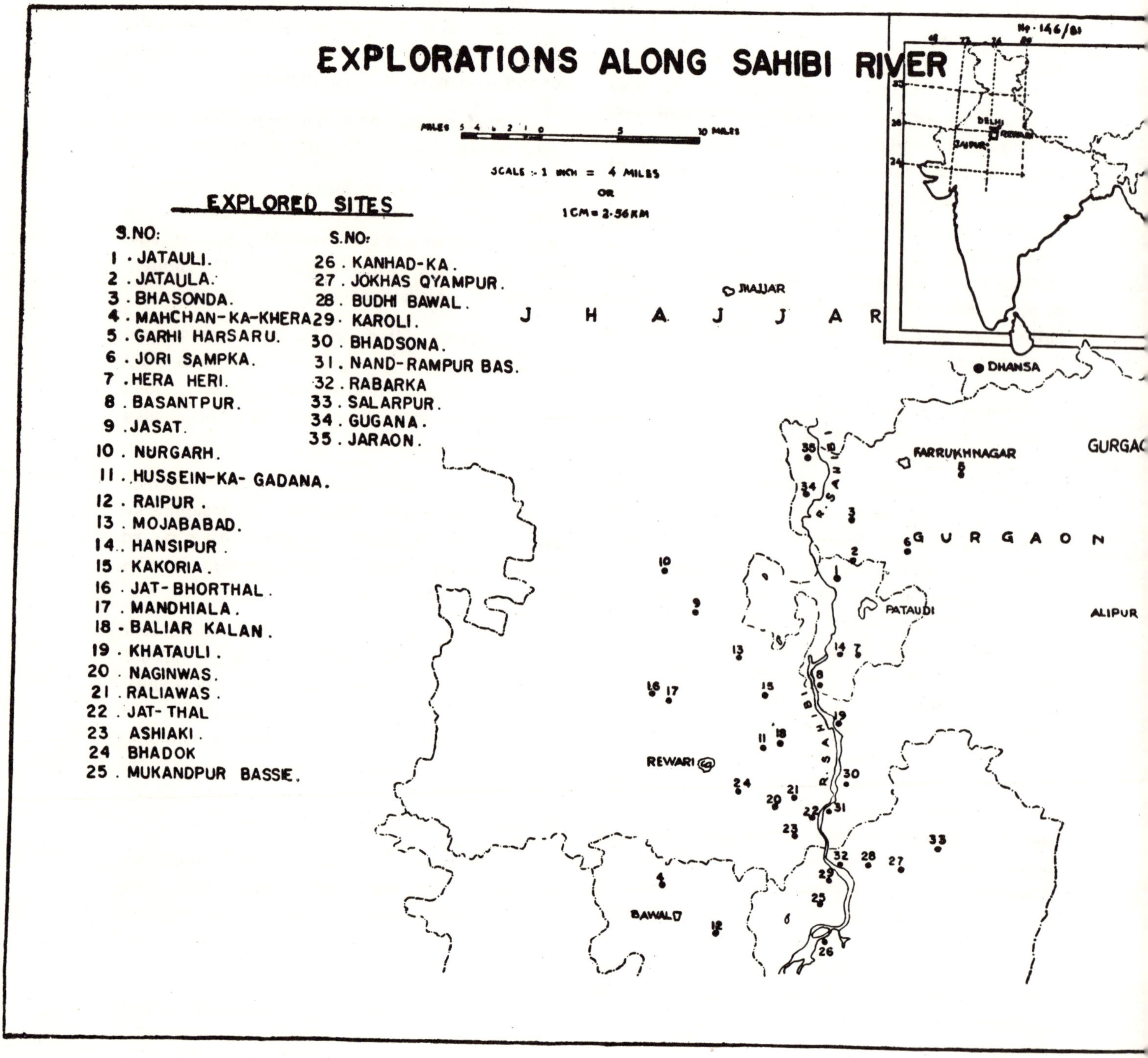

EXPLORATIONS ALONG SAHIBI RIVER
SCALE :- 1 INCH = 4 MILES
OR
1 CM = 2.56 KM
EXPLORED SITES
S.NO:
1 . JATAULI.
2 . JATAULA.
3 . BHASONDA.
4 . MAHCHAN-KA-KHERA
5 . GARHI HARSARU.
6 . JORI SAMPKA.
7 . HERA HERI.
8 . BASANTPUR.
9 . JASAT.
10 . NURGARH.
11 . HUSSEIN-KA- GADANA.
12 . RAIPUR .
13 . MOJABABAD.
14 . HANSIPUR .
15 . KAKORIA .
16 . JAT-BHORTHAL .
17 . MANDHIALA .
18 . BALIAR KALAN .
19 . KHATAULI .
20 . NAGINWAS .
21 . RALIAWAS .
22 . JAT-THAL
23 . ASHIAKI .
24 . BHADOK
25 . MUKANDPUR BASSIE.
S.NO:
26 . KANHAD-KA .
27 . JOKHAS QYAMPUR .
28 . BUDHI BAWAL .
29 . KAROLI .
30 . BHADSONA .
31 . NAND-RAMPUR BAS.
32 . RABARKA
33 . SALARPUR .
34 . GUGANA .
35 . JARAON .
JHAJJAR
J H A J J A R
DHANSA
FARRUKHNAGAR
GURGAON
G U R G A O N
PATAUDI
ALIPUR
REWARI
BAWAL
R. SAHIBI
DELHI
JAIPUR

are comparable to Rang Mahal pottery. The western portion of the mound is occupied by modern houses.

7. *Hera Heri* :—This is nearly 3 km. to the south of Hailey Mandi by road. The mound lies in east-west orientation and measures 100 m. × 50 m. The height of the mound is 5 m. The site has yielded eerly historical ceramics mainly red ware.

8. *Basantpur* : The village is located 11 km. from Pataudi. It has a high mound, measuring 100 m. × 50 m. in north-south orientation.

9. *Jasat* : It is located on Pataudi-Rewari road. The village is partly situated on the ancient mound. The western part of the mound, in east-west orientation, is open. The mound yielded fine red ware of medieval period.

10. *Nurgarh:* The village is situated on plain level land along the road leading to Pataudi in north-west. An ancient mound measuring 300m × 10 m. is located to the west of the village. This is exclusively a Rang Mahal culture site, having a deposit of atleast 6 m. or so. Locally the mound is known as Baloch-nagar. Rang Mahal ceramics are represented by red ware vases etc. Medieval pottery is represented by *handis* found in large numbers.

11. *Hussein-ka-Gadana*: It comprises two villages, Hussein-ka and Gandana. A road divides the two villages; Gandana has no mound but Hussein-ka has an early historical mound of insignificant height, in north-south direction.

12. *Raipur* : The village is 7 km. south of Hailey Mandi. The mound is located 2 km. east of the village. It is of level with ground. The pottery from the site is late medieval.

13. *Mojababad* : It is located on Pataudi-Rewari road. The mound measures 100 m. × 200 m. × 5 m. It is oval in shape and has yielded medieval pottery. The area is badly damaged.

To the north of the mound on rocky elevation, a three arched mosque having vaulted roof is built with *lakhauri* bricks in lime concrete mortar. It is a late medieval mosque.

14. *Hansipur* :—This mound known as Hansipur, measuring 200 m. x 100 m. x 4 m. is located in the jurisdiction of the village of Galawas Pottery recovered is distinctly medieval. Galawas falls in Pataudi tehsil.

15. *Kakoria* :—It is located 16 km. from Pataudi. The mound is located on Pataudi-Rewari road and measures 100 m. x 50 m. x 5 m The deposit of the mound is clearly medieval represented by *handis*, vases, lids etc.

16. *Jat-Bhorthal* :—The suburb of the village has an ancient mound, of oval shape measuring 100 m. x 100 m. x 5 m. The habitation deposit is around 3 m. Kushan pottery, comprising typical spouts, vases, *handis*, basins and lid with external knob, was recovered from the site.

17. *Mandhiala* :—The village lies about 10 km south of Pataudi. The mound in north-south orientation is located on the road side. The shape of the mound is rectangular, its sides being 100 m, x 50 m with a height of 4 m. The pottery consists of the kushan red ware, represented by vases with obliquely cut rims.

18. *Baliar Kalan* :—It is located 6 kms. from Rewari in the southern direction. The ancient mound is near Hansi Kalan and measures 100 m. x 50 m. The top of tbe mound has a grey and sandstone pilaster. The ceramics recovered from the site are of late medieval variety.

19. *Khatauli* :—The mound No. 1, which is located to the south of the village, has yielded pottery of late variety. Mound No. 2 lies to the south-east of the village on the river bed. It is a circular mound measuring 35 m. x 35m. having a deposit of 1. 80 cm. Pottery recovered from the site is Chalcolithic in character. It is a single culture mound.

20. *Naqinwas* :—The village is located on an elevated ancient mound besides which a dam is being built to control the water of the Sahibi river. The pottery recovered from the mound is of late Medieval period.

21. *Raliawas* :—The mound is 10 m. high from the surrounding plan and measures 100 m. x 100 m. The northern outskirts of the mound have village houses. The ceramics belong to the early centuries of the Christian era. A Siva temple of late medieval tradition with fluted arch entrances is built on the mound.

22. *Jat-Thal* :—The village is located on an ancient mound measuring 200 m. x 100 m. with a height af 10 m. In the east lies the newly-built dam on Sahibi. The pottery recovered from the site belongs to the early historical period.

23. *Ashiaki* :—A mound is located to the east of the village nearly one km. away from the Sahibi dam. This is an imposing mound with a height of nearly 10 m. The sides of the mound measures 200 m. × 100 m. The ceramics recovered is red ware of Rang Mahal type consisting of vases, basins, storage jars etc.

24. *Bhadok* :—The ancient habitation is of the late Medieval period. It is located on a high sand dune.

25. *Mukandpur Bassie* :—The ancient mound is located by the side of the Sahibi dam and measures 50 m. x 5 m. The pottery recovered is of Rang Mahal culture represented by vases of Red ware with top of rim painted in black bands.

26. *Kanhad-ka* :—The village, is located on an undulating landscape. It has a low circular mound of nearly 2 m. height with a diameter around 50 m. Pottery explored from the site is of Rang-Mahal culture. A few sherds resemble the proto-Historic ceramics of Katauli.

27. *Jokhas Qyampur* :—The ancient mound located along the river bank is about a km. to the south-west of the village. It is partly eroded by the river. In the present shape it measures 30 m. x 50 m, x 3m. The ceramics belong to the Medieval period.

28. *Budhi Bawal* :—Antiquarian remains comprise a *chhatri* supported on eight pillars and having a fluted dome. There is a *samadhi* of a Hindu Saint. Paintings were observed on the intrados of the dome and also on the spandrels of the arches. It dates possibly to the late Medieval times.

29. *Karoli* :—Huge twin mounds measuring 300 m. x 200 m. are located towards east of the village. A rain-gully divides the twin mounds. The maximum height is 15 m. The pottery is mostly of Rang Mahal type represented by painted vases, basins, storage jars, lids etc. Kushan red ware sherds of vases have also been found from the site.

30. *Bhadsona* :—It is located on Bhadsana-Halapur road. The mound 1. 5 m. high and measuring 20 m. x 20 m. is located one km. to the east of the village. Pottery is of late Medieval period.

31. *Nand Rampur Bas* :—The village has four mounds. Mound no. 4 is on the outskirts of the village. It has yielded pottery of late Medieval period. Mound no. 2 is located 1.5 km. to the west of the village and is known as Theurwala Khera. Its height is 5 m and area 100 m. x 100 m. The pottery yielded is mainly of the proto-historic period. The sherds of vases of Rang Mahal period were also picked up. Mound no. 3 is known as Raniwali Khera. It measure 30 m. x 15 m. If belongs to the late period. Tradition supports this conclusion. Mound no. 4 is Majrewala Khera. It has yielded pottery of early historical period.

32. *Rabarka* :—The village is located on plain level land. Nearly one km. to the north-west of the village lies the high ancient mound, 5 m. in height measuring 100 m x 100 m. Ceramics belong to the early centuries of the Christian era represented by red ware vases, storage jars, basins, etc

33. *Salarpur* :—Nearly 3 km to the east is an ancient mound measuring 30 m. x 30 m. x 4 m. Pottery types include vases with splayed-out rim, basins, bowls, lids etc. of Rang Mahal culture.

34. *Gugana* :—An ancient mound lies towards south-east of the village. It is mostly covered by houses and partly remains untouched. Its orientation is north-south and area 100 m. x 50 m. The site has ceramics of Rang Mahal culture with incised decorations and paintings on the neck of vessels. The main types are vases, jars etc. The other types are bowls, lids, vases etc.

35. *Jaraon* :— It is located on Hailey-mandi-Siwari road. The entire mound is occupied by the

village. It has yielded red ware, painted in black pigment resembling Rang Mahal pottery. Pottery types are *handis* lids, bowls and storage jars.

DISCUSSION

The term conclusion is deliberately eschewed, because, (a) some area on both sides of Sahibi is yet to be explored (b) and, the work done so far has raised a few more vital problems.

The archaeological sites that have yielded protohistoric ceramics are: Khataoli, Nandrampur Bas and Kanhadka. All these sites including Jodhpura (District Jaipur, Rajasthan) and Dhandsa (Delhi) explored by the Rajasthan Government and Kurukshetra University respectively are located on the eastern bank of the river bed. It appears that migrations took place along the eastern bank of the river in the proto-historic period when the river had shrunk in size and was flowing a little to the west.

During exploration from Kot-Qasim to Siwari Painted Grey Ware sites are conspicuous by their absence. The PGW sites are found along the western bank of the Yamuna, east of Aravalli range at Mathura. It appears that from Jodhpura people followed the small tributaries like Banganga and entered into Bharatpur, Dig, Kaman and proceeded northward along Yamuna. The Aravalli ranges which cut through the district provided cultural barrier between the east and the west.

The PGW people were accustomed to live in open lands along the banks of rivers. The land along Yamuna is sandy and fertile In contrast to the Bairat region it is marked by hilly tracts, comprising of bare and treeless mass. (Gupta, 1977). Hence from Jodhpura the PGW people adopted an eastward course.

After the early historical period, represented by the associated types of NBP and Kushan red ware, the area witnessed a spurt of population during the Gupta Period, represented by Rang Mahal pottery.

Quantitatively the Rang Mahal sites are profusely distributed a little away from the river beds. The mounds are as high as 10 m. and deposit is not less than 6 m. The area of the mounds is quite extensive : for example, Ashiaki and Nungarh mounds are 300 m. x 200 m. They could have accommodated a pre-industrial town. The sites are located at a distance of 10 kms. from each other. This proximity indicates a rise in population. The present exploration reveals that Rang Mahal culture was not a localised culture of Bikaner region but had extensions in north-east as also in the Kutch region and Gujarat in south.

References

Agarwala, R.C. 1981 "Fresh light on Ochre Coloured pottery from Rajasthan" *Madhu*, New Delhi, p. 77.

Gazetteer, Punjab 1908 Government : *Gurgaon District*, Vol. IV.A. *The Imperial Gazetteer of India*, 8 XII pp 401-412.

Ghosh A 1952 "The Rajputana desert : its archaeological aspect' *Proceedings of the Symposium on Rajputana desert, Bulletin of the National Institute of Sciences of India*, New Delhi-, 1 pp. 37-42.

Gupta, S.P. 1977 "Painted Grey Ware sites in relation to old river beds in Rajasthan" in *Ecology & Archaeology in Western India*, (Ed.) Agrawal, D.P. and Pande, B.M. (New Delhi) pp. 7a ff.

Jagatpati Joshi 1966 "Explorations in Northern Kutch, *Journal of Oriental Institute*, 16. pp. 62-69, Pl. 1-7, map. 1

"Explorations in Kutch and Excavations at Surkotada and New light on Harappan migration, 22 (1972) pp. 98-144.

Margabandhu, C. 1979 "Early Historic Rang Mahal culture, its origin and diffusion in north-west Rajasthan", *Vishveshvaranand Indological Journal*, XVII. pp 206-15.

Pal, S.K. 1978 "Sahibi *nadi* catchments and issue of flood hazards, *Man and Environment*, II.

Rydh, Hanna 1959 *Rang-Mahal*. (Lund) Sweden.

Neolithic of Western Sub-Himalaya

G. C. MOHAPATRA
Panjab University, Chandigarh

The western Sub-Himalayan zone is well known for its distinctive Palaeolithic Culture which goes by the name Soanian. Scores of sites yielding different industries of this culture in Jammu, Himachal Pradesh, Punjab and Haryana Sub-Himalaya attest to the occupation of this area by man continuously from Middle Pleistocene onward. Scattered over this submontane terrain are also the neolithic sites mostly located at those places, that were formerly palaeolithic stations. Therefore, artifacts of both Palaeolithic and Neolithic types occur together on the surface at every such place.

Dehragopipur in the valley of the Beas in Kangra provided the first evidence for the presence of a Neolithic Culture in this region. A stray polished stone celt was picked up from a ploughed field adjecent to the trenches which were being excavated by the author for ascertaining the stratified context of the Early Soanian artifacts found abundantly on the surface of all the three terraces in the neighbourhood (Sahni and Mohapatra, 1964, Mohapatra, 1966). Although more than a hundred Early Soan tools were recovered from the trenches, no other veidence of the Neolithic was found; neither in the stratified deposits recorded during the excavation nor from anywhere else on the surface of the terraces.

Based on this observation, the 'presence of both the palaeolithic and the neolithic artifacts at one and the same place should appear as a matter of mere superficial superposition. But critically looking into the problem of the absence of a Mesolithic Culture in western Sub-Himalaya, nay in the whole of N.W. India, the matter of locational convergence of the two cultures cannot be dismissed as just coincidence.

Notwithstanding the handicap of lack of details, at least two simple deductions can be made out from this. One is the departure from the conventional lithic cultural chronology in the western Sub-Himalaya and the other, more or less linked to the first, is the continuation of a type of specialized hominid habitat pattern in this submontane terrain ecology despite the initiation of a techno-economic change. Some discussions about these two points will be made in the sequel.

However, out of the four palaeolithic industries in the western Sub-Himalaya i.e. the Acheulian, the Early, Late and Final Soan, with which the neolithic celts occur, the Final Soan belonging to the end of the Pleistocene is chronologically the latest. At present although some circumstantial evidence like the absence of the mesolithic, leads to the conclusion that the neolithic succeeded the late Pleistocene industry of Final Soan, there is no direct means to ascertain whether this happened as a continuous evolutionary process or there was a time culture gap in between.

The sites

Fifteen sites yielding polished stone celts ring-stones and grinding stones have been reported so far which are located in the Jammu Sub-Himalaya (Mohapatra and Saroj, 1968-69; Saroj, 1974; Mohapatra' mss, 1981), in Kangra valley (Sahni and Mohapatra, 1964; Mohapatra, 19 6) and in the Nalagarh-Pinjore *dun* in Himachal Pradesh (Mohapatra, 1974; Mohapatra and Singh, 1979), in the Hoshiarpur Siwalik Range in the Punjab (Mohapatra and Singh, 1978; Mohapatra, 1981), and on the outer slopes of the Siwalik Frontal Range near Chandigarh (Mohapatra, 1979).

In Jammu the sites are Gudapatan on the Chenab River in Akhnur district, Kurro and Mah on the Ravi River, Dyalachak on the Tarnah and Kuta on the Ben streams all in Kathua district. In the Kangra valley Baroli and Dehra on the Beas River and Ror on the Banganga stream, and in the Nalagarh-Pinjore *dun*, Basawal, Marhanwala, Baddi, Dhang Nihli and Palasi are the other neolithic find-spots. In the Hoshiarpur Siwalik Range, Aitbarapur, recently coming into prominence for its rich yield of Acheulian artifacts, provides only one celt. On the slopes of the Siwalik Frontal Range near Chandigarh, Karor Uparla is the onlv site so far.

The artifacts

None of the sites have been excavated, therefore, their complete artifactual repertory is yet unknown. However, at two sites, Ror in Kangra valley and Dhang Nihli in the Nalagarh-Pinjore *dun* which are by far the two most potential sites, some occurrence of pottery, animal bones etc., is noticed. But due to their intensely weathered and fragile nature it is difficult to distinguish them from those of the later cultures without stratified evidence. Specially at the site of Dhang Nihli where the ruins of Harappan and early historic cultures are also found on the surface, the problem is acute.

The lithic artifact assemblage consist of six main types. These are axe, chisel, pick, axe-hammer, ring-stone and grinder-muller.

Axe: Triangular form, rounded butt (occasionally approaching a blunt-point), elliptical to lenticular longitudinal section, bifacially polished sharp edge are the most salient characteristics of the axes. In length they vary between 9 to 21 cm. The most common is the size between 10 and 13 cm. the width at the edge which is usually the broadest part of the axe, ranges between 4.5 to 8.5 cm; the most common being those between 5 and 6 cm. The polished adge is straight median and in outline it is convex. Besides these generalised characters, there are certain minor departures seen on some specimens like flaring and oblique edge, convex sides, slender-longish or squat-thick body etc.

Chisel: These have parallel sides due to which the width at the butt is same as at the edge; the body outline thus becomes rectangular. Most of them have plano-convex cross-section with incipiently bevelled edge. The largest intact specimen measures 12.5 cm long and 5.4 cm broad.

Pick: These are characterised by long slender sturdy body, straight slopping sides and semicircular exquisitely polished and sharpened median edge. The butt is narrow but symmetrically rounded. The edge is approximately three times of the butt in breadth. The ratio of body length to breadth is 2.5 : 1. Polishing is mostly confined to the edge. The rest of the body shows rough grinding. Cross-section at the edge is thin biconvex at the middle and at the butt, oval.

Axe-hammer: As the name implies, these artifacts probably served dual functions. Necessarily therefore, they have to have squat heavy body which the specimens do. In addition, they show highly battered and blunted butt and edge, perhaps because of their use for rough purpose. These are only ground and never polished. The cross section is elliptical at the broader end and almost circular at the narrower end or the butt. The squat body is in the ratio of 2 : 1 to the breath. Its longitudinal section is elongated oval or elliptical. The heaviest specimen weighs nearly 1,700 grams.

Ring-stone: These artifacts variously interpreted as net - sinkers, mace – heads, digging - stick weights etc. are comparatively smaller and thinner than their counterparts in Kashmir or peninsular India. The largest has a diameter of 9 cm. with a bore of 3 cm wide which slopes to an actual hourglass perforation of 15 cm only. It weighs 500 grams. While all the specimens are only ground some of them have thin sharp edges and are very light (less than 250 grams) and are without polish.

Grinder-muller: Not being typical Neolithic types these are very much indistinguishable from those occurring in Chalcolithic and other later contexts. No quern or whetstone has been found from any site. The only indication that they may be Neolithic is their association with the celts at the same site. The average length of these is about 26 cm. The circular cross-section on average is of 9 cm. diameter.

The raw material used for these artifacts was either hard grey shale or the trap depending on what is available in the neighbourhood.

IN RETROSPECT

Prior to the discovery of the western Sub-Himalayan Neolithic Culture, sometimes also designated as the 'Siwalik Neolithic Culture' (Mohapatra, 1977), the protohistoric early peasant village culture of hill-flanks and plains of the Greater Punjab (Indo-Pak) was considered as the earliest representative of a food-producing culture in North western India. Thus on economic consideration alone, which incidentally fitted very well to a pattern of cultural chronology at that time, these incipient food-producing settlements could pass on as neolithic (Krishnaswami, 1960). But by the discovery of the neolithic and that too so widely spread in the Sub-Himalayan region, a reassessment of the position of these early peasant settlements has become necessary.

ASSESSMENT OF PRESENT DATA

As noticed above, data available regarding archaeological attributes of the western Sub-Himalayan Neolithic are very scanty. Therefore, conclusions arrived at solely by means of these attributes are bound to be deficient in many respects. However, if the archaeological attributes are interpolated with those related to the present geographical location and ecological condition of the sites, significant conclusion as regards the habitat-a very important aspect of the study of early food-producing cultures–are likely to emerge.

In a study undertaken on these lines it is essential at the first instance to identify those factors that have direct bearing on the basic morphological and ecological elements of the terrain over which each site is located at the present, Recording of these elements individually at each site and observing their frequency of recurrence in one or more combination will help in determining the dominant traits. These on the other hand could be tested against the varying density of site clusters for the purpose of concluding the optimum conditions that might have been sought after in the Sub-Himalaya by the authors of this culture.

Some results obtained from a preliminary analysis on these lines are as follows :

1. All the sites occur in the well defined geo-environmental zone i.e. the Sub-Himalayan low hilly terrain,
2. Seven out of fifteen sites are located at a height of 300 to 350, two between 350 and 400. another two between 400 and 450, and three between 450 and 500 metres from the mean sea level. Therefore, as a single largest group 300 to 350 metres height might indicate certain locational advantage or preference.
3. As regards terrain type, thirteen sites are located on loamy/loessic terraces within the submontane valleys (*duns*) and on the outer alluvial slopes of the Siwalik Frontal Range at or near their outlets to the plains. Only one site is located on a mountainous slope which is at a height of 450 to 500 metres and another at the same height but on a water-divide within a submontane valley.
4. Five sites which are minor in nature yielding one of two celts only are located close to the channels of the main Himalayan rivers like the Ravi, the Chenab and the Beas. Six sites that can be considered important from many angles occur on wide open terraces of medium size perennial (fordable in summer) tributary streams. Remaining four sites are associated with seasonal ephemeral streams or runnels (choes) mostly within the Siwalik Range or on its outer slope.

Therefore, it is clear that there was a preference for the terraces in the valleys of small tributary streams like the Tarnah, the Ben, the Sirsa, the Chikni, the Banganga and some of the major Siwalik chos. In this context it may be interesting to note that valleys of the major antecedent Himalayan rivers held no great attraction for this culture. Thus a line can probably be drawn between the habitats during the experimental manipulation of the biotope as was probably the case with the Neolithic, and those at the time of effective production of the peasant village stage.

5. The precipitation chart shows that all the sites are situated within the 1,500 fo 1,000 mm. rainfall zone,
6. In twelve cases the vegetation around the site can be classified as mixed-deciduous and only in three cases it is sub-tropical dry thorny scrub. For the latter type the sites are either situated at comparatively higher levels of a water-divide or on the desiccated outer slope of the Siwalik hills.
7. The mean annual temperature at present at seven of the sites is between 60.0° F and 69.2° F with a range of 28.5°F, of another seven it is 67.6° F with a range of 27.1° F, and of the rest one site it is 68.5° F with a range of 28.0° F.

Gleaning from the precipitation, vegetation and temperature data all the sites come under the *Cawg* climatic type (Koeppan). Notwithstanding occasional minor oscillations there is no evidence of a drastic departure from the present type of environmental condition during the past five or six thousand years in the western Sub-Himalaya.

Thus in summary and substance the Neolithic Culture in the western Sub-Himalaya appears to have preferred the alluvial terraces on the banks of medium size perennial streams within small submontane valleys located at heights between 300 to 350 metres from the mean sea level. These place at present have mixed-deciduous type of vegetation in a over all *Cawg* type (Koeppen) of climate.

In the light of this the locations of the early peasant village settlements of the protohistoric period project a radically different type of habitat. The technical attributes of the Neolithic artifacts being so obviously different from those of these early village cultures further leave little doubt that to cope with a different type of biotype different method or technique of subsistence had to be adopted. In the context of early food production in the subcontinent this ecological and technological difference between the two has far greater implication than their superficial economic similarity.

For ascertaining the age of the western Sub-Himalayan Neolithic Culture is no direct means at present. If the matter of locational convergence of both palaeolithic and neolithic is given careful consideration in the light of the absence of a Neolithic Culture in this region, some guess about the probable chrono-cultural position of the neolithic can be made. It is a certainty that the Neolithic in the western Sub-Himalaya has no mesolithic precedence. Hence it is likely to have succeeded the palaeolithic directly. The sites and the ecology being the same, it appears that the area continued to provide natural attractions for both the cultures. As there are some faint indications available for the continuance of final Soan Culture beyond the limits of Pleistocene (Mohapatra, 1979), it is likely that the food-gathering stage of man represented by this culture was replaced by an incipient food producing one i.e. the present Neolithic without much time gap. This appears as a reasonable hypothesis in view of the rapid desiccation of almost the whole of north-western India immediately after the Pleistocene which must have hastened food-production without going or having an opportunity to go through a transitional stage like the mesolithic hunting. The ideal environment provided by the secluded valleys at the mountain flanks had reasonable scope to nurture such a change quite early in Holocene.

Reference :

Krishnaswami, V.D. 1960. The Neolithic pattern of India. *Ancient India* 16, pp. ; 25-65.

Mohapatra, G.C. 1966. Preliminary report of the exploration and excavation of Stone Age sites in Eastern Punjab. *Bulletin of Deccan College Research Institute* 25 : 221-37.

Mohapatra, G.C. 1974. Lithic industries of Himachal Pradesh, in *Perspectives in Palaeoanth-*

ropology. Edited by A.K. Ghosh, pp. 199-212. Calcutta : K.L. Mukhopabhyay.

Mohapatra, G.C. 1977. The Siwalik Neolithic Culture," in the *Dictionary of Indian Archaeology*. Edited by A. Ghosh. New Delhi : Indian Council of Historical Research (in press).

Mohapatra, G.C. 1979. Pattern of cultural growth in prehistoric north-west India", in *Early Man in North-West India*. Edited by S.R.K. Chopra pp. 107-33. New Delhi : Allied Publishers.

Mohapatra, G.C. 1981. Acheulian discoveries in Siwalik Frontal Range, Punjab, India. *Current Anthropology* 22 (5).

Mohapatra, G.C. (*mss*). 1981. Environment and culture of Early Man in the valley of the rivers Chenab and Ravi, Western Sub-Himalaya. *Xth Congress of the International Union of Prehistoric and Protohistoric Science's Commission on Environment and culture of Fossil Man in Asia*. 10-25 October 1981. Mexico City.

Mohapatra, G.C. and H.M. Saroj. 1968-69. Discovery of lithic artifacts in Jammu Area. *Puratattva* 2 ; pp. 11-12.

Mohapatra, G.C. and Mukesh Singh. 1978. Stratified occurrence of lithic artifacts in the Siwalik Frontal Range of western Sub-Himalaya. *Panjab University Research Bulletin (Arts)* IX (3-4).

Mohapatra, G.C. and Mukesh Singh, 1979. Prehistoric investigations in a Sub-Himalaya valley, Himachal Pradssh, India. *Current Anthropology* 20 (3) ; pp. 600-02.

Sanhi, M.R. and G.C. Mohapatra. 1964. The first record of small flake-tools and polished stone celts in Kangra district, E. Punjab. *Current Science* 33 ; pp. 178-80.

Saroj, H.M. 1974. *Lithic industries of Jammu*. Doctor of Philosophy dissertation. Chandigarh : Punjab University Library.

An Archaeological Reconnaissance in Birbhum

DILIP K. CHAKRABARTI, A. K. NAG AND SUBRATA CHAKRABARTI
Department of Ancient Indian History, Culture and Archaeology,
Visvabharati University

This paper summarizes the results of a brief archaeological exploration in Birbhum in January, 1981 under the leadership of the first author. The purpose of this reconnaissance was to assess the over-all archaeological potential of the district.

Lying between 23°32′30″N-24°35′N and 88°1′40″—87°5′25″E the modern district of Birbhum comprises about 4550.94 sq. km. and is bordered by the districts of Santal Parganahs (on the north and west), Burdwan (on the south) and Murshidabad (on the east). Geologically this shows a succession of Archaeans (followed by an unconformity), Lower Gondowanas, Upper Gondowanas, Rajmahal traps, Tertiary rocks, Old and New alluvium. Geographically the main interest of this district lies in the fact that it is one of the Bengal districts which are a continuation of the Chotanagpur plateau, gradually merging into the Gangetic alluvium. The general gradient is from the west to the east, with local variations. From the south to the north, the major rivers are the Ajay, Kopai (known as *Sal* in the upper reaches), Bakreshwar, Mayurakshi, Dwaraka. Brahmani and Bansloi. There is also a large number of minor rivers and *nullahs* (locally called *kandars*). Generally the rivers flow in mere trickles in summer but carry a lot of water during the rains, often resulting in floods. Before the introduction of modern irrigation canals irrigation depended on the rains, rivers and tanks. Tanks, in fact, constitute a major source of irrigation in Birbhum. According to the local information a tank of standard size can irrigate about 20 acres of land. The local people tend to classify land available for cultivation into the following types: *entel* (a sticky, brownish clay, suitable only for rice, if manured), *metel* (a clay soil suitable for the *aman* or autumnal rice, sugarcane, wheat and a few pulses), *bagha entel* (heavy, reddish soil,) suitable only for rice, if manured), *palimati* (alluvial deposition, suitable for a wide variety of crops), *bindi* (a sandy soil), *doansh* (mixture of clay and sand, suitable for a wide variety of crops), *kankar* (a reddish, loose, lateritic soil with ferruginous concretions), *bele* (a whitish, loose, friable soil) and *bastu* (a rich blackish soil, suitable for a wide variety of crops). Rice is the most important crop of the district. The average annual rainfall is 1100 — 1600 mm, most of it in June-September. The temperature ranges between 45/46° (the maximum point in summer) and 6/7° (the maximum point in winter).

Birbhum has had a tradition of local antiquarian investigation, the results of which have been discussed (in Bengali) by Mahima Niranjan Chakrabarti (1323 B.S./1916 A.D.; 1326 B.S./1919 A.D.; 1334 B.S./1927 A.D.), Gourihar Mitra (1343 B.S./1936 A.D.; 1345 B.S./1938 A.D.) and Deb Kumar Chakrabarti (1379 B.S./1972 A.D.). The recent investigations have been dealt with by Deb Kumar Chakrabarti (1972) and Durgadas Majumdar (1975). All references to recent reports in the present paper are based on these two publications.

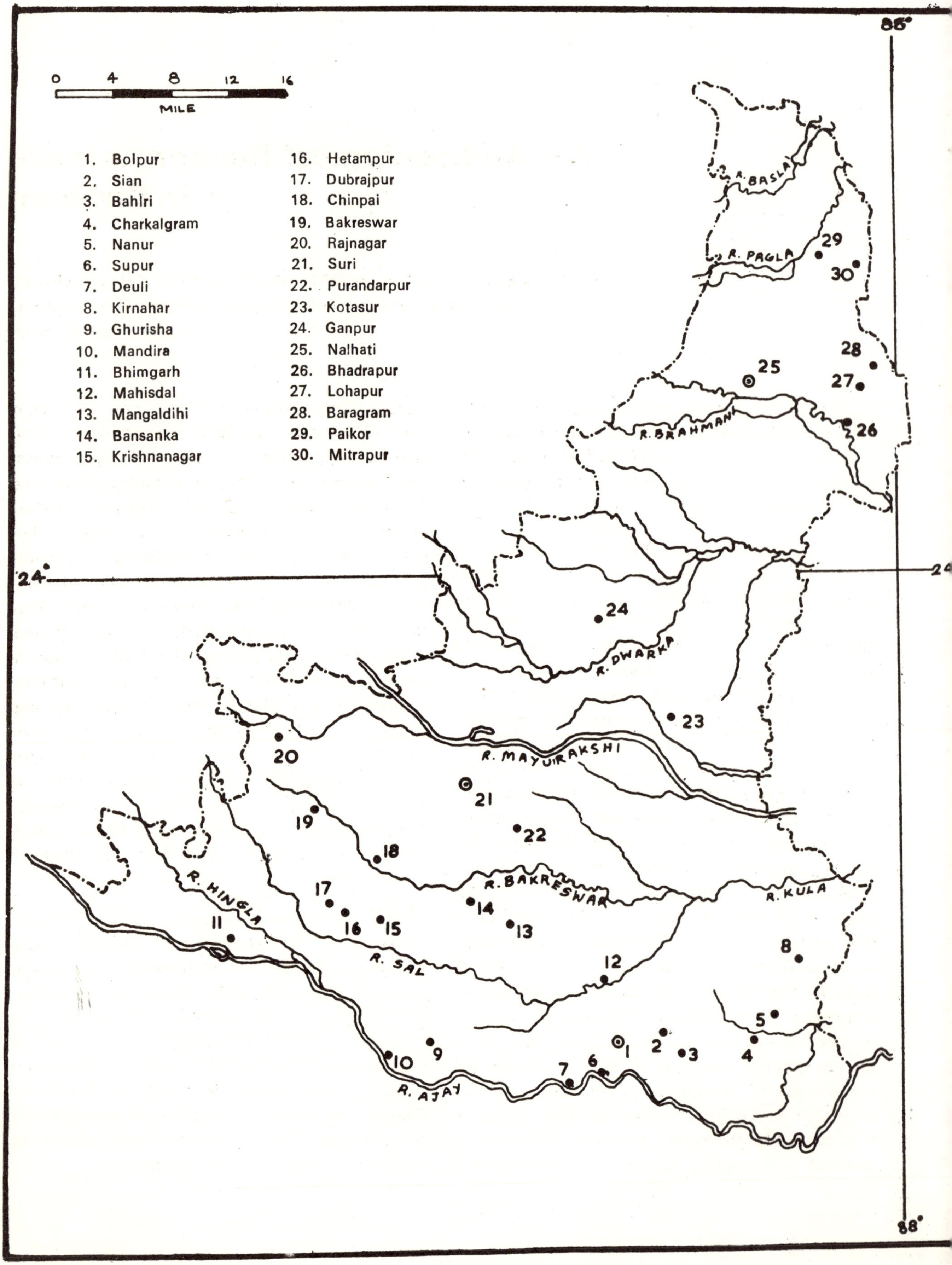
0 4 8 12 16
MILE
1. Bolpur
2. Sian
3. Bahiri
4. Charkalgram
5. Nanur
6. Supur
7. Deuli
8. Kirnahar
9. Ghurisha
10. Mandira
11. Bhimgarh
12. Mahisdal
13. Mangaldihi
14. Bansanka
15. Krishnanagar
16. Hetampur
17. Dubrajpur
18. Chinpai
19. Bakreswar
20. Rajnagar
21. Suri
22. Purandarpur
23. Kotasur
24. Ganpur
25. Nalhati
26. Bhadrapur
27. Lohapur
28. Baragram
29. Paikor
30. Mitrapur
R. BASLA
R. PAGLA
R. BRAHMANI
R. DWARKA
R. MAYURAKSHI
R. BAKRESWAR
R. KULA
R. HINGLA
R. SAL
R. AJAY
24°
88°

SKETCH PLAN
OF
KOTASUR
SCALE 0 25 50 METRES
FORTIFICATION WALL
FORTIFICATION WALL
FORTIFICATION WALL
FORTIFICATION WALL
TO SAINTHIA HIGHWAY
POND
POND
POND
MODERN STRUCTURES
N

The Sites

1. **Bahiri** : the place is about 7 km east of Bolpur on the Bolpur-Palitpur road. There are three mounds in the village of Bahiri. One of them roughly measures 90 m (north-south) and 70 m (east-west). The circumference is roughly 250 m and the height is about 3 m trom the surrounding plain level. The surface does not yield any identifiable pottery type but the general impression is that the mound is of the Gupta-post-Gupta periods. The local primary school is located on the top of this mound. The second mound is on the other side of the Bolpur-Palitpur road and close to the modernl irrigation office. This is a low mound, hardly a metre above the plain level, but is quite extensive, roughly 300 m in circumference. Late historical pottery is strewn on the surface but one can also pick up occasional black-and-red ware pieces. This mound is comparatively undistrubed. The third mound at Bahiri is locally known as *Chandra Hazrar Danga* ('the mound of Chandra Hazra"). This roughly measures 80 m (north-south) and 70 m (east-west). The circumference is roughly 250 m and the height about 2 m. There is a large tank to the southwest of the mound and there is a smaller tank to its south. On close investigations it is found that this smaller tank, in fact, has been cut into an old occupational area and the earth has been dumped on the surface of *Chandra Hazrar Danga*. The central section of *Chandra Hazrar Danga* yields a considerable amount of black-and-red pottery all of which is actually from the earth dumped from the pond. The northern section has been considerably cut into and does not yield any black-and-red sherd.

   The Ajay flows about 6 km to the south of Bahiri. It may be added that the *Chandra Hazrar Danga* section of Bahiri and the contiguous pond area have been probed by the first author (D.K.C.) and S. Jamal Hasan on behalf of the Archaeology and Museum Unit of the Department of History, Delhi University, in March, 1981. The report will be published in due course.

2. **Beluti**: the place is about 15 km to the northeast of Bolpur on the Bolpur-Nanur road. The mound is in the compound of local high school which lies immediately to the north of Bolpur-Nanur road. From a discussion with the teachers of the local school it appears that the original height cf the mound could well be about 6 m. The present heig'h is hardly 1 m from the level of the school compound. The mound is basically destroyed, but on the existing surface the alignment of a number of burnt brick walls is clearly visible. These exposed walls, are primarily rubble walls, comprising bricks dug up from the earlier levels. The general impression is that of a monastic building. The total exposed area measures roughly 27m (north-south) and 31 m (east-west). The standard brick-size is 34by 24 cm. The general impression is that of the Gupta bricks. In this connection it may be noted that the place has an association with the Gupta period in the local legend. The association is with the goddess Saraswati and the poet Kalidasa. The local school is, in fact, called "Kalidasa Memorial School". On the other side of the road there is a modern temple of Saraswati on the top of a low and small mound with an adjacent small pond which is called *Saraswati Kunda*. A fair is held at this spot on the *Saraswati Puja* day every year (in the month of January-February). The Saraswati image inside the modern temple is supposed to be an old one but it is in fragments and covered with a piece of cloth. Because of the absence of the local priest this could not be inspected. The Ajay now flows about 8 km to the south of this place.

3. **Nanur:** about 20 km northeast of Bolpur on the Bolpur-Kirnahar road the mound at Nanur within the village of Nanur is about 8m

high and measures 100 m (north-south) by 50 m (east-west). This measurement is valid only for the preserved southern section of the mound. The northern portion is considerably levelled and has a number of 18th-19th century terracotta temples (14 Siva temples in all, including the main *Bansuli* temple which has a small and exquisite Saraswati image in the Pala style). The mound was excavated by K. G. Goswami on behalf of the Ashutosh Museum, Calcutta Uuiversity (*Calcutta Review*, March, 1950). Black-and-red sherds have been recently reported but the present exploration could not find any such sherd on the surface. There are fragmentary sculptures in the Pala-Sena style on the top of the mound.

4. **Charkalgram** : a few km to the southeast of Nanur, Charkalgram has been reported to have yielded black-and-red sherds. The present exploration failed to corroborate this report, despite careful search.

5. **Suratheswar Siva temple mound** : this is a fair-sized mound at the spot where the road to the village of Supur branches off from the Bolpur-Ilambazar road. This contains the Suratheswar Siva temple on the top. The temple is of the recent period but a lintel and a broken piece of sculpture in the 11th-12th century regional style have been reported from this place. Some pieces of iron slag and apparently historical pottery lie scattered on the surface. Black-and-red ware has been reported from this mound but the present exploration could not corroborate this report.

6. **Suratheswar mound at Supur** : this mound, again a fair-sized one, is located in the village of Supur and yields apparently historical pottery on the surface. No sherd could be related to the early historical period. This mound is about 2 m high from the plain level. ' Suratha" of the Supur area has bean related to the king Suratha of the *Devimahatmya* section of the *Markandeya-purana*. It may be mentioned that this site has yielded black-and red ware, although the present exploration did not find any such sherd on the surface. However, its occurrence has been vouchsafed by Mrs Madhusree Nag who claims to have handled the material.

7. **Kankutia** : a village beyond Supur, south of the Bolpur-Ilambazar road, this has a large dissected mound in its outskirt. The impression is that this is unlikely to be earlier than the 11th-12th century.

8. **Deuli** : further south of Kankutia, this is on the bank of the Ajay and protected from it by an embankment. A chalcolithic site with black-and-red ware is reported to have existed here but the Ajay floods and the construction of the embankment have completely ruined the site. Not a single piece of black-and-red sherd could be collected during the present exploration. The place has also an association with the mediaeval Vaishnava poet Lochandas who is said to have been buried at the spot. One notices a stone lintel on the top of his burial. There are also a few sculptural pieces the most remarkable of which is a large (182 cm long and 84 cm broad) *Mahisamardini* figure of black stone in the 10th-12th century style.

9. **Mandira** : this is a deserted village on the bank of the Ajay near Jayadev-Kenduli. A chalcolithic site is said to have existed here but the site has now been destroyed by the Ajay floods.

10. **Ghurisa** : a village on the Ilambazar-Dubrajpur road, this is more famous for its terracotta temples but one also notices a few fragmentary pieces of mediaeval sculpture including a Jain *tirthankara* figure. A few well-cut blocks of laterite suggest the existence of an earlier temple made of lateritic blocks.

11. **Hetampur, Garh Danga** : in the outskirt of the modern town of Hetampur, Garh Danga shows primary laterite right on the

surface. Microlithic flakes and chips in a cherty material could be collected from the surface in a very limited quantity. There is also clear evidence of iron-smelting at the spot.

12. **Jashpur-Pochera-Krishnanagar** : the whole area, roughly to the east of Hetampur, has a spread of primary laterite and shows huge deposits containing remains of pre-industrial iron-smelting. Nothing else was found in this area, despite an earlier report of the occurrence of microliths.

13. **Chinpai** : this village on the Dubrajpur-Suri road is reported to have yielded microliths but the present exploration found none.

14. **Jibdharpur** : Early and Middle Palaeolithic tools and microliths have been reported from this area on the Dubrajpur-Suri road (a few km souheast of Suri) but the present exploration, despite careful search, failed to locate any evidence of this kind except microlithic chips and flakes in a very limited quantity. The sequence here shows primary laterite below surface humus. There is also no locally available raw material. There is a small river called *Chandrabhaga* in this area. Exploration along its banks as well as along the banks of a small *nullah* proved futile.

15. **Mahammadpur-Ganpur-Deucha** (on the Suri-Rampurhat road) : the whole area shows extensive lateritic spread and remains of pre-industrial iron-smelting in the form of ashy deposits, slag and outlines of furnaces. The pre-industrial blacksmiths were called *Saluis* (derived from *Sal* i.e., furnaces) a large number of whom are now settled at Deucha.

16. **Bergram** : (on the Bolpur-Suri road) : there is an unpublished report of black-and red ware from this area but the present search did not reveal any black-and-red ware or any other evidence of ancient occupation in this area.

17. **Mangaldihi** (on the Parui-Batikar road, branching off from the Bolpur-Suri road) : there is a spread of black-and-red ware and other types of pottery over about an acre of ploughed-up land to the west of this village. The site has been destroyed. The local people report the find of many pieces of antler from this spot.

18. **Batikar** : a polished stone celt was collected from the sacred ground of a local deity called *Dharmathakur* and a fragment of a pointed butt axe was observed at a different spot in the vicinity. The local report indicated the existence of 20 such celts in this area but all of them except these two have been stolen,

19. **Banshanka** : the village of Alipur near Banshanka, a little to the northwest of Mangaldihi, revealed a small mound on the bank of the Bakreshwar river. There was no identifiable pottery type but the mound apparently belongs to the historical period.

20. **Potanda** (off the Purandarpur-Sainthia road) : there is a report of black-and-red pottery, microlithic flakes and 4 polished stone celts from this place. The present investigation revealed that the celts were collected from the place of a village deity and that there was a small mound within the village, which has subsequently been destroyed. There was no evidence of black-and-red ware and microlithic flakes.

21. **Purandarpur** (on the Bolpur-Suri road via Parui) : the area shows a primary lateritic spread on the surface of which it is possible to pick up microlithic chips and flakes in a limited quantity. A large part of this area has been destroyed by the construction of a factory.

22. **Bhimgarh** (to the southwest of Dubrajpur, on the bank of the Ajay): in the local Bhimeswar Siva temple there are 5 Neolithic celts around the *lingam*. There is an earlier report of 8 such celts. The celts are described below :

(a) length 19 cm : breadth 10.5 cm. : thickness 5 cm; slightly rectangular and rounded butt end, oval in mid-section, broad cutting edge; (b) 12:2.5:4 cm ; pointed butt; (c) 3.5 : 2.5 : 1 cm, butt end slightly rectangular and round, lenticular in mid-section, broad cutting edge; (d) 9:5:1 cm, pointed butt. (e) 11.5 : 5.5 : 1 cm, pointed butt. The celts are all of basaltic material.

23. **Kotasur** (a few km northeast of Sainthia) : the most impressive feature of this site is a mud fortification wall which is about 1 km in circuit. The modern village of Kotasur largely overlies the ancient site but the outline of the fortification is clearly visible. This is near the Mayurakshi and it is said that the Mayurakshi floods have done considerable damage to the site. On the southern and northern sides there are apparently two openings in the rampart, both properly oriented to the true north and south with 10° variation in both cases. At a somewhat undamaged section in the southern side the fortification wall is about 10 m wide. To the east of the site there is a low-lying canal-like ground which may well be the part of an original surrounding moat. The central part of the site is dominated by a Siva temple (locally known as *Madaneshwar Siva Temple*) which is located on the top of a 6 m high mound. There are two pieces of mediaeval sculpture (Surya and Vishnu) near the temple. In the exposed tank sections early historical pottery occurs in abundance. It was also possible to collect a polished stone celt. Black-and-red ware has been reported from the site but the present exploration was unable to corroborate the evidence.

24. **Lalateswari hill, Nalhati**: this large lateritic hill behind the Lalateshweri temple (a *pitha* where the elbow of *Sati* is supposed to have fallen) is said to have yielded early and middle Palaeolithic tools and microliths but a careful search failed to reveal such evidence. However, a few microlithic flakes and chips in a cherty material could be picked up from the surface.

25. **Bhadrapur** (east of Nalhati, on the Nalhati-Raghunathganj road) : there is a large historical mound, possibly not earlier than the 10th-12th century A.D., in the *Shasthitala* area of the village. The mound has been cut into a number of places and the exposed sections are full of potsherds. An exposed road section is about 9 m high. There is a similar mound in the neighbouring village of Simlandi.

26. **Baragram** (in the same area) : there are three major clusters of fragmentary pieces of sculpture in the village : *Pirtala*, *Burapirtala* and local *Durgapuja* temple. All these pieces belong to the 10th-12th century style and all except one are in black basaltic stone. The exception is a female figure in sandstone. It is easy to see extensive occupation deposits, perhaps not earlier than the 10th-12th century A.D., in the village. An interesting feature of Bara is the occurrence of a number of decorated black stone lintels, possibly belonging to a mosque. According to the Arabic inscriptions on these slabs a mosque was built at this place in 1460 A.D. The images from Bara are well-known in West Bengal and have been mentioned in a number of publications.

27. **Birnagar** (west of Rajgram, north of Nalhati) : the area as a whole enjoys the local reputation of containing old remains but the present exploration failed to locate any such evidence except extensive remains of pre-industrial iron-smelting.

28. **Paikor** (east of Murarai, north of Nalhati) : two places in the village, *Narayan Chattar* and *Burasivtala*, contain a number of mediaeval sculptures. The most important object on the bank of the tank called *Narayan Chattar* is an inscribed pillar containing the name of the Chedi king Karnadeva of the 11th century A.D. The inscription refers

to the installation of the stone image of a female deity. An image at this spot shows *Narasimha* killing an *asura* and perhaps belongs to the 12th century A.D. The images at *Burasivtala* contain a few Vishnu figures and a figure of Surya, among other things. One also notices extensive occupation deposits (perhaps not earlier than the 10th-12th century A.D.) at Paikor.

29. **Tarapith** (east of Rampurhat): archaeologically this famous pilgrim centre of West Bengal is unimportant except that two extremely fine Vishnu images of the 10th-12th century A.D. are kept in an adjunct of the main temple.

30. **Bakreshwar** a little away from the pilgrim centre of Bakreshwar, on the bank of the Bakreshwar river, one notices extensive deposits of pottery of unidentifiable varieties. An unpublished report mentions black-and-red ware at this place, which, however, the present work failed to corroborate.

31. **Sian** : a large village on the Bolpur-Nanur road, Sian is noted for its Pala inscription (inscribed in two black basaltic slabs which are set in the walls of a local *maqbara* (*Pir Baba Maqdum Sahib*) but there is also evidence of mediaeval occupation, although not of black-and-red ware, as reported.

32. **Kirnahar** : There is a low mound at the burial spot of the Vaishnava poet Chandidas in Kirnahar. This mound did not reveal any identifiable pottery but another mound in the area is said to have revealed black-and-red ware.

OBSERVATIONS

The present reconnaissance is limited in scope but a few generalizations can be made. First, the present evidence is not enough to support the idea of a prehistoric period in the district. The reports of early and middle Palaeolithic tools are unsubstantiated. Microlithic tools do occur but there is no assurance that these represent a Mesolithic age and are not contemporary with the later food-producers of the district. Even the polished stone celts cannot be made much of. Even the early historic site of Kotasur has revealed one of these celts. It is not that true prehistoric sequence cannot be obtained in Birbhum; the general geomorphological features do suggest the existence of prehistoric men. What is being emphasized is that the present evidence is not adequate to suggest this. That Birbhum had a Chalcolithic period is proved by the evidence from Mahisdal but it should be admitted that the mere occurrence of black-and-red sherds is not enough to suggest a Chalcolithic stage because this pottery type obviously continued well into the later periods. The sequence from the Chalcolithic to the Pala-Sena periods is clear in different areas of the district and one may suggest that the general concentration of settlements was in the major river valleys of the district. Birbhum would repay closer investigations but what is known is enough to indicate that this region was not a backwater in the cultural development of West Bengal.

References

Chakrabarti, Deb Kumar 1972. *Birbhum Jelar Purakirti* (in Bengali). Calcutta.

Chakrabarti Bahadur, Maharajkumar Niranjan 1323 B.S. *Birbhum Bibaran* (in Bengali), vol I. Hetampur.

———1326 B.S. *Birbhum Bibaran* (in Bengali), vol. II. Hetampur.

———1334 B.S. *Birbhum Bibaran* (in Bengali), vol. III. Hetampur.

Majumdar, Durgadas 1975. *West Bengal District Gazetteers, Birbhum*. Calcutta.

Mitra, Gourihar 1343 and 1345 B.S. *Birbhumer Itihas* (in Bengali), vols I and II Suri,

Note : the sketch plan of Kotasur in this article has been prepared by A.K. Nag. However, the work was done as a part of Delhi University's field-programme in Birbhum in March 1981 under the leadership of the first author of this article.

New Archaeology and the Indian Situation

M. K. Dhavalikar
Deccan College, Poona-6

Revolutionary changes have been taking place in archaeological theory during the last two decades as a result of which archaeology is now gradually being elevated to the status of a scientific discipline. What is more, some universities in the west have instituted courses in archaeological science. At the same time, however, it should be remembered that a great debate (Flannery, 1967) is still going on in the west whether archaeology is a science and there are still some authorities who think that archaeology is an "undisciplined discipline" (Clarke, 1979 : 109) Not long ago an eminent archaeologist observed: Archaeology *perse* is no more than a method and a set of specialised techniques for the gathering of cultural information. The archaeologist, as an archaeologist, is really nothing but a technician" (Taylor, 1948 : 43).

There is no point in denying the fact that archaeology has no systematic body of philosophy and no clearly defined concepts and methodology. Perhaps that is why some educationists in America insisted that it should be included as a tool course which really belonged to in the curricula of vocational schools and not of those of a university. It is therefore high time that we do some soul searching by analysing the state of archaeology as in independent discipline and see if we can remedy the situation in India by instilling a modicum of discipline and scientific rigour in its methodology.

We have come a long way since Walter Taylor (1948) wrote his *Study of Archaeology*. Since then and particularly during the last two decades, a sort of revolution is taking place in the method and theory of archaeology and its beginning is to be traced to Taylor's work only. He was first to advocate a conjuctive approach to archaeological problems. He called his approach conjunctive because it contrasted the summing of objects of a single type and function which had been popular earlier, with the connecting of different objects into a single complex necessary to reveal their functions. This method is also known as contextual since the objects are to be studied in their proper contexts. Taylor discarded the representation of culture as a mere list of traits and called for the study of the functions and of functional connection of objects in a context. He explains it as: "The conjuctive approach... has as its primary goal the elucidation of cultural conjunctives, the associations and relationships, the affinities, with the manifestation under investigation. It aims at drawing the completest possible picture of past human life in terms of human life and geographic environment" (Taylor 1948 : 95-96).

Although Taylor propogated his 'conjunctive' approach to archaeology in 1948 it was L.R. Binford (1972) who initiated the great debate in archaeology with his paper "Archaeology as Anthropology" (Binford, 1972 : 20-32) which was followed by many more writings, and he is therefore justifiably described as the high priest of what is now known as New Archaeology. It should be confessed that much of the literature on New Archaeology, more particularly that by Binford, is hard to comprehend, and this fact has been noted by the doyen of American archaeologist, Robert Braidwood (1973 : 45). Binford too agrees on this point for when he wrote his first paper "Archaeology as Anthropology" and read it to his students, they offered to translate it into English (Binford, 1972 : 10). This was the first paper in which he set out his revolutionary ideas and after this he put forth one paper after an other. Binford was deeply influenced by his teacher Leslie White, a great exponent of the evolutionary theory of culture and of cultural ecology which forms the basis of Binford's approach. He soon won many adherents and they have been branded as the "Binford Mafia." It should, however, be stated that the practioners of New Archaeology are also recognised as belonging to the "Processual School" as they are interested more in the evolutionary process of culture and the explanation of culture change.

Binford (1972 : 20-32) begins by surveying the state of archaeology and shows that archaeology is nothing but a hobby like stamp collecting. He concludes from the survey that : (1) There is general acceptance of the three aims of archaeology viz. reconstruction of cultural history, reconstruction of past lifeways, and the delineation of cultural process, and (2) there has been increasing despair over the feasibility of achieving the third aim. He criticises the normative theory of culture which is based on the assumption of a culture centre from where culture spreads to surrounding areas. This diffusionist approach, according to him, is the aquatic view of culture. He describes culture as "man's extrasomatic means of adaptive system that is employed in the integration of a society with its environment and with other socio-cultural subsystems". He is of the opinion that culture is not shared but participated in and hence, as explanation of culture change influences and migration are discarded and processual explantion, that is, internal mechanisms of systems were advanced.

The ultimate goal of archaeolgy, according to Binford (1972 : 78-104) is the formulation of laws of cultural process which is to be attained by the explanation of cultural similarities and differences. To him, this is neither difficult nor impossible to apply to archaeological situations because human behaviour is patterned and this can be recovered by proper excavation. This, according to him, can be achieved by system approach. The General Systems Theory or Systematics is a framework for analysing life process and living systems which came to be applied in the fields of physical and social sciences, for the basic presumption is that there are in existence systems so basic that they operate in every sphere of life. Essentially, the General Systems Theory seeks the underlying rules that govern the relationship that we observe in the real world. In archaeology, therefore, culture is a system consisting of a number of subsystems such as settlement pattern, subsistence techniques, social organization and religious beliefs. Since all the material remains of an archaeological site are highly patterned or structured the first task of the archaeologist is to define the archaeological structure or pattern of a site and then from that infer the organisation of the society and aspects of behaviour.

The hypothetico-deductive method advocated by Binford (1972 : 78-104) consists in framing a hypothesis and then applying the deductive method. This method has a very wide application in different disciplines and Binford (1972 : 79-96) has given excellent examples of both inductive and deductive methods, Scholars, however, differs on the relative value of the deductive approach for it is observed that in the conduct of research, inductive and deductive procedures are always interrelated.

On the other side of the Atlantic, a number of young archaeologists were attracted towards New Archaeology among whom David Clarke was in the forefront. Clarke's first paper appeard in the same year in which Binford published his seminal essay "Archaeology as Anthropology" in 1962. His *magnum opus, Analytical Archaeology* appeared in 1968. Unfortunately he died young at the age of 36, but his several longish papers are remarkable in that they illustrate the application of new methodology and are shining models of British scholarship. His work is also written in the jargon which, according to him, is inevitable when scientific methodology is employed in any discipline (Clarke, 1979 : 83-105). One must therefore agree with him that "Yesterday's jargon is tomorrow's prose" (Clarke, 1979 : 75).

In one of his longish essays Clarke (1979 : 21-81) has given the clearest possible exposition of New Archaeology. According to his, the new methodology consists of :

1. Morphological paradigm
2. Ecological paradigm
3. Anthropological paradigm
4. Geographical paradigm.

Thus it is the methodology of diffirent scientific disciplines which has been borrowed for archaeology and Clarke has himself shown how fruitfully it can be applied to archaeology. The morphological paradigm consists of detailed study of artifacts assemblages using computer techniques. It is intimately involved with the numeral, statistical and taxonomic approaches. In his doctoral dissertation on "The Origin and Development of British Beaker Pottery" Clarke has demonstrated how the matrix analysis can be profitably applied to archaeological problems. In fact considerable work had already been done on beaker pottery and we are told that Lord Abercrombie had already published a massive volume early in the century that included a simple classification based on shape in particular of the neck of the vessel. But Clarke showed that beakers were neither simple nor easy to analyse; many other characteristics apart from shape existed including the motifs, combinations and disposition of decoration, and far from falling into three large and clearly defined classes, these vessels possessed a bewildering range of similarity and difference from one to another and by applying the sophisticated technique of matrix analysis, he could elucidate significant combination of characteristics.

The second, the ecological paradigm, is most remarkably illustrated in Clarke's "Mesolithic Europe-The Economic Basis" which he contributed to Professor Grahame Clark Felicitation Volume (Clarke, 1979 : 207-262). The title of the paper is a combination of elder Clark's renowned works with the article 'the' deliberately added by David Clarke. This paper instantly became so famous that it has now been published as a separate monograph. Grahame Clark had postulated that the mesolithic economy was mainly based on hunting-fishing, but David Clarke, after reexamining the vast plethora of evidence, has convincingly established that the fact other way round, that is, 80% of the subsistance was based on plant foods, the balance being made up by hunting-fishing. Clarke's ingenuity lay in the functional analysis of the microlithic blade tools which supports his thesis.

The anthropological paradigm is illustrated by Clarke (1979 : 363-434) in his scholarly paper "A Provisional Model of an Iron Age Society and its settlement system". It is a reexamination of the evidence from Glastonbury excavations which were carried out in the beginning of the century. The recording of the evidence by the earlier excavators was so thorough that it should even now serve as a model for us. The critics of New Archaeology often brand it as old wine in new skins implying thereby that there is nothing new in it. But the late David Clarke has shown how a new archaeologist can interprete evidence and how he is different from the traditional archaeologist. What Clarke did was that he studied the old records of the Glastonbury excavations and reinterpreted the evidence. The most noteworthy feature of the recording of the Glastonbury excavations was that each house was excavated carefully and everything found in it was meticulously recorded. From the recorded evidence Clarke has identified various structures and has located the different activity areas. He has constructed a brilliant catchment model which is firmly tied with the yearly cycle of activities in the immediate neighbourhood of the site. Clarke has discussed the spatial, structural and artefact relationships and has succinctly traced the development of the site. He could identify in each complex the major house, minor house, ancillary backing hut, granaries, stables etc. The study began with a typological analysis of the buildings on the site and a structural analysis of their relationships. This procedure resulted in the identification of male and female activity areas, the socio-economic position of the occupants etc. From this, the study expanded to consider the site in the regional context. The work is remarkable in that it shows how far-reaching conclusion can be drawn.

Clarke's paper on "Spatial Information in Archeology" (1979: 453-482) is a superb example of the geographical paradigm and shows what can be done in the way of obtaining information from spatial relationships. It is a stimulating review of the different aspects of spatial analysis. The geographical paradigm consists of settlement pattern studies which have now become an important part of archaeology, Gordon. R. Willey (1974 : 149-178), the pioneer of settlement pattern studies in archaeology has explained how he conceived and executed his Viru Valley project in the forties. Since then, a number of interesting studies have appeared (Chang, 1968).

The Indian Scene

We simply marvel at the advance made by the Binclarke school in archaeological theory and method in the western world but when we look at the condition in India, the picture appears to be dismal. It required a Marshall to take back the antiquity of our civilisation to the third millenium and a Wheeler to build up culture sequences, but again we are back into our shell and have not progressed much beyond Wheeler. Perhaps because of him we are complacent for he once declared that "No part of world is served better in archaeology than India". There is no doubt that technically our excavations are not lacking ; the trenches are so nicely dug that they look like, what Flannery (1976 : 2) calls, ice cube trays. But that is all. We do not do anything more. Most of our excavations have been vertical digs only for building culture sequences, and we have developed a weakness for what is known as Wheeler's trench. Many of us are not aware that Wheeler has been criticised for not including a botanist, a geomorphologist and a zoologist in the list of staff for an excavation (Woodbury, 1973 : 312)

Excavation activity is in full swing in India and a number of excavations are carried out year after year, and perhaps that is why Indian excavators were compared to hounds (Bacon, 1961; 220). There are colleagues who take pride in digging two or three sites every season, but there is no accountability. This sad state of affairs is bound to perpetuate if we do not change our research methodology and if our research goals are not defined clearly. The question that then arises is : How far is the new methodology applicable in India? This is all the more important in view of the fact that the New Archaeology has been vehemently criticised, but for this, it is the practioners of New Archaeology who are responsible. It is therefore necessary that we should adopt the new methodology and see for ourselves whether it is in any way different from the traditional one. In our own way, we have employed it in our excavations at Inamgaon and there is no doubt that it leads to interesting results.

Clarke (1979: 21-82) has discussed the new methodology in great detail. He emphasises that all excavation should be problem oriented and thus we are all very assiduously following since the time of Wheeler. But we do not have all the facilites to employ the scientific aids recommended by Clarke such as air photography in the exploration of ancient sites and since the situation is not likely to improve in the near future, we do not know whether we will be able to use it at all. It may however be interesting to know that recently a colleague at the Deccan College carried out resistivity survey at NaiKund (Dt. Nagpur, Maharashtra), a megalithic site, where he could locate an iron-smelting site of the megalithic period (Gogte, 1980)

Another new technique is that of site sampling which was first employed by Binford and later perfected by Redman and Watson (1970) at Cayonu, a bronze age site in Turkey, where the results of sampling were later confirmed by excavation. The method is said to be an extremely useful technique for determining where to dig, but can also be employed on sites where excavation is not possible for lack of funds. We tried this technique at the chalcolithic site at Walki (Dt. Poona, Maharashtra), but the results were not very encouraging since it was a multi-culture site. It appears that the sampling may be profitable in the case of single culture sites.

A most important technique for the recovery of charred grains from excavation is that of floatation which is now very widely employed in the west. When running water is not available at the excavation site froth floatation is carried out in laboratory. It is a very economical technique which can be carried out on most of our sites as they are located near some perennial source of water which is required for floatation. Agriculture, whicn forms the basis of subsistence of the early farming communities, has been completely neglected in India and hence the importance of this technique. We have floated vast quantities of earth from our Inamgaon excavations for the last several seasons with the result that it is one of the most heavily floated sites in the annals of archaeology. It is only because of this that we now have an almost complete record of agriculture of the first farmers of Maharashtra. Here, in the first cultural period barley was the predominent cereal whereas wheat was introduced in Period II only when the facility of irrigation was available. In the third cultural period, agriculture was on the decline and the people began to subsist more on animal food as they had resorted to a semi-nomadic existence. The most distinguishing feature of agriculture was double cropping. The monsoon (*Kharif*) crops included bajra, sorghum, black gram, hyacinth bean and horse gram whereas the winter (*rabi*) crops were wheat, barley, lentil, grass-pea and field-pea (Kajale, 1978; Dhavalikar 1978).

The matrix analysis of the Jorwe pottery from three sites—Inamgaon, Chandoli and Nevasa—revealed that the pottery from Inamgaon and Chandoli was closely related whereas there was much difference between the pottery from these two sites and that from Nevasa. It could be concluded from this that the Inamgaon potters were supplying pottery to Chandoli which being a small village, could not have afforded the services of a full time potter. The discovery of two pottery kilns at Inamgaon, respectively of 15th and 13th cent. B.C. is significant in this connection. Colleagues at the Deccan College have also applied statistical techniques to the study of stone artifacts (Joshi & Marathe, 1977). New Archaelogy is gradually finding support in India too (Sankalia, 1977; Agrawal, 1970).

We have so far exposed over a hundred mud-houses belonging to different cultural periods from *Circa* 1600 B.C. to Inamgaon. Our careful recording has enabled us to identify the houses of different craftsmen such as potter, lime-maker,, lapidary etc. as also that of the ruling chief. This shows that it was a class structured society. The change in the house plan from rectangular to circular in Period III led us to conclude that the people enjoying settled life in the earlier periods were forced to be semi-nomadic in Period III. It is again from the house plans that it could be inferred that the earlier society was characterised by extended families and, if ethnographic parallels are any indication, we may as well say that the late Jorwe society was probably polygamous. This would underline the overriding role of ethno-archaeology, more so in India, here there are several tribes whose exploitative technology is almost prehistoric. The importance of ethno-archaeology can never be overestimated because "the ethnographic present, in a loosely defined way, provides the archaelogist with a set of controlled or "laboratory" condititions within which he can evaluate and sharpen his own analytic techniques" (Yellen, 1977 : 11).

Our work on the subsistence pattern (Dhavalikar, 1978) illustrates the utility of the ecological paradigm for we could establish that the chalcolithic farmers did cultivate the black cotton soil. The site catchment analysis, pioneer pioneered by Vita-Finzi and Higgs (1970) is being carried out for Inamgaon.

Settlement pattern studies constitute an important part of the New Archaeology. Our own study of the chalcolithic settlement pattern may be mentioned in this connection since it indicates why the concentration of chalcolithic sites in the Tapi valley is not on the banks of Tapi itself but on the tributaries as is the case today (Dhavalikar, 1978). The micro-settlement pattern of Inamagoon was characterised by the concentration of the dwellings of craftsmen in the western part of the principal habitation area wheras in the central part were located the houses of the ruling chief and well to-do people. This could be done because of the contextual study of the artifacts recovered from the excavations.

The foregoing discussion about the tenets of New Archaeology and its applicability in India amply shows that it is high time that we adopt the new methodology in order to find solutions to the multitude of problems in Indian archaeology. It may also be remembered that New Archaeology also has its own drawbacks and has therefore come under heavy criticism not only from the traditional scholars (Braidwood,1973) but from the practitioners of New Archaeology as well (Flannery, 1973). One of the basic aims of New Archaeology, that is, the formulation of laws, has been especially singled out, for a number of scholars are of the opinion that this is perhaps one goal which can never be achieved. Sometimes very ridiculous laws have been formulated and hence they have been branded as Micky Mouse Laws (Flannery, 1973). The hypothetico-deductive mothod has no doubt its own merits and has to be recommended if we have to subject our hypothesis to scientific rigour. The same is the case with systems theory or the ecological approach which was pioneered by Grahme Clark in the forties. Scientific methods have to be applied with scientific rigour and we need not be unduly pessimistic and wait for the end of this "love affair with science". In the end we can only appeal to fellow archaeologists to employ the new methodology or else we are bound to remain only potsherd chroniclers.

References

Agrawal, D.P. 1970 Archaeology and the Luddites. *Antiquity*, 44, pp. 115-29

Bacon, Edward 1961 *Digging for History*. London

Binford, L.R. 1972 *An Archaeological Perspective.* New York.

Braidwood, Robert J. 1973 Archaeology—View from Southwest Asia. In Charles Redman (ed.), *Research and Theory in Current Archaeology.* New York. pp. 33-46.

Clarke, David 1979 *Analytical Archaeologist-Collected Papers of David Clarke.* London.

Chang, K.C. 1968 *Settlement Archeology.* Palo Alto.

Dhavalikar, M.K. 1975-76 Settlement Archaeology of Inamgaon. *Puratattva*, No. 8, pp. 44-54.
1978 Early Settlement and Subsistence Patterns in the Deccan. A paper read at the International Seminar on Problems in Indian Prehistory, Poona. 1978.

Dhavalikar, M.K. & Possehl, Gregory 1974 Subsistence Pattern of an early farming community in Western India. *Puratattva,* No. 7, pp. 39-46.

Dhavalikar, M.K. & Marathe A.R. 1978-79 Jorwe Pottery—A statistical study. *Bull.of the Deccan College Res. Inst.,* Vol. 38 pp. 17-22

Flannery, Kent V. 1967 Cultural History vs Cultural process—A Debate in American Archaeology. *Scientific Amercian,* 217. pp.119-122.

Flannery, Kent V. 1973 Aracheology with a capital 'S'. In charles Redman (ed), *Research and Theory in Current Archaeology.* New York.

Flannery, Kent V. (ed) 1976 *An Early Mesoamerican Village.* New York.

Joshi R.V. & Marathe, A.R. 1977 Metrical Avalysis of handaxes from Chirki-on-Pravara. *Puratattva,* No. 8 pp. 3-12.

Kajale, M.D. 1978 Bio-archaeology of the Ghod Vallsy, Maharashtra. Ph.D. Thesis submitted to University of Poona.

Redman, Charles L. & Watson, Patty Jo 1970 Systematic Intensive Surface collection, *American Antiquity.* Vol. 35. pp. 279-291.

Sankalia, H.D. 1977 *New Archaeology and Its Scope and Application to India.* D.N. Majumdar Lectures. Lucknow.

Taylor, Walter 1948 A *Study of Archaeology.* Philadelphia.

Vita-Finzi, C. and Higgs, E.S. 1970 Prehistoric Economy in the Mt. Carmel Area of Palestine : Site Catchment Analysis. *Progs. of the Prehistoric Soc.,* Vol. 36. pp. 1-37.

Willey, Gorden R. 1974 The Viru Valley Settlement Pattern Study. In Gordon R. Willey (ed), *Archaeological Researches in Retrospect* Cambridge. Mass. pp. 149-178.

Woodbury, Richand B. 1973 Getting Round Archaeologists out of Square holes in Charles Redman (ed), Res. & Theory in Current Archaeology N Y. pp 311-20.

Yellen, John E. 1977 *Archaeological Approaches to the Present.* London.

Chronology of Mathura—An Assessment

M. C. JOSHI & A. K. SINHA
Archaeological Survey of India, New Delhī

As an archaeological site, Mathura (27 31″ north and 77 14″ east) was subjected to archaeological investigations much earlier than most of the Indian cities mentioned in ancient literature. Dates of the early settlements of this ancient town were assigned on the basis of events referred to in the traditional literature and archaeological material like the coins, epigraphs, sculptures, etc. In fact, most students of ancient Indian history, because of popular literary inference from *Anguttar Nikaya*, regarded Mathura around sixth century B.C. as a well established city of Surasenas, which could hardly be a fact in the light of archaeological data available. Similarly, the believers in the Brahmanical epic lore tried to push back Mathura's antiquity to a hoary period without much archaeological substance.

In 1954-55, M. Venkataramayya and Ballabh Saran of the Archaeological Survey of India (*AIR*, 1954-55) carried out a small scale excavation at Katra mound and revealed a cultural sequence ranging in date from *circa* 600 B.C.[1] to A.D. 600 according to their own estimate.

With a view to reassessing the antiquity and nature of early settlements at Mathura, the Archaeological Survey of India conducted excavations (Joshi and Sinha, 1981) for four seasons from 1973-74 to 1976-77, and nearly fourteen sites located in different parts of the present town of Mathura were excavated. It has also to be noted in this respect that only during these excavations Painted Grey Ware at Mathura could be found in stratified context in only one site at Ambarish Tila (MTR-8). A sequence divisible into following cultural Periods was brought to light as a result of the excavations:

Period I : from *circa* sixth century B.C. to closing decades of the fourth century B.C.

Period II : from closing decades of the fourth century B.C. to *circa* second century B.C.

Period III : from *circa* second century B.C. to about the end of the first century B.C.

Period IV : from the beginning of the first century A.D. to about the third century A.D.

Period V : from *circa* fourth century A.D. to the close of the sixth century A.D.

Material relating to the later Periods was found in some sites but it was not possible to date the same in precise terms within a specified chronoframe.

The dates of the Periods specified above have been assigned in accordance with the conventional archaeological methods based on relative stratigraphy including analyses of finds and deposits.

The evidence obtained from the excavations suggested the beginning of Mathura as a hamlet of PGW using people in Period I which was located in the northern part of the present town at Ambarish Tila (MTR-8). Period I itself has been further divided into two phases A and B on the basis of the finds and their location.

---

1 According to our observations on the subsequent excavations the earliest remains at Katra area could not be older than the closing decades of the 4th century B.C.

A deposit of nearly 80 cm. thickness comprising, structurally, a mud floor superimposed by a mud-platform represented Period IA (first phase) which was characterized by the use of Painted Grey Ware and associated plain grey, red, and just three sherds each of Black-Slipped and degenerated black-and-red wares. Period IB (second phase), which was also marked by mud floors, apart from PGW, had some seventeen sherds of Northern Black Polished Ware within it along with terracotta figurines of a bird and animal as important finds. In fact, phase B of Period I represented the overlap of PGW and NBPW.

The tiny habitation (in MTR-8), represented by PGW turned by first half of Period II into an extensive settlement (Joshi, 1979) fortified by a massive mud-wall (*Dhūlkot*) which was planned as an oblong-crescent with river Yamuna on the east as a protective boundary. The mud fortification had lost its utility in Period III, but the size of the settlement remained the same as during the previous period. A notable feature of Mathura of Period III was the foundation of a Jain establishment (at Kankali Tila) outside the mud fortification in the later part of the period.

During Period IV (Saka-Kushan age), the mud fortification was not only revived, enlarged and repaired but an inner fortification or high-walled enclosure, now represented by long elevated earthen pile in Katra area, was also constructed.

In Period V Mathura seems to have lost much of its importance as a politico-cultural seat in comparison to the previous Period, and perhaps it flourished mainly as a centre of arts and crafts and religious establishments.

It may also be necessary in the present context to assess the radio-carbon dates relating to the cultural chronology of Mathura, for some nine charcoal samples (*IAR*, 1976-77) belonging to different levels of the excavated areas were examined by the Physical Research Laboratory, Ahmedabad for ^{14}C dating and the dates calculated are as under :

PRL-333

MTR-8, B1-Qd2	2490±140 B.P.
Pit 3, S.B. (5)-3.18 m.	(540±140 B.C.)
Late Level of Period II	2560± 150 B.P.
(NBPW)	(610±150 B.C.)

PRL-334

MTR-10, A1-Qd4	2600±150 B.P.
(9)-1. 45m.	(650±150 B.C.)
Mid Level of Period III	2680±150 B.P.
(NBPW)	(730±150 B.C.)

PRL-336

MTR-8, B1-Qd2	2540±90 B P.
(6)-3.00m.	(590±90 B.C.)
Mid Level of Period II	2610±100 B.P.
(NBPW)	(660±100 B,C.)

PRL-337

MTR-11, T.T.	2340±100 B.P.
Pit 5 S.B. (20)-5.45m.	(390±100 B.C.)
Mid Level of Period II	2410±100 B.P.
(NBPW)	(460±100 B.C.)

PRL-338

MTR-11. T.T.	2280±100 B.P.
(18) -4. 70m.	(330±100 B.C.
Late Level of Period II	2350±110 B.P.
(NBPW)	(400±100 B.C.)

PRL-339

MTR-8, B1-Qd3	2380±100 B.P.
Pit 2, S.B. (3)	(430±100 B.C.)
Mid Level of Period III	2450±100 B.P.
	(500±100 B.C.)

PRL-340

MTR-8, A1-Qd4	2390±150 B.P.
(11)- 4. 20m.	(440±150 B.C.)
Mid Level of Period IB.	2460±150 B.P.
(Overlap phase of PGW and NBPW)	(510±150 B.C.)

1 In PRL ^{14}C Date list 1/1977, this sample has been shown as associated with the deposit of the overlap phase of PGW and NBPW, which is a mistake crept in inadvertently. At this site there is no such deposit indicating cultural overlap. The position can be very well varified from our summary reports for each year from 1973-74 onwards published in *Indian Archaeology-A Review*.

DATES RELATED TO MATHURA EXCAVATIONS (1973-74—1976-77)

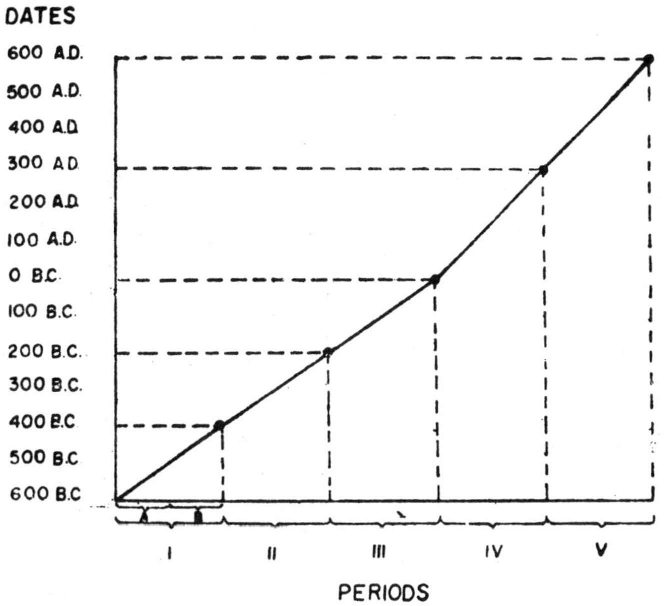

Fig. a

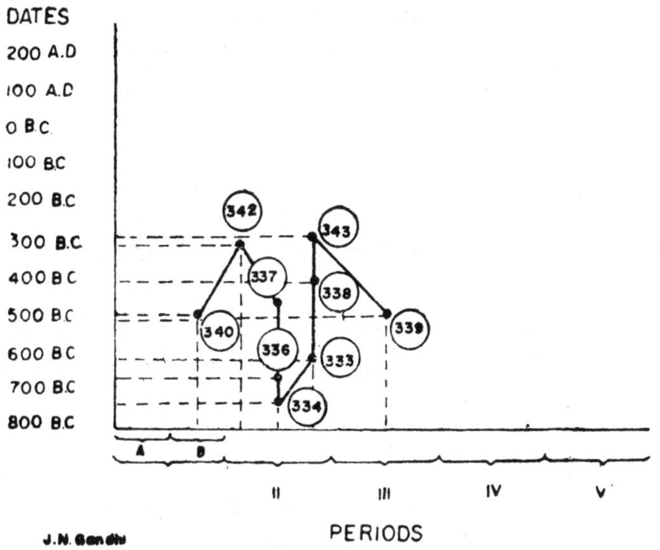

Fig. b

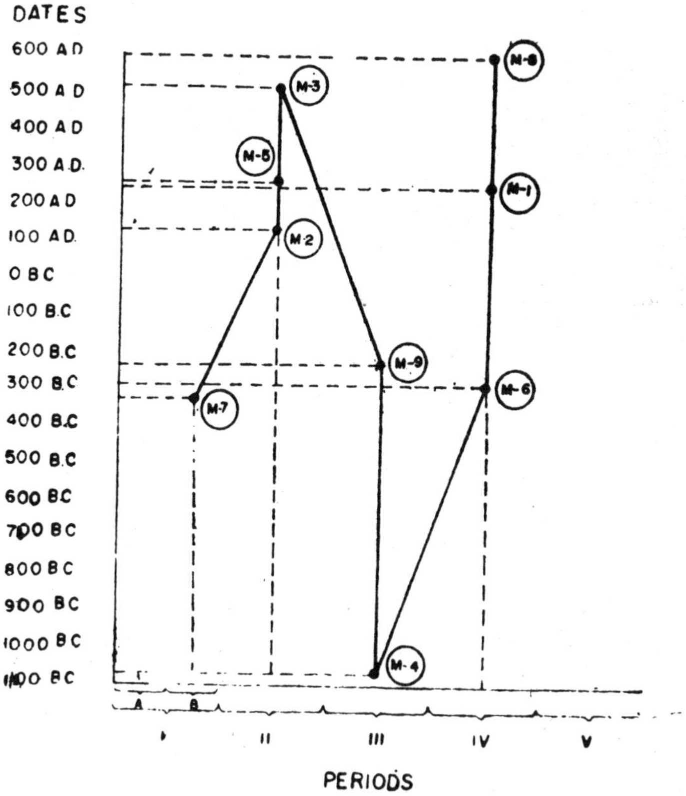

Fig. c

Fig.—a. Based on archaeological methods
Fig.—b. Based on ^{14}C method
Fig.—c. Based on thermoluminiscence age estimation

PRL-342

MTR-8, B1-Qd2	2180±160 B.P.
Pit 8, S.B. (8)-3.65m.	(230±160 B.C.
Early Level of Period II	2250±160 B.P.
(NBPW)	(300±160 B.C.

PRL-343

MTR-11, T.T.	2150±100 B.P.
(18)-4. 02m.	(200±100 B.C.)
Late Level of Period II	2220±100 B.P.
(NBPW)	(270±100 B.C.

A perusal of the above table would show that from amongst the nine samples (from Mathura excavation) subjected to ^{14}C test as many as seven belong to various levels of Period II and only one each to Period I (in its later phase) and Period III. It may be stated again in the present context that from the excavation at Mathura, the Painted Grey Ware in the stratified context was found only at MTR-8 (Ambarish Tila) and all the remaining sites located within the fortified area of that city had only the NBPW and associated pottery in their lowest levels. The cultural overlap between the PGW and NBPW thus was available only at Ambarish Tila. Similarly another important site Kankali-Tila (MTR-5), located immediately outside the ancient mud-fortification, which had no NBPW within it, showed its beginning only in the later part of Period III.

Coming back to ^{14}C dates (fig-b) listed above, we may say that some of them coincide precisely or broadly with the time bracket ascribed by us to different Periods pertaining to ancient Mathura. There are, however, some other dates which do not tally at all with our periodization.

The solitary sample (PRL-340) to Period IB indicates two central dates viz., 440 and 510(±150) B.C. which are almost close to the time bracket of Period IB as assigned by us. Amongst the other dates from MTR-8 the dates indicated by PRL-342, related to early level of Period II, go well with our time span.

The dates provided by the sample PRL-333, PRL-336 and PRL-339 are not acceptable to us on account of the fact that although these are from upper levels, they indicate dates which go even earlier to Period IB (*vide* sample PRL-340) forming lower deposits at MTR-8 itself. Even the archaeological materials from the levels from where the above samples were collected suggest a date later for them than that of the overlap phase of Painted Grey and Northern Black Polished Wares.

In the same way sample PRL-334 from MTR-10, which was associated like the earliest level of MTR-2, MTR-9, MTR-4, MTR-7 or MTR-13 with the mid levels, of Period II characterized by the use of NBPW, cannot be ascribed to 650±150 B.C. and 730±150 B.C. at all, the reason being that the material as well as the general stratigraphy of the site go against these dates. Does it not suggest that 650±150 B.C. and 730±150 B.C. may be the date of the pre-Period II charcoal which somehow might have got deposited along with the later deposits of MTR-10 ?

The samples collected from MTR-11 (100m. west of Yamuna, in the main area of the city) *i. e.* PRL-337, PRL-338 and 343 have indicated three dates 390±100/460±100 B.C., 330±100/400±100 B.C., and 200± 100/270± 100 B. C. respectively, which broadly tally with our time bracket of Period II. We do not preclude the possibility of variation to a limited degree in the chronology of the cultural Periods proposed by us as well as in ^{14}C dates.[1]

[1]The undernoted chart relating to dates derived from various ^{14}C samples, collected from a trench MTR-8/BI-Qd-2 is also of interest to us :

PRL-333	Pit 3 S.B. (5)	540± 140 B.C.
	-3.15 m.	610± 150 B.C.
PRL-336	(6)	590± 90 B.C.
	-3.00 m.	660± 100 B.C.
PRL-342	Pit 8 S.B. (8)	230± 160 B.C.
	-3.65 m.	300± 160 B.C.

It would be seen from this table that the date of sample PRL-342 is later to the date calculated for PRL-336 and PRL-333 though [stratigraphically it is earlier and therefore it should have given an early date too (contd.).

For the assessment of the chronology of the Cultural Periods of ancient Mathura, it has to be remembered that its archaeology/history has a gap-less (cultural) continuity ever since the first settlement was founded here. Any one who probes into the past of such a habitation has to proceed from a known to an unknown direction taking into account various datable factors like epigraphs, coins, terracotta plaques/figures, ring-wells, etc. Keeping in view such datable antiquities there may not be any serious dispute in regard to the date of Period III even of period II, for the latter almost had its beginning with the emergence of terracotta ring-wells, representative pottery of the Period being NBPW and associated ceramics. Period II itself was preceded by IB *i.e.* the overlap phase containing PGW and only seventeen sherds of NBPW distributed in about half a dozen layers. We felt that these limited fragments of NBPW could only be parts of imported pots to Mathura from an area where they were originally produced *i.e.* the eastern U.P, and western Bihar. It may also be mentioned in this connexion that somewhat similar to the terracotta animal figurines of Period IB and early levels of Period II (of Mathura) were also found at Sravasti (Sinha, 1967) where they have been placed in Period I (*circa* 300 B.C. to 600 B.C.), marked by the presence of NBPW, the origin of which is regarded by most of scholars to be somewhere in the sixth century B.C. in the mid-eastern India; its transportation to Mathura (from estern India) might have taken considerable time in those days. Therefore we dated Period IB around 500 B.C.

In respect of the date of Period IA, the above mentioned factors have to be be taken into account for the deposit of Period IA is superimposed by that of Period IB. Further the occurrence of PGW togather with very limited quantity of Black-Slipped and coarse black and red wares, and evidence of only two structural levels in Period IA, it is difficult to push back its antiquity much beyond 600 B.C. What is significant in this regard is that even other PGW sites of neighbouring areas, viz., Atranjikhera (Gaur, 1968), Bateshwar (*IAR*, 1975-76), Khalua (*IAR*, 1965-66), Jakhera (Sahi, 1978), Allahpur (Dikshit, 1973), Noh (*IAR*, 1970-71) and Jodhpura (*IAR*, 1972-73), the quantity of Black-Slipped and black and red wares, gets less and less and loses significance in the later levels of the Painted Grey Ware Culture which further lends strength to a later date for the PGW deposit at Mathura.

Incidentally, we may also like to mention the dates obtained as a result of 'TL' tests carried out on the pottery samples from Mathura excavations by Dr. K.S.V. Nambi of Health Physics Division B.A.R.C., Bombay. The details of the dates are as under :

M-1
MTR-9 (6) 1688 (±—, 14%) B.P.
Period IV

M-2
MTR-8 1811 (±17%, ± 17%) B.P.
Period II

M-3
MTR—8 (11) 1420 (±—, ± 17%) B.P.
Period II

M-4
MTR—8 (2) 3018 (±—, ±17%) B.P.
Period III

M-5
MTR—8 (5) 1682 (±—, ±14%) B.P.
Period II

M-6
MTR—8 (2) 2227 (±—,± 19%) B.P.
Period IV

In another case, three samples from a trial trench (MTR-11) when subjected to radio-carbon tests, gave the following results :

PRL-337	Pit 5 S.B. (20)	390± 100 B.C.
	-5.4 m.	460± 100 B.C.
PRL-338	(18)	330± 100 B.C.
	-4.70. m.	400± 100 B.C.
PRL-343	(18)	200± 100 B.C.
	-4.02 m.	270± 100 B.C.

It may be observed from the above table that two samples collected from one and the same layer (18) have given two dates with a difference of more than a hundred years.

M-7

MTR—8 (13) 2262 (± 5%, ± 13%) B. P.
Period IB

M-8

MTR—5 Tank-Complex (brick) 1335 (±—, ±17%) B. P.
Period IV

M-9

MTR—4 (6) 2175 (±—, ± 16%) B. P,
Period III

According to Dr. Nambi two errors are specified for each age : the first is the standard error on the mean 'TL' age estimate (when more thae one is made) and the second is the predicted percent accuracy of the age estimate. The predicted accuracy ranges from ±9% to ± 17% in these samples because of a generous assumption of all possible values for the water content in the pottery and soil samples over the archaeological period, (quoted from a letter of Dr. Nambi dated 16th February 1979).

Out of nine samples, examined by Health Physics Division, B.A.R.C., only two samples M-1 and M-9 are in fair agreement with our datings. The dates of samples M-2, M-6 and M-7 are nearer to the agreement within the predicted accuracy limits. The 'TL' age estimation (fig.-c) of the remaining samples does not coincide with the time bracket arrived at by us. We have no specific comments to offer further in this regard as we have already explained our stand in respect of the chronology, we have adopted for Mathura (fig.-a). It would however be an impossibility to have a date in the beginning of the first millennium B.C. for a potsherd of first-second century B.C. as indicated by sample M-4.

References

Dikshit, K.N. 1973 The Allahpur Evidence and the Painted Grey Ware Chronology *Radiocarbon and Indian Archaeology* (ed.) D.P. Agrawal and A. Ghosh, pp. 148-153.

Gaur, R.C. 1969 The Painted Grey Ware at Atranjikhera — An Assessment, *Potteries in Ancient India* (ed.) B.P. Sinha, pp. 185-187.

Indian Archaeology-A Review, 1954-55, pp. 15-16; 1965-66, pp. 41-42; 1970-71, pp. 31-32; 1972-73, pp. 29-30; 1973-74, pp. 31-32; 1974-75, pp. 48-50; 1975-76, pp. 42-43; 1976-77, pp. 54-56, pp. 88-89.

Joshi, M.C. 1979 Mathura as an Ancient Settlement Paper submitted in the Mathura Seminar (in press).

Joshi, Munish Chandra and Ashok Kumar Sinha, 1981 Puratattvik Sakshya Aur Prachin Mathura ki Khoj. Puratattva anka, *Uttar Pradesh* (Hindi), May, Lucknow.

Sahi, M.D.N. 1978 New Light on the Life of the Painted Grey Ware People as Reflected from Excavations at Jakhera (Dist. Etah) *Man and Environment* Vol. II pp. 101-103.

Sinha, K. K. 1967 *Excavations at Sravasti—1959* Varanasi, pp. 55-56, pl. XVI-7.

Was Ayodhyā A Mythical City ?

B. B. LAL
Indian Institute of Advanced Study, Simla

It is common experience that the moment one chooses to tread on an unbeaten path or tries to open up an altogether new one through a dark jungle, one takes the calculated risk of exposing oneself to the likely dangers that beset such a venture. This is as much true in research-work as in real life, and archaeological research is no exception Thus when in 1950 the present writer started off to find out if the historicity of the *Mahābhārata* epic, which has been regarded by some as wholly true and by some others as a mere figment of the imagination, can at all be tested on the touchstone of archaeology, he knew full well the risk he was running. As is well known, this epic has got inflated eleven times, from the *Jaya* of 8,800 verses through the *Bhārata* of 24,000 verses to the *Mahābhārata* (the now-available form) of nearly 100,000 verses. Archaeological excavations and explorations of the sites associated with the *Mahābhārata* story have, however, thrown up some pieces of evidence—such as the existence of the same type of material culture (viz. the Painted Grey Ware Culture) at all these sites, which binds them together broadly during the first quarter of the first millennium B.C.; the destruction of the PGW settlement at Hastinārpura by a flood, which finds a reference in the literature ; the continuance of the PG Ware in its devolved form at Kauśāmbī, which again lends an indirect support to the literary evidence about the capital being shifted from Hastināpura to Kauśāmbī after the flood-debacle ; and so on—which suggest that the epic may not have altogether been a fiction, but in all probability had a kernel of truth which, of course, got immensely magnified over a period of nearly one-and-a-half thousand years when it assumed its present shape (Lal, 1976). While many scholars have accepted the foregoing deductions (Gupta and Ramachandran, 1976), there still are a few who would like to have inscriptional or some other 'solid' evidence in support of it, though they themselves are aware of the fact that at this period of our history writing was not in vogue. (Barring the Indus Civilization, with which we are not concerned in the present context, archaeological evidence of writing is not available in the country prior to the 3rd-4th centuries B.C. Thus we have to sift carefully other kinds of evidence to see which way they point.)

Be that as it may. The writer has invited another trouble by trying to find out the archaeological potential of the sites associated with the Rāmāyaṇa story. The *Rāmāyaṇa* of Vālmiki gives very clear references to sites like Ayodhyā, which was the capital of Rāma, Śriṅgaverapura, where he crossed the Gaṅgā during his exile, Bhāradvāja Āśrama, where he sojourned for a while, and so on. Though the project is yielding useful results which are being processed for publication, it is rather amusing to note that doubts are being expressed even about some very fundamental things. For example, it is being made out that Ayodhyā was a *mythical* city and, therefore, there is little sense in subjecting to excavation the site known today as Ayodhyā (near Faizabad in Uttar Pradesh). In this context I might draw attention to a paper by M. C. Joshi (1978), wherein he says :

"Both Sankalia and Lal appear to be absolutely

sure about the identification of ancient Ayodhyā with the modern town of the same name, but an early reference to this city gives a different picture. The original text is as under:

Ashṭāchakrā navadvārā devānām pūrayodhyā
Tasyām hiraṇmayaḥkośaḥ svargo loko jyotishāvṛitaḥ
Yo vai tām Brahmaṇo veda amṛitenāvṛitām-purrim
Tasmai brahma cha Brahmā cha āyuḥ kīrtim prajām daduḥ
Vibhrājamānām hariṇīm yaśasā samparivṛitām
Puram Hiraṇmayīm Brahmā viveśāparājitām
(*Taittarīya Āryaṇyaka*, 1, 27)

Ayodhyā (impregnable), the city of the gods, consists of eight circles (also cycles) and nine entrances; within it there is the golden treasure-dome the celestial world, everilluminated with light (north pole). Whoever knows it as the Creator's city ever surrounded with nectar will have long life, fame, and offspring bestowed on him, by Brahma (the sun), and Brahmā (the moon). Into this city ever shining, moving, and pervaded with *yaśas* (fame and lusture), the creator has entered."

Joshi then quotes Shamasastry (1940), from which the following is an extract:

"Rāma, the son of Daśaratha, the friend of Indra, is an incarnation of Vishnu, the sun-god. He lives in Ayodhyā which is formed by the seven intercalary month-circles and becoming 19 years old, he leaves it at the behest of his father for the forest world of Daṇḍaka and Laṅkā. He wanders there for 14 years. Reaching Laṅkā on or near the equator, he destroys the Rākshasa Rāvaṇa, their chief, and returns at the completion of 33 years to Ayodhyā of the Devaloka. The same work is repeated in every cycle of 33 years. This is the original real Kalpa which the authors of the *Purāṇas* and the Siddhāntas magnified into 43,20,000 years. *The word Zodia or Zodiac seems to be philologically akin to Ayodhyā.* Accordingly the story of the Rāmāyaṇa appears to be a development of an early Zodiacal myth ?"

(Italicing by the present writer.) Thereafter Joshi adds his own comments, as follows:

"One may accept or reject Shamasastry's surmise, but it is certain that the time when the *Taittarīya Āraṇyaka* was composed the memory of the Ayodhyā of the mortals was wholly forgotten, if it existed at all. Ayodhyā with nine portals, eight circular enclosures and a surrounding pool of nector appears to be purely a mythical city which could be compared to some extent with Samavasaraṇa and Nandīśvara-dvīpa (central part) of the Jaina mythology. Thus, it is probable that modern Ayodhyā and its association with Rāma is of a later origin."

Since Joshi has not pressed that we should accept Shamasastry's "surmise", the present writer would also not waste energy on demonstratting the invalidity of Shamasastry's stand. However, he cannot resist commenting on the tendency to make all sorts of deductions in the name of philology, such as the one when Shamasastry says: "The word Zodia or Zodiac seems to be philologically akin to Ayodhyā." Indeed, it has been well said that sound-philology is not always sound philology'.

In his above-quoted comments, Joshi, however, makes the following three proposition :--

(i) "When the *Taittarīya Āraṇyaka* was composed the memory of Ayodhyā of the mortals was wholly forgotten if it existed at all";

(ii) "Ayodhyā appears to be purely a mythical city"; and

(iii) "modern Ayodhyā and its association with Rāma is of a later origin".

By his first proposition Joshi means to say that if there ever was on this *terra firma* a real city called Ayodhyā it must have existed very much before the time of the composition of the *Taittarīya Āraṇyaka* since, according to him, by that time it had been forgotten. This statement of Joshi goes counter his third proposition wherein he says that modern Ayodhyā as well as its association with Rāma are *both* of later origin. Although

Joshi has not spelt out 'later than what?', yet he seems to mean later than the *Taittariya Āraṇyaka.* One really wonders as to how Joshi envisages his Ayodhyā of the materials' on the one hand to have ceased to exit *long before* the composition of the *Taittariya Āraṇyaka* and, on the other, to have come into being *well after* the same *Āraṇyaka.* Further, Joshi has to answer: "Who was this Rāma and why and when did he come to be associated with 'modern' Ayodhyā?" Anyway, from the foregoing discussion the highly presumptive nature of the first and third propositions becomes self-evident, but the matter may be left at that since the main purpose of the present paper is to discuss Joshi's second proposition, viz. that Ayodhyā was 'purely a mythical city'.

This requires a very close and critical study of the Sanskrit text itself. The verses quoted by Joshi from the *Taittariya Āraṇyaka* which contain the word 'Ayodhyā', also occur in the *Atharvaveda,* though their *inter se* arrangement is somewhat changed :

> *"Ūrdhyo nu sṛishtāstiryaṅ nu sṛishṭāḥ*
> *sarvā diśaḥ purusha ā babhuvāṅ*
> *puram yo brahmaṇo veda yasyāḥ purusha*
> *uchyte* 28
>
> *Yo vai tām brahmaṇo vedāmṛitenāvṛitām puram*
> *tasmai brahma cha Brāhmāścha chakshuḥ prāṇam*
> *prajām daduḥ* 29
>
> *Na vai tām chakshurjahāti na prāṇo jarasaḥ purā*
> *puram yo brahmaṇo veda yasyāḥ purusha*
> *uchyate* 30
>
> *Ashṭāchakrā navadvārā devānām pūrayodhyā*
> *tasyām hiraṇyayaḥ kośaḥ svargo jyotishāvṛitaḥ.*
> 31
>
> *Tasminhiraṇyaye kośe tryare tripratishthite* 32
> *tasminyad yakshamātmātmanvat tadvai*
> *brahmavido-viduḥ.*
>
> *Prabhājāmānām hariṇīm yaśasā samparivṛitām*
> *Puram hiraṇyayīm Brahmā vivesāparajitām* 33
>
> *(Atharvaveda. x, 2, 28-33)*

William Dwight Whitney's English rendering of the foregoing verses runs thus :

"28. Was he now created upward (*ūrdhva*) ? (or) was he now created crosswise? did man grow unto (*a-bhū*) all the quarters ?- he who knoweth the *brahman's* stronghold from which man is (so) called,

29. Whoever indeed knoweth that *brahman's* stronghold, covered with *amrita* —unto him both the *brahman* and the Brahmans have given sight, breath, progeny.

30. Him verily sight doth not desert, nor breath, before old age, who knoweth the *brahman's* stronghold (*pur*), from which man (*purusha*) is (so) called.

31. Eight-wheeled, nine-doored, is the *impregnable* stronghold of the gods ; in that is a golden vessel, heaven-going (*swarga*), covered with light. (Italicising of the word 'impregnable' by the present author.)

32. In that golden vessel, three-spoked, having three supports-what soul-possessing monster (*yakṣa*) there is in it, that verily the knowers of the *brahman* know.

33. The brahman entered into the resplendent, yellow, golden, unconquerred stronghold, that was all sorrounded with glory."

It would be seen that Whitney has takan the word *Ayodhyā* not in the sense of a proper noun, i.e. not as the name of a city, but as a compound word consisting of two parts, viz., *a* + *yodhyā.* The first part has a negative meaning, and the second is derived from the root *yudh* the meaning of whole word being 'impregnable'. That this is the only correct interpretation is absolutely clear from the context in which the word occurs. The *Sūkta* is captioned as *'Brahmaprakāsanam'* in which more than half of the verses are devoted to the raising of highly searching and fundamental questions, such as 'who created this or that, ?; while the remaining verses attempt the answer. Herein the word *'pur'* clearly means the body, and what dwells in it is the *purush.* The use is in the same sense in which the words *deha* and *dehin* have been used in the *Bhagvad-Gita* (II, 30). Thus, what the above-quoted Mantra 31 means to say is that the body *(pur)* wherein the *purusha* resides is impregnable (*a+yodhyā*), having eight chakras (*ashṭā-chakrā*) and nine doors (*nava-dvārā*). Within it is the golden vessel (*hiraṇmayaḥ kośaḥ*) covered with light *jyotishāvṛitaḥ*) The reference in this last part is obviously to the effulgent light that the mystic experiences within himself when in deep meditation. The eight *chakra* are the eight plexuses, beginning with the *mūlādhāra* at the base and ending up in the *sahasrāra* at the crest of the head. The *nava-dvāras* or nine gates of the human body are : the two eyes, two nostrils, two ears, the mouth, the rectum, and the opening in the sex-organ. The *Bhagvad-Gita* (V, 13) also refers to these 'gates' when it says : *'nava-dvāre pure dehī naiva kurvan na kārayan'*. The *dehin* i.e. the embodied soul dwells in the nine-doored *pura* i.e. the human body, neither working nor causing work to be done.

It seems necessary also to examine if in any other Vedic text the word *ayodhyā* has been used in the sense of a town or city. A reference to *Chaturveda-Vaiyākaraṇa-padasūchī* by Vishva Bandu (1960, p. 97) shows that the foregoing is the only occurrence of the word *ayodhyā* in all the *Vedas*. However, cognate forms do occur at three other places in the *Atharvaveda* itself. (In the other Vedas even a cognate form does not occur. One of the occurrences in the *Atharvaveda* is as follows :

"Achyutachyutsamado qamishṭho
mṛidho jetā pura-etāyodhyaḥ
Indreṇa gupto vidathā nichikya-
ddhṛiddyotano dvishatām yāhi śibham.
(V, 20,12)

"Stirring *(chyu)* the unstirred, going oftenest into contest conquering scorners, going in front. *unsubduable* made safe by Indra, nothing counsels (*vidatha*) burning the hearts of our adversaries, go thou quickly." (Translation by Whitney).

The above *Sūkta* deals with the war-drum (*dundubhiḥ*). In it the drum is praised by saying it thunders loudly like a lion, it overpowers the foes, and so on. It is in this context that the word *"a+yodhyaḥ'* has been used, which has rightly been translated by Whitney as *'unsubduable'*. The word is not in the least a proper noun and thus there is no posibility whatsoever of its having to do anything with a town or city.

Two cognate forms, viz. *a+yodhyena* and *a+yodhyaḥ*, occur in *Kāṇḍa* 19 of the *Atharvaveda* The relevant texts and translations are given below:

"Saṅkrandanenānimishəṇa jishṇunāyodhyena
duschyavanena dhṛishṇunā
Tadindreṇa jayata tatsahadhvam
yudho nara isbuhastena vṛishṇā

"With the roaring, unwinking, conquering, *invincible*, immovable, bold one—with Indra thus overpower the fighters, O men, with the arrow—armed bull (*vṛishan*) (XIX, 13, 3)

"Abhi gotrāṇi sahasā gāhamāno-
adāya ugraḥ śatamanyurindrah ।
Duśchyavanaḥ pṛitanāshāḍayodhyo-
asmākam senā avatu pra yutsu ॥

'Plunging with power into cow-stalls, Indra, pitiless, formidable, of hundred-fold fury, immovable, overpowering fighters, invincible—let him favour our armies in the fight." (XIX, 13, 7)

The *Sūkta* is primarily a prayer to Indra who is beseeched to help the devotee to overpower the enemy and win the wars. Hundreds of adjectives have been used in the praise of Indra, and the word *a+yodhyaḥ* (*invincible*) in Mantra 7 is just one of them. Because of the construction of the sentence, the same adjective occurs in the *tritiyā vibhakhti* (*a—yodhyena*) in Mantra 3, but the meaning there also remains the same.

Lest it should be misunderstood that the present writer has dwelt only upon the occurrences of the word *ayodhyā* or its cognates in the *Atharvaveda* and not on the one in the *Mantra* quoted by Joshi from *Taittariya Āraṇyaka*, it may be emphasized that that even Sāyaṇa in his commentary on this *Mantra* confirms the same meaning. He says : *"Pūriti-śarīramuchyate"* i.e. the word *pur* has been used for the body. Further, he adds : *"ayodhyā=karmagatimantareṇa kenāpi prahartumaśakyā"* (Phadake and Apte 1926 : 103)

From what has been discussed above, it is absolutely clear that in all the foregoing instance *ayodhyā* has been used as a compound word, consisting of two parts, viz. *a+yodhyā*, and the same is the case with its variants, viz. *a+yodhyaḥ* and *a+yodhyena.* In all the cases the meaning is *"invincible". Not even in single case has the word been used as a proper noun. Thus, it would be patently wrong to think that it refers to a city, and at that a mythical city.*

We do have a non-mythical town on the *terra-firma* called Ayodhyā, situated on the bank of the Sarayū, near Faizabad in Uttar Pradesh. Why should we fight shy of excavating it in order to find out its antiquity and to ascertain if and what light it can (or even cannot) throw on the historicity of the *Rāmāyaṇa* ? Why should a scientific attempt to find out the truth-be it palatable or unpalatable-be scuttled by throwing up baseless suggestions like the one that Ayodhyā was a mythical city?

References

Apte, V.G. (ed.), 1926. Taittarīya Āraṇyaka of *Krishna-Yajurveda* with commentary of Sāyaṇa Āchārya, Anand Ashram, Pune.

Gupta, S.P. and K.S. Ramachandran (eds.) 1976. *Mahābhārata : Myth and Reality—Differing Views,* New Delhi.

Joshi, M.C. 1978. 'Archaeology and Indian Tradition—Some Observations', *Purātattva,* no. 8 1975-76, pp. 98-102.

Lal, B. B. 1954-55. 'Excavations at Hastinapura and other explorations, 1950-52', *Ancient India,* nos. 10-11, pp. 4-151.

Lal, B.B. 1976. *Mahābhārata and Archaelogy', in* Mahabharata: *Myth and Reality; Differing Views,* S.P. Gupta and K.S. Ramachandran (eds.)

Santabolekar, 1938. *Atharvaveda Samhitā,* Svadhyaya Mandal, Audh. S.D. (ed.)

Shamasastry, R. 1940. 'Ayodhya, the City of the Gods', in *D. R. Bhandarkar Volume,* Calcutta, pp. 17-18.

Vishva Bandu. 1960. *Chaturveda-Vaiyākaraṇa-Padasūchi,* Vishveshvaranand Vedic Research Institute, Hoshiarpur.

Whitney, W.D., 1905. Atharvaveda Samhitā (tran.) Harvard University.

Symbiosis and Traditional Behaviour in the Subsistence Economies of the Kunchapuri Yerukulas of South India : A Predictive Model

M.L.K. MURTY
Deccan College, Poona

Introduction

The inland plateau regions on the southeast coast of Andhra Pradesh are inhabited by a few ethnics, notable among them being the Yanadis, the Yerukulas and the Boyas. Traditionally, they are all hunter gatherers favouring forested/semi-forested/scrub jungle riverine zones. Owing to the encroachment of agricultural, pastoral and trader communities into their native ecosystems, these ethnics came under interaction with advanced castes and are in varying stages of acculturation. That apart the consequential depletion of floral cover and faunal biomass in their original habitats forced on them a readaptation of their subsistence behaviour, which they have achieved by striking a symbiotic adjustment to suit the village based economies. This fact notwithstanding, there is enough ethnographic evidence to predict that the culture core of these ethnics preserved its traditional fabric and that their hunting and foraging habits help to evaluate the archaeological patterning of economic behaviour in hunter gatherer ecosystems of the region under consideration.

The economic behaviour of Kunchapuri Yerukulas (also called as Kuncha Yerukulas), discussed below, makes an interesting case study to interpret the aspects of traditional behaviour and resource scheduling of a subethnic group under the selective pressures of symbiotic organization.

The Kunchapuri Yerukulas

The name 'Yerukula' (spelt variously as Erakala, Erukala etc.) is derived from the traditional occupation of this ethnic, the sooth saying (Telugu, yeruka). The Yerukulas are divided into as many as 14 subethnics each named after its specialized occupation (Hassan, 1920 : 185-95 ; Pratap, 1975 : 46-48). The occupation of Kunchapuri Yerukulas is making of weaver brushes (Tel. : Kuncha, brush). In the same way, there are Dabba Yerukulas (bamboo basketry), Itha Pullala Yerukulas (wild date basketry), Nara Yerukulas (rope making). Uppu Yerukulas (trading in salt), Eddu Yerukulas (carring merchandise on bullocks), Karivepaku Yerukulas (selling the leaves of Murraya koenigii), Kavali Yerukulas (watchmen), Voora Yerukulas (pig rearing and agricultural labour), etc. These occupational names obviously reflect their varied adaptations through the course of history. Some of them, especially in the coastal districts, are also known for their notoreity as dacoits and highway robbers and attempts to wean them away from crime, made from the British times are still continued (with no impressive success) by the Government. Each subethnic is again divided into four exogamous clans (*gotra*) and each clan is further subdivided basing on the house name (Tel. : intiperu). All the Yerukula subethnics speak Telugu, the local language, but they have their own common language. The Yerukula language has the linguistic features of Tamil, Telugu and Kannada with a heavy emphasis on Tamil (Guru Reddy 1968 : 45-50). It seems to be related to the languages of other nomadic ethnics like Koravas, Koramas and Korachas of Karnataka, and Kaikadis of Maharashtra (Ibid ; Bhat 1968 : 4). Likewise, the language of Koramas has affinities to that of Yerukulas and Kaikadis and seems to be a corrupt form of Tamil. It is interesting to note that some of the bird names like-*andri, pennara, maccanara, sanganara* etc. used by the Yerukulas have their equivalents in the Korama language.

In the region under consideration there are two subethnics : the Dabba Yerukulas and Kunchapuri Yerukulas, both leading a symbiotic life with the peasant and village communities. Unlike the sedentary Dabba Yerukulas, the Kunchapuri Yerukalas are semi-nomadic, moving seasonally in small bands comprising two to six families and living in the outskirts of villages. While the Dabba Yerukulas exploit a variety of wild plant foods, big and small game, avifauna, aquatic fauna and honey, the Kunchapuri Yerukulas exclusively depend on avifauna. The occassions when they included animal meat in their diet are very rare and even on these rare occasions they ate animals like squirrel (*Funambulus palmarum* Linn.), fox (*Vulpus Bengalensis* Shaw), *bush* rat (*Golunda ellioti* Gray) and monitor lizard (*Varanus monitor* Linn.) but not the usual game preferred by the other traditional hunter gathers. The favourite meat animals commonly preyed upon (because of their availability) by other groups are hare (*Lepus nigricollis ruficaudatus* Geoffrey), porcupine (*Hystrix indica* Kerr), wild bear (*Sus scrofa cristatus* Wagner), the giant squirrel (*Ratufa indica* Enxleben), jungle cat (*Felis chaus* Guldenstaedt) and pangolin (*Manis crassicaudata* Gray).

The Ecosystem

The region falling under the range of movement of the small band of the Kunchapuri Yerukulas under discussion here (Fig. 1) is situated in the Nandyal Basin of Kurnool District, Andhra Pradesh. It is a low limestone plateau country fringing the Erramalais (also Erramala, a chain of the Eastern Hill ranges) with narrow valleys and gorges drained by seasonal streams criss-crossing the plateaux. It is a semi-arid landscape with a mean annual rainfall of 523.24mm (20.60") recorded at Banaganapalli, which is situated almost in the centre of their range of movement. The geological formations are represented by the rocks of the Cuddapah and Kurnool series and chiefly comprise horizontal beds of massive limestones, flaggy limestones, shales, argillaceous limestones and quartzites. A common geomorphological feature of this region is the occurrence of extensive terraces of limestone and limestone structural benches due to differential weathering. The limestone surface is fretted and fluted and Lapies surface or limestone pavements due to surface karstification are also common. Sink holes, swallow holes and dolines leading to underground caverns are frequent and there are zones with a well developed subterranean drainage system. There are a few lakes in the low lying basins of such zones which receive considerable discharge during the monsoon and go dry in summer (from February to July). The vegetation on the fringes of hills and the plateaux is typical of scrub jungle and shrub savanna with grasses, xerophytic plants and occassional dry deciduous trees. The soil cover comprising mostly red sandy loams and occassional patches of black loams is thin and is of low marginal utility for agriculture. The land is best suited (other than for sheep and cattle pastoralism) for dry farming and the cultivated crops are the great millet (*Sorghum vulgare* Pers.), the Itallian millet (*Setaria Italica* Beauv.), bajra (*Penisetum typhoides* Stapf.), black gram (*Phaseolus mungo* Linn.), red gram (*Cajanus cajan* Millsp.), green gram (*Phaseolus radiatus* Linn.), groundnut (*Arachia hypogea* Linn.). safflower (*Carthamus tinctorius* Linn.), rice (*Oryza sativa* Linn.), cotton (*Gossypium herbaceum* Linn.), and tobacco (*Nicotiana tabacum* Linn.). These are cultivated on limestone terraces, hilly slopes and flanks and valley bottoms but the crop pattern is purely dependent upon the monsoon cycle. However, some areas as at Muchchatla and Mudduleti, having tanks fed by perrennial springs pro-

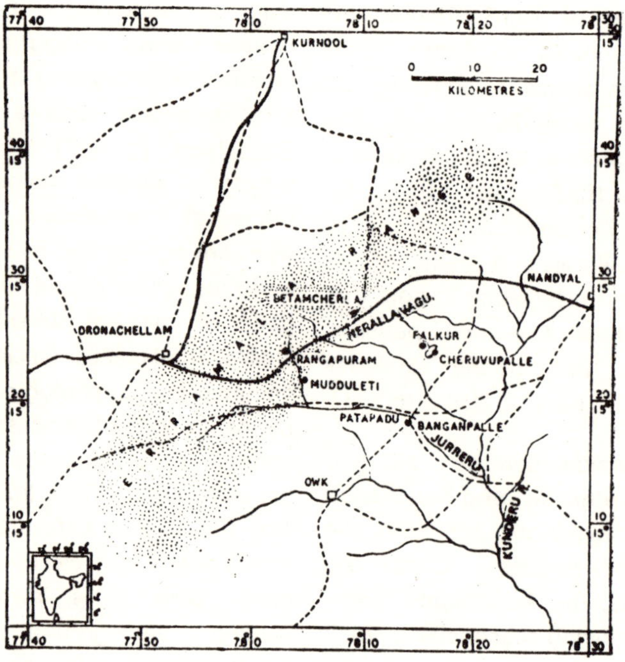

Fig. 1

vide some irrigation facilities for the rice crop. There are vast stretches of uncultivable rough terrain with thorny bushes, shurbs and xerophytic plants in which the terrestrial birds abound taking shelter under the boulders or in bushes.

Symbiotic Relationship with other Communities

The economic activity of the Kunchapuri Yerukulas is essentially dependent on the village and forms a subsidiary unit of the agricultural economy. Their chief occupations are the sale of cattle and pig dung as manure to the farmers, for which they maintain herds of cattle and piggery, and working as farm labourers at the time of harvest. They also sell pigs and pork. They eat pork frequently but the right time when they get the best pork is after *ugadi* (Telugu New Year's day which falls around the end of March or beginning of April), because, by this time, the pigs put on good fat, having fed for nearly three months on the remnants of the groundnut crop in the fallow fields. Pork is more frequently eaten in this season than in the others.

No matter what their chief occupations during the present times are, bird hunting is their speciality. They possess a remarkable knowledge of the habits and habitats of resident and migratory birds which is lacking with the agricultural and other advanced communities. Bird hunting is carried on regularly throughout the year, barring the bad weather days in the months of monsoon, *provided it does not interfere with their chief occupations.* This is because their symbiotic association with the agricultural castes demands a greater part of their time in tending the cattle and pigs, to supply manure as per the farming schedules of the various villages. This symbiotic association has become an economic tradition for the Kunchapuri Yerukulas as it assures guaranteed returns in cash as well as in kind. They have forgotten their traditional occupation, the making of weaver brushes, as there is no demand for these brushes now. Apart from selling manure, they work as farm labourers, especially for the harvest of the second crop of rice at the time of *ugadi*. Further, their women beg food in the evenings from a few households in whichever village they camp and they are never discouraged.

The small band of Kunchapuri Yerukulas under consideration here consists of two families of brothers and an aged mother, the father having died recently. Their base camp consists of three rectangular huts, approximately 4m in length, 2m in width and 2m in height. These huts are portable and are made of large screens made from the reeds of the grass *Cymbopagan martini*. For making a hut, two or three bamboo arches are pegged into the ground in a row and the reed screen is tied around and on the top forming the walls and roof of the hut, respectively. One side of the hut is kept open and it can be closed by rolling down the screen. Close to the huts, the cattle are tied to the pegs and the pigs are kept in a small enclosure. They also keep a few mules which are essentially used for transport. A rearrangement of the huts is made once in a fortnight when the surroundings get dirty with cattle and pig dung and camp litter.

These two families always live and move together and their movement is confined to the villages of Palkur, Betamcherla, Rangapuram and Patpadu and the small hamlets within the vicinity of these villages (see Fig. 1).

During the monsoon they always camp at Palkur, a lake side village, for about four to five months between August, and December. For the rest of the year they move between the villages on the plateaux. At the Palkur camp they are joined by two families : those of their brothers-in-law. The latter go on their own way when the camp is shifted from Palkur. Roundabout December they shift from Palkur to Betamcherla and stay there until March. Between March and August they move between Rangapuram, Patpadu and the neighbouring hamlets and return to Palkur by time of monsoon.

All these villages practise fallow swidden cultivation and the seasonal nomadism of the Kunchapuri Yerukulas between these villages is determined by the demand for the sale of manure, opportunities for agricultural labour and availability of feed for the pigs. For instance, their arrival at Betamcherla coincides with the completion of the first harvest of millet and groundnut crop and their pigs are allowed to stray into the fields to feed on the leftovers of the groundnuts and other roots. But they have no difficulty in finding grazing grounds of their cattle, whereever they camp, as the region has good pastures.

The semi-nomadism of the Kunchapuri Yerukulas, it is true, is linked with the symbiotic orientation of their economy. Nevertheless, it plausibly seems to have primarily been determined, in antiquity, in keeping with the habits and habitats of the resident and migratory birds. Thus, the practice of establishing the camp at Palkur, during the season of monsoon every year. might come into vogue primarily in pursuit of the migratory aquatic birds like flamingoes and storks. It must have been their subsistence behaviour in pre-contact times, which is being continued despite the new orientation in their economy. Their belief that being the best place for trapping flamingoes, storks and other waterside birds is the Palkur lake, and monsoon the best season, further lends support for such a reasoning. The rest of the terrain within their semi-nomadic range abounds in terrestrial birds; and they schedule bird hunting in such a way that it does not upset other occupational commitments.

Traditional Behaviour

Their traditional economic behaviour can be distinguished in the bird hunting habits. Bird hunting is exclusively conducted by the males; the females, other than attending to household chores, assist the males in tending of pigs and cattle, and collection of pig and cattle dung and making it into heaps of measured quantities for sale.

The birds that are commonly hunted by the Kunchapuri Yerukulas belong to the following species.

Order/Family	*Zoological Name*	*Common English Name/ Vernacular Name*
Pelicaniformes		
Phalacrocoracidae	*Ibis leucocephalus (Pennant)*	Painted stork/*sanganāra*
Phoenicopteridae	*Phoenicopterus roseus* (Pallas)	Flamingo/*tenamā, samudrapu ciluka*
Ciconiformes		
Ardeidae	*Hrdeola grayii* (Sykes)	Paddy bird or pond heron/*guḍḍi konga*
Ciconiidae	*Ciconia episcopus* (Boddaert)	White necked stork/ *nalla konga, maccanara*
	Ciconia ciconia (Linnaeus)	White stork/*battameka, pennāra*
	Leptoptilos dubius (Gmelin)	Adjutant stork/*vode koraku*
Threskiornithiadae	*Pseudibis papillosa* (Temminck)	Black ibis/*kullāyandri*
Anseriformes		
Anatidae	*Tadorna ferruginea* (Pallas)	Brahminy duck *saraga*
	Anas acuta Linnaeus	Pintail/*dāra*
Galliformes		
Phasianidae	*Francolinus pictus* (Jardine & Selby)	Painted partridge/ *kakkarāvu*
	Francolinus pondicerianus (Gmelin)	Grey Partridge/lāruka
	Coturnix coromandelica (Gmelin)	Blackbreasted or rain quail *konamgoi n̄itikoḍi*
	Coturnix coturnix (Linnaeus)	Common or grey quail/ *elise*
	Peridicula asiatica (Latham)	Jungle bush quail/*kerja*
	Galloperdix sapadica (Gmelin)	Red spurfowl/*cedalakovi*
GRUIFORMES		
Turnicidae	*Turnix tanki* Blyth	Indian or yellow legged button quail/*kanju*
	Turnix suscitator (Gmelin)	Common or blue legged bustard quail/*kanju*

Rallidae	*Gallinula chloropus* (Linnaeus)	Indian moorhen/*temba*
Charadriiformes		
Charadriiformes	*Vanellus indicus* (Boddaert)	Redwattled lapwing/*kardi*
	Vanellus melabaricus (Boddaert)	Yellowwattled lapwing/ *tikkatītuva*
Columbiformes		
Pteroclididae	*Pterocles exustus* Temmink	Common sandgrouse/ *bellagādu*
Columbidae	*Columba Livia* Gmelin	Blue rock pigeon/ *pāvuramu*
	Chalcophaps indica (Linnaeus)	Emerald or bronze winged dove/*pacca pāvuramu*
Caprimulgiformes		
Caprimulgidae	*Caprimulgus asiaticus* Latham	Common Indian nightjar/ *gurdemuka, cappatagādu*
Coraciformes		
Upupidae	*Upupa epops* Linnaeus	Hoopoe/ *raju pitta, juttu, Pitta, juttu kunja*
Passeriformes		
Alandidae	*Ammomanes phoenicurus* (Franklin)	Rufostailed finchlark/ *polaka*
Timaliinae	*Turdoides malcolmi* (Sykes)	Large grey babbler *goyyagadu*

Hunting Methods

The Kunchapuri Yerukulas hunt birds with ease. Their hunting strategy involves neither any elaborate planning nor cooperative activity; it is just a family affair. The hunt requires the action of two or three male members, most often an adult and a younger member, who set off with the traps in the early hours of the morning around 0600 hours and return to the camp with the catch within three or four hours. No strict time schedule is observed though the preferred timings are between dawn and forenoon. Birds are hunted by two methods : (1) with a multiple noose trap (a bigger one for large aquatic birds like flamingoes and a smaller one for the terrestrial birds) and (2) with a tubular net trap using a cow for camouflage.

Multiple Noose Trap

This noose trap is called urla padi[1]. This is a simple but effective device consisting of multiple slender pegs, each peg having a noose. The pegs, which are thin and elongated, are cut out of bamboo staves, and the end that is pegged into the ground is painted. About two-thirds of the length of the peg, leaving about 3 cm bare at either end, is twined with a cotton thread. At the upper end, just at the point where the twining of of the cotton thread ends, is tied a strand of horse tail terminating in a noose. This horse tail noose goes off laterally from the pegs and stands floating in the air above the ground. Several such pegs of the same dimension, each with a noose, are tied at regular intervals to a long cord at the pointed end (at the place where the twined thread on the body of the peg terminates). For instance, a multiple noose trap with about 20 pegs, tied to a cord at intervals of 30 cm, covers a length of 6 m.

The multiple noose trap used for capturing large aquatic birds comprises pegs of 30 cm length, with the number of pegs varying between 30 and 40: thus they can be spread to a length of 10m to 12m. In these bigger traps, the gut used for tennis rackets is used instead of the horse tail for the nooses, as it is thick affording better strength. The size of the pegs used in the traps for the smaller land birds is about 20 cm and only horse tail is used for making the nooses.

Multiple noose trap for water birds is laid across in a marshy ground either along the margin of a lake or a tank, or in the fields close to a lake or a tank where the birds move feeding, advancing in rows. Traps for terrestrial birds are laid in a fretted, boulder strewn limestone terrain, where several of them move in groups hopping or walking around in search of grub. These smalier traps are also laid along the margins of shallow waterpans into which some of the birds tread for drinking water. More than one multiple noose trap is laid if the birds are located in l.rge numbers.

For laying the multiple noose trap, one of the loose ends of the long cord to which the pegs are tied is firmly secured to a boulder or a bush. Stretching the cord from this end, the pointed ends of the pegs are firmly pressed into the ground one after another in a line, the nooses of the respective pegs are widened, and the other end of the cord is also tied firmly. The trap, with several nooses floating in the air just above the ground in the path of the unwary birds, is now ready, and the trappers wait keeping a safe distance so as not to disturb the approaching birds. This multiple noose trap is most effective for the large aquatic birds like white storks and flamingoes which move in several pairs in a row feeding on the ground. There is every possibility of atleast two or three birds getting their legs or legs or necks entangled in the nooses of one multiple noose trap at a time. When the entangled birds try to fly away, the noose gets tightened and through the pegs come off the ground the birds cannot escape since the cord to which the pegs are tied is firmly secured at either end. Seeing the birds trapped, the trappers in wait rush to the spot, tie both the legs together of each bird, loosen the noose and carry them home. The smaller land birds are made immobile by breaking their leg joints and are carried home in a flat circular basket of about 30cm radius with a stretch-open mouth of 6cm radius at the centre.

---

1. *urla-pa:ḍi* (*uri* 'snare' of DED 564: Telugu *uri* 'snare', *uralu* 'to be caught in a snare'. *pa:ḍi* could be ascribed the meaning 'object fixed in the ground at regular intervals' of. DED 3363: Malayalam *pa:kuka* 'to lay things regularly on the ground, fix in the ground regularly'. DED - Burrow, T. and Emeneau, M.B. 1961. *A Dravidian Etymological Dictionary.* London: Oxford University Press.)

Tubular Net Trap and Camouflage

This method is most commonly used for capturing the smaller land birds as it affords to catch several at a time. By this method, birds like partidge, finch lark, quail, babbler, pipet, spurfowl. lapwing and nightjar fall and easy prey.

The tubular net of the trap is about 2.5m long with a wide mouth tapering to a closed end. The tubular shape of the net is brought about by the support of broad oval shaped frames of bamboo staves, varying from 6 to 8 in number, kept in position at intervals of 0.3° to 0.4°m within the tube. The frame that supports the tube at the mouth gives to it a widh of about 0.45m and a height of 0.30m; the frame at the closed end makes a width of about 0.30m and a height of 0.20m. These bamboo frames, other than supporting the tubular net for keeping it in position, also help in closing-in the tube by bringing them together and making it convenient to carry.

Associated with the tubular net on either side of the mouth are foldable rectangular notted frames, also made of bamboo staves. There are about four such on either side each with a width of about 0.6m and a height of 0.30m which are stretched laterally. This trap when laid across with the rectangular frames stretched laterally from either side of the mouth of the tube cover a length of 5.20m. These frames stand vertically and barricade the forward movement of birds and lead them into the tubular trap. The tubular trap is only the outfit. For trapping the birds the trapper ties a flat square hat (a square piece of 30cm x 30cm cut out of a gunnysack fixed to a frame made of bamboo staves) to cover his head and uses a cow for camouflage.

The Kunchapuri Yerukulas set out in the morning with the folded trap, the hat and a cow. No prior reconnaissance is made to determine the place for laying the trap; the decision is taken on the spot after arriving at a niche and spotting the birds. They now lay the trap with the rectangular frames extended on either side at a safe distance from the birds without being noticed by them, but in the direction of the forward movement. The cow is kept standing at a close distance in front of the trap and the trapper wearing the square hat remains concealed behind the cow. The unwary birds keep only the cow in sight, the presence of which does not deter their movement, and fail to notice the trapper behind the cow. They advance towards the trap skulking or in zig-zag spurts feeding on the ground. At this moment the trapper moves the cow around, himself taking cover behind the cow and leads the cow on to the birds from sideways Since the birds are not frightened of the cow, they never fly away when the cow (with the camouflaged person behind it) is moving around. As the birds move on towards the barricade of the rectangular netted frames, their onward movoment is obstructed and with the cow being made to advance slowly on them from sideways, they move towards the centre, enter the tubular trap and try to escape through the closed end. By this method quite a few birds (as many as ten sometimes) can be driven into the tubular trap. Once the birds are in the trap, the mouth of the trap is closed by pushing the erect standing bamboo frame backwards, thus closing the net between the first and second frames at the mouth. By pulling the remaining frames close to the mouth, the birds struggling to escape from the rear are brought within the reach of hand at the closed mouth-end and are taken out one by one. As soon as a bird is removed from the trap, its knee joints are dislocated to make it immobile and all the birds are conveyed to the circular basket to be taken to the base camp for their own consumption and sale.

Traditional Behaviour : an Archaeological Perspective

The exploitative territory of the Kunchapuri Yerukulas, as of today, is shared by (1) other traditional broad spectrum groups like the Dabba Yerukulas and Boyas ; (2) sheep pastoral groups like the Kuruvas ; and (3) village based farming cum pastoral communities. Archaeologically speaking, there is ample evidence indicating that this region was originally inhabited by Stone Age hunter gatherer bands (Isaac 1960 ; Murty 1974 ; Murty and Reddy 1976) and that from *circa* third millenium B.C. (Neolithic-Chalcolithic) populations geared to agriculture and cattle pastoralism moved into these zones. For an appraisal of the archaeological evidence to understand the ontogeny of the ethnoeconomic ethology (this being crucial to hypothesize the hunter gatherer adaptive strategies), it is essential to take stock of some of the unique features of the ethnics in the study area.

One of the striking features of these ethnics that distinguishes them from the advanced communities is their expert knowledge of the biological environment. The Kunchapuri Yerukulas enumerate the names (in their own vernacular) of resident and migratory birds, their habits and habitats. The Dabba Yerukulas cite a list of wild plants within the habitation range and explain their food, economic and medicinal value (Murty, in press). The Dabba Yerukulas and Boyas, as well as Chenchus on the higher hill ranges and Yanadis along the coastal tract are expert trackers : they identify the animals by looking at their footprints and trail them to their abodes. Within the habitation range of the ethnographic present there are Palaeolithic and Mesolithic occurrences ranging from occupation scatters with home bases to transitory sites. Such a contiguity makes it imperative that hunter gatherer ecosystems that were exploited by the prehistoric bands and whose structures although have now become vestigial yet continue to support hunting and foraging societies. As a theoretical excercise, if we eliminate the agricultural/pastoral/trader systems that are intrusive, there will be none else than the hunter gatherer and such a reasoning suggests a link in the ethnoeconomic traditions from the prehistory to the ethnographic present. Suffice it would to say that archeological evidence supported by oral traditions of the sheep pastoral groups (Murty and Sontheimer 1980) and references in the contemporary literature of as late a period as the medieval times (12th-14th centuries A.C.) provide fascinating examples on the culture core of the hunter gatherer peoples and their interaction with the advanced societies. These instances indicate continuity in hunter gatherer traditions and that the basic patterns of their culture core continued their originality throughout the developmental phases of the ethnographic present.

By analogy with the dietary habits of the ethnics (foragers, collectors and subsistence agriculturists) adapted to varied ecosystems in this geographical region, it can be safely conjectured that broad spectrum subsistence strategies were the rule, during normal years, right from the Stone Age times. The questions that naturally arise then are : (1) what were the causative forces that made the Kunchapuri Yerukulas restrict almost exclusively to bird meat that can be regarded as a narrow spectrum adaptation? and (2) what could be the antiquity of such an adaptation?

Temporary periods of relying on narrow spectrum diet by all the groups during Stone Age times must have been a recurring phenomenon under unprecedented conditions of environmental instability, when the food chain in the biome gets jeopardized triggering competition between different groups for exploitation. Even today, these ecosystems on the southeast coast periodically witness bad weather vagaries like cyclones and droughts and the ethnics adopt various strategies in the hunger years. Both the long run and short run climatic shifts of the Pleistocene and early Holocene, apart from upsetting resource availability, must have also hindered and discouraged hunting and foraging activities inducing the Stone Age bands to reschedule their exploitative strategies plausibly confirming to a narrow spectrum diet. Upon the reversion of the environment to the original conditions, the subsistence strategies also might have been reversed to the usual broad spectrum pattern, as is happening with the ethnics in these zones today. Nevertheless, a narrow spectrum strategy like hunting and greater reliance on bird meat, if proves to be more advantageous, may be favoured by cultural selection and become an imortant means of food procurement for some groups, an economic adaptation, under changed conditions of demographic-ecosystem equilibrium. It is hypothesized here that bird hunting as a specialized adaptation plausibly has been developed by the ancestral groups of Kunchapuri Yerukulas under some such environmental pressures, and this finally became an economic tradition as it suited their symbiotic way of life. Presumably, from the time the ancestral groups of Kunchapuri Yerukulas became symbiotic with the village based groups, they have had to devote a major part of their time in the management of cattle and piggery (as today) which makes it difficult to keep away indefinitely from the base camps in pursuit of game. Bird hunting is an ideal strategy in that it can be carried out without disturbing their time budget to supplement their dietary requirements.

An endeavour towards reduction of effort is the other important guiding principle underlying the bird hunting strategies of the Kunchapuri Yerukulas. Hunting of game requires elaborate planning, cooperative activity and is tedious. Even then, there is no guarantee that the hunt always ends successfully. Instances are not infrequent when the Dabba Yerukulas and Boyas returned exhausted and empty handed after having spent about two or three days (with traps) in pursuit of even small game like hares, porcupines and pangolins. On the other hand bird hunting is relatively much easy, safest, the chances of success being the highest and the efficiency of capture is maximal even with simple traps. A single individual would suffice, when more manpower is required to look after the cattle and pigs, in bird hunt and no cooperative activity is involved. Birds are the most reliable source of food available throughout the year; their meat tastier (a delicacy for the advanced communities who obtain them from the Kunchapuri Yerukulas either by barter or cash purchase) and long distance trekking and indefinite chase is required. No other groups in this area surpass the Kunchapuri Yerukulas in their knowledge of avian ethology; and cultural inheritence perpetuates the code bird habits and habitats in their memory bank, generation after generation.

Thus with minium effort : (1) by setting a base camp in proximity to a bird habitat ; (2) by shifting the base camp according to the seasonality of the resident and migratory birds; and (3) by using simple traps, the Kunchapuri Yerukulas meet the demand of food supply, as and when required. Further and most important, as the other broad spectrum groups do not exploit bird sources to the same degree, competition and possible friction with other groups within the exploitative territory is minimal.

It can be predicted, borrowing the concept of 'deviation amplifying' process of Maruyana (1963: 164) (all processes of mutual casual relationships that amplify an insignificant or accidental initial kick, build up deviation and diverge from the initial condition) that what was originally an accidental deviation in the subsistence strategies of hunter gatherer groups, eventually became an important subsistence activity for the (ancestral groups of) Kunchapuri Yerukulas. What is more, the operation of selective pressures towards greater bias for specialized adaptations, on atleast some groups, must have increased with the moving in of immigrant Neolithic populations into these hitherto undisturbed hunter gatherer ecosystems. For this region with a low mean annual rainfall and poor red/black sandy loam cover and limited irrigated facilities (gravity flow irrigation is the predominant type) is only of marginal utility for farming operations. And the new populations, with the emergence of Neolithic-Chalcolithic settlements, have had to find ways and means to support themselves, which the achieved by placing greater reliance on cattle pastoralism, supplemented by hunting, as attested by the Neolithic-Chalcolithic settlements in the southern Deccan (Allchin, 1963).

The management of mountain pasture and encroachment into the hitherto undisturbed forested zones from the Neolithic times must have affected the wild fauna, forcing them to retreat into the higher forested mountain ranges of the Erramalais, Nallamalais (also Nallamal) Velikondas etc., where they survive in protected reserves to this day. Thus the introduction of pastoral and agricultural economies brought into force population pressures, impoverishment in the game and what is more, a share in the latter to supplement the dietary requirements of the Neolithic groups, dislocating the ecological balance struck by the hunter gatherer groups. All these factors must have necessitated varied readaptations and demographic realignments to the eclogical milieu, and this must have forced (the ancestral groups of) Kunchapuri Yerukulas to develop a symbiotic orientation with the agricultural groups, in addition to bird hunting.

It would be worthwhile to examine at what stage the Kunchapuri Yerukulas acquired the tradition of using cow for camouflage. Two possible conjectures can be offered on theoretical considerations.

First, this tradition might have developed sometime in late Pleistocene or early Holocene times itself. It may not be wrong to assume, on the basis of central Indian cave paintings that some prototypes of traps, snares and other hunting aids of the ethnographic present were certainly known during the Stone Age times and that avifauna were exploited. As mentioned earlier, this region is characterized by Middle and Upper Palaeolithic findspots. While the Middle Palaeolithic occurrences are typical streamside occupations (eg. : right on the bank of the river Jurreru near Banaganapalli), those of the Upper Palaeolithic Mesolithic are cave and plateau occupations, majority of them being transitory sites indicating restricted wandering within a homerange.

That during the late Pleistocene and early Holocene times, there were atleast two varieties of *Bos* sp. extant In this region is indicated by the faunal remains occuring in the excavated cave sites (Murty 1975). The man-animal relationships may not always necessarily have been that of the hunter-and-prey; there must have been, obviously. face to face no-harm-intended encounters with the wild cattle. Such a contact might have given rise to some sort of man-animal association leading to taming of wild cattle possibly on a limited scale. The causative process that must have favoured taming or wild cattle is the symbiotic associotion between the cattle and the terrestrial birds, and the realization that cattle can be used as an aid in trapping birds. Evidence as yet may not be available in the study area to substantiate this explanation but archaeological instances indicating man-animal relationships from the Palaeolithic times are known from a few regions of the Old World (Higgs and Jarman 1969: 38-39).

The second possibility is that the (ancestral groups of) Kunchapuri Yerukulas, being as they were familiar with the bird-ungulate association. started making use of cattle for camouflage in bird hunt, after having adopted domestic cattle from the times they established contact with the Neolithic groups and developed symbiotic organization.

Conclusions

The Kunchapuri Yerukulas inhabit an ecosystem that was originally hunter gatherer and share it with other traditional hunter gatherer groups like Dabba Yerukulas and Boyas. The occurrence of Palaeolithic and Mesolithic scatters within the exploitative range of these hunter gatherer groups, and the procurement strategies (exploitation of wild plant foods, game, avifauna, aquatic fauna and honey) of the Dabba Yerukulas and Boyas in the study area and Yanadis and Chenchus in the neighbouring zones, provide indirect evidence to hypothesize that similar broad spectrum dietary patterns must have been the case in the Stone Age past. Ethno-economic behaviour during hunger years in these ecosystems further point out that, reliance on narrow spectrum diet must have been a recurrent phenomenon in the prehistory, as one of the strategies to tide over food shortage periods under conditions of environmental instability. It is predicted here, basing on the concept of deviation-amplifying process of Maruyama that, excessive exploitation of birds as a source of food, which must have been originally resorted to as an accidental deviation during periods of ecological duress (when the regular food supplies were affected) became a principal subsistence activity for the (ancestral groups of) Kunchapuri Yerukulas, The operation of selective pressures on some groups for specialized adaptations must have become intense with the moving in of Neolithic populations from about third millenium B.C. and this must have caused (the ancestral groups of) Kunchapuri Yerukulas to develop a symbiotic organization with the agricultural groups, in addition to bird hunting.

The ingenuity of Kunchapuri Yerukulas lies in their method of hunting birds using the tubular net trap and a cow for camouflage. It is suggested here that some sort of man-animal associations were possible during late Pleistocene and early Holocene times and wild cattle were plausibly tamed on a limited scale for use as aids in bird hunting during prehistoric times. The tradition of maintaining small herds of cattle (and pigs) as a regular source of returns might have emerged as an important part of their economic organization from the times of their symbiotic association with the Neolithic stocks.

References

Allchin, F.R. 1963. *Neolithic Cattle Keepers of South India.* Cambridge : Cambridge University Press.

Bhat, D.N.S. 1968. A Survey of the Mysore District. *The Linguistic Survey Bulletin No. 1,* pp. 1-6 Poona : Deccan College (cyclostyled copy).

Guru Reddy, C.V.R. 1968. The Erukala language. *The Linguistic Survey Bulletin No. 4,* pp. 45-50 Poona : Deccan College (cyclostyled copy).

Higgs, E.S. and Jarman, M.R. 1969. The Origins of Agriculture : A reconsideration. *Antiquity.* LXIII (172) : 31-41.

Hassan, Syed Siraj ul. 1920. *The Castes and Tribes of H.E.H. The Nizams Dominions 1,* pp. 185-95. Bombay.

Isaac, N. 1960. *The Stone Age Cultures of Kurnool.* Unpublished Ph. D. Thesis, Poona University.

Maruyama, M. 1963. The second cybernetics : Deviation-amplifying mutual casual processes. *American Scientist.* 51 pp. 164-79.

Murty, M.L.K. 1974. A late Pleistocene cave site in south India. *Proceedings of the American Philosophical Society.* 118 (2) pp. 196-230.

Murty, M.L.K. 1975. Late Pleistocene fauna of Kurnool caves. *In Archaeozoological Studies,* pp. 132-38. Amsterdam.

Murty, M.L.K. and Thimma Reddy, K. 1976. The significance of lithic finds in the cave areas of Kurnool, India. *Asian Perspectives.* 38 (2) pp. 214–26.

Murty, M.L.K. u.d. Use of plant foods by some hunter gatherer communities on the southeast coast of India : Its possible relevance to prehistory. Presented at *Symp. Recent Adv. Indo-Pac. Prehis.,* 1978, Pune.

Murty, M.L.K. and Sontheimer, G.D. 1980. Prehistoric background to pastoralism in the southern Deccan in the light of oral traditions and cults of some pastoral communities. *Anthropos* 75 pp. 163-84.

Pratap, D.R. 1973. *Occupational Structure and Development Priorities of the Scheduled Tribes of Andhra Pradesh.* Hyderabad : Tribal welfare Department, Govt. of Andhra Pradesh.

Mesolithic-Megalithic Links— New thoughts for Study in India.

K. V. SOUNDARAJAN
Archaeological Survey of India, New Delhi

Our concepts on Megalithic culture in India had been based on the considerations of structural architecture, black and red ware and its antecedents or variations and the Iron Age syndrome wherein we found its greatest elaborations. Our early attempts to study them in India, in the days of Meadows Taylor, Carllyle, Breeks and Logan had been to envelope it in a mystique and to consider individual examples of their in the concerned regions as standing for exclusive types. Alongside, whatever European megalithic studies had been imbibed in India, prior to independence had been mainly to consider them as a post—Neolithic introduction, as a diffusionist pattern of propagation and virtually a magnificient eschalogical display of a Worldwide inter-relationship in style. In the era of Wheeler—notwithstanding the fact he himself was no deep specialist of Megalithic lore of Europe and the British Isles and was, in the ultimate analysis, one of the most perfected methodologists of archaeological techniques and tools the world of archaeology had been fortunate to process-our first attempt was to survey and screen not merely the variegation, but also the pattern of variegation of the monumental character of it, in different parts of South India especially, and to establish-to the extent possible at that stage when studies had not even emerged as a chronological computer for archaeology— the relative dates for the same in the expanding linked sequence of the Neolithic-chalcolithic Iron Age Culture framework.

The bottom of the complacency which such a world wide situation on Megalithic culture and its supposed links had with the burgeoning Neolithic revolution, has been knocked out by the concerted attempts made by Irish and Swedish archaeologists working in that remote insular region of islands and islets in Ireland and between the British Isles and the Scandinavian peninsula, especially the north sea coast line. The trends created in sustained excavations at Carrowmore and the Boyne valley 50 km north of Dublin and Co Sligo and the megalithic graves of South Sweden and Denmark by Goran Burenhult (1977-79), which placed 'students of European archaeology and Irish archaeologists in particular deeply in debt'. This has been one of the largest archaeological excavations in progress in Europe at the moment, and with most important results according to Glyn Daniel, writing in *Antiquity* (1981) editorially recently. He appends also an astounding chart compiled on the Radiocarbon dates for Megalithic tombs in Ireland and Britain. The gist of what he has to say is best put in his own words on this most extraordinary situation.

"While not producing certain conclusion, they do question the existing model now used to explain the origin and chronological inter-relations of the two main types of Irish megaliths viz. the Court cairns and the passage graves. Until recently, the accepted view was that the court cairns were the earliest Irish megalithic monuments and that the passage-graves represented a new and later wave of Neolithic people. Our present evidence therefore dates the court cairns between 3300-2000 B.C. The Swedish team excavated two monuments at Carrowmore that yielded surprising dates. Carrowmore 7 was dated to 4200 B.C. and Carrowmore 27 to 4190-3900 B.C. Here is Burenhult revolution in Irish Prehistory. 34 Radio-carbon dates described with justifiable pride as the "largest complex of C-14 dates from any archaeologically investigated area in Ireland". The important new date from site 4 at Carrowmore is 3800±80 B.C. which on the Suess calibration is 4580 B.C. The radiocarbon dates for Carrowmore of 4580-3710 B.C. make it, we are told "the earliest known megalithic cemetery in Europe" (But, we ask, is the date of 4700 B.C. for Kercado in Brittany been forgotten ? Or are we perhaps dealing with the use of different curves ?). "The traditional stereotype : forming community-megalithic monuments, can no longer be upheld, and a *development within a pre-existing mesolithic population* (emphasis ours) has been put forth as a preliminary madel of the socio economic background to the chambered-tombs at Carrowmore. Tnis idea is supported by offering of unopened sea shells in the excavated monuments".

Commenting on how such a *denoument* was seen coming by another perspicacious veteran archaeologist Grahame Clerk, Glyn Daniel (1981) quotes from the former's paper, on the pursuit of fish and the importance of exploitation of coastal resources during the first period of megalith building, hinting already thereby at a mesolithic background for the first megaliths ; and he goes on to say; 'we look to the mesolithic hunters and fishers of South Portugal, and the coasts of Brittany, Sligo, Sjael-land and Sweden to initiate the megalithic architecture of western and northern Europe.

Basing on the above revealing situation, it is becoming ever so urgent to examine the situation in India and South Asia. While the South Asian Neolithic, as in Indonesia, had also nurtured certain megalithic types, we are not in a position to link them in any manner with the Indian ones, notwithstanding the Neolithic links that could well have ushered the Eastern Indian food-gathering stages, at their earliest working from Thailand and Burma. But the more important aspect is that even on those new elements of megalithism seen on the west coast of India northern Karnataka (Sundara, 1975) in the Dharwar District, as at Halingali, Terdal, etc., already chambered tomb types had been seen with a possible association with pre-Iron Age culture, monument-wise and artefacts-wise. If so, can any economic base be established for these people of these periods who also should have had, on modern anology, a thriving fishing occupations on the rivers on the bank of which these sites are found ? We found that chambered tombs and certain types of dolmens have been particularly prevalent in South Canara District and the adjacent Anjanad valley further south in Malabar area of Kerala. The rock-cut tombs of Malabar and rest of Kerala had again been fitful either in their associated materials of pottery, of Iron implements etc., and often are without any such. The Kerala situation, besides, is persuasively anologues in its architectural tracts to the megalithic cultures of Spain and Portugal and further in Kerala, we do seem to have an essentially mesolithic situation earlier also, in the Stone Age notwithstanding the notice of sporadic palaeolithic-looking tools in North Kerala. What further research will hold out for a mesolithic-preNeolithic base for megalithic tombs in Karnataka and Kerala will depend largely on scientific future excavations. That many of these tombs in these two regions besides have coursed stone masonry built tombs, both for the cruciform passage tombs of the former including the surrounding oblong enclosure walling and the lintel corbel method of raising the central chamber, would hold out clear typological possibilites at least of an independent architectural beginning for such devices long before either. Neolithic or Iron Age constructions and the latter have not shown within their ambit of creations in construction, any coursed or corbelled and dry masonry structures. In every way, the air has been cleared by the inspired presentation of the Irish sites at Carrowmore and on the Boyne valley for considering an economic Mesolithic beginnings of these communities who could have initiated the chamber tombs, as seen in India in north Karnataka. Our present relevant Chalcolithic situation for these tombs - at present dichotomising the Neolithic with their own beginning - may itself be capable of further review by a careful study of the pottery, skeletal remains and even other secondary vestiges, if any, of sea shells and the like. The need for separating the Iron Age efflorescence of megaliths as seen in the rest of lower southern India from its antecedents and separating also incidentally the black and red ware consanguinity with most of the megalithic stages of development in the Iron Age in this process also appears to be calling for imaginative investigations. A scientific reassessment of the material from north Karnataka (with its devolutions, if any, in coastal Malabar of Kerala would appear to hold out possibilities of yielding interesting results for our understanding the economic flash-point that should have triggered the truly megalithic architectural inception. It may place the whole of the upper Deccan, central Indian and southern tip megaliths outside the ambit of this diagnostic situation and will be perhaps amenable to being represented by a divergent evolutionary process.

Even for the Vindhyan mesolithic, grading into a series of rich microlithic culture assemblage it is possible, by discerning fresh studies, to find the socio-economic base upon which it could not evolve into the Neolithic situation but was becoming degenerate and stagnant and somehow might have caused some megalithic creations, unrelated to any Neolithic Culture development. The focus is thus on both the better understanding of the Mesolithic of India and its links with the Neolithic, on the one hand, and the developing megalithic constructional architecture, on the other. Of course, the ideal situation for a viable economic vocation, as found in the Scandinavian and Irish sites, cannot be said to be existing as yet in the central Indian inland context. But such a study can still clearly help to identify the material vestiges of the communities which throne *before* the advent of Megalithic architecture of certain standardized patterns in south India.

The megalithic studies of Sundara (1975) show that the passage chamber builders who created the Greek Cross and Latin Cross plan types at Terdal and Halingali had preferred mostly the river valley areas in the hilly terrain; that they are a regional and an almost circumscribed manifestation; that the port-hole cist types are comparatively later to the passage-grave types, in a typological sense; that owing to the impact of these passage-grave builders, the local people in the Neolithic-Chalcolithic stages gradually developed the megalithic styles like the round barrows, cairn circles, cist burials, etc.; that red ware pottery is predominant in the passage tomb culture ; that post-firing graffiti is not found in the passage chamber types and perhaps were borrowals from the Chalcolithic Cultures ; that Iron technology was not a feature of the passage grave builders and had not diffused from north into lower deccan and south India, but were locally and indigenously developed coevally in the Karnataka region ; that the megalithic builders of the passage grave type are intrusive into Neolithic society of the lower Deccan and south India, which included the Dravidian and the proto-Australia people and were perhaps racially comparable to the Seytho-Iranian stock coming from Mediterranean region and thus megalithism was heralded for the first time in Karnataka only ; that the megalithic cultures, wherever seen in northern India, are different from those of the south and was relatively *later* to the latter. We find that Narasimhayya (1980) has examined the lower southern Megaliths of Tamil Nadu etc., in terms of its pottery and also seems to feel that the red ware pottery has a distinctive usage among certain types of megaliths, namely, the cairn circles and barrows, as different from the dolmen and cist-using types, given to black and red ware and all-black ware profusely. It is perhaps therefore possible that the key to the understanding of the first introduction of Megaliths lies in our isolating the red ware using Megalith builders (of the passage chamber types) in north Karnataka, in order to find if there could be a priority or overlaps between them and the Neolithic-Chalcolithic people. Sundara found that the barrow type at Terdal gave exclusive pre-Iron Chalcolithic-Neolithic elements including microliths of chert etc. It has not been possible for him to test what has been the relationship between the barrow or cairn circle users and the passage form users in that area. [Red ware is also seen dominantly associated with a Neolithic stratum at the site new Mettur Dam, Tamil Nadu]. It is, however, seen by him that the latter have an admixture of both the red ware and black and red ware in certain parts of the chamber, as excavated, and the tombs excavated seem also to be disturbed. Whether this is disturbance or re-use has not also been tested so far. We have, therefore, a possibility still of showing that the barrow types underlay the passage-grave type in North Karnataka and together triggered the typical megalithic development in Central and South Karnataka subsequently, and led to the diffusion of the same into Tamil Nadu, by at least the 7th century B.C., as indicated by the Payyampalli (*IAR*, 64-65) evidence. We note that even in the Irish cases at knowth on the Boyne, the barrows which indeed contain the passage-graves underlay the longer barrows tombs in that area, as excavations have shown. It is, therefore, essential that the North Karnataka area along with the continuous chains of high altitudes hilly areas of the ghats towards South Kanaras and North Malabar should be ideal for a re-examination of the typical characteristics of the passage-grave users and the pottery that specifically characterised them, isolating, in this process, the hybrid later use of passage graves with port-holed cists, and subsequently separating the cist builders and passage grave builders and the evolved cairn circle users. Until that is done successfully, the hope will remain that the coastal North Karnataka on the Krishna valley has the claim of first introduction of Megaliths. through passage-grave builders, during or before Neolithic societies, and without Iron essentially. We have seen also that post-firing graffiti is a typical characteristic of the later Megalithic cist, dolmen etc. in Karnataka and Tamil Nadu as well as upto Tapti valley, as at Ranjala (*IAR*, 60-61) and Bahal (*IAR*, 56-57). The links between Mesolithic cultures and the lithic antiquities found in the passage-graves will also bear close examination, besides the possibilities of any secondary feature like the availability of shells etc. as seen already in full, with perforation found from a disturbed round barrow and anthropomorphic figures, as at Rajamkolur and Mettur, in Andhra Pradesh and Tamil Nadu respectively in these graves indicative of their vocational predilections.

In terms of date, Sundara has suggested an anterior date upto 1200 B.C. for the inception of the passage grave builders of Terdal and Halingali. It remains to be seen if this could be divested of its Neolithic Chalcolithic links and shown as directly related to the indigenous late Mesolithic societies, with certain impulses, moving from the west. The situation places the entire Karnataka and North Kerala coast open for a fresh review and study, in respect of the megalithic monuments seen there, specially those which show (a) passage graves; (b) cyclopaean build of the tombs in coursed masonry and with enclosing walls around them, and (c) the red ware pottery usage seen in them and continuing along with the Neolithic - Chalcolithic and Iron Age black and red ware pottery, in later stages. The association of Megaliths with Iron Age essentailly in India has been, in any event, contested, in this process; and the pre-Iron (and if possible) a pre-Chalcolithic base for the adoption of Megalithic passage and chamber tombs of the South as in North Karnataka has been revealed as a distinctive possibility, highlighting the need for the first introduction of pottery itself (possibly of the red ware) in the later Mesolithic stages in these areas which around in Mesolithic assemblages.

References

Burenhult, G. u.d, *The Archaeological Excavation at Carrowmore, Co Sligo, Ireland (1977-79)*,

Institute of Archaeology' University of Stockholm (ed.) Mats. P. Malmer.

Daniel, Glyn. 1981; Editorial, *Antiquity*. July 1981.

Indian Archaeology—A Review, 1956-57, 1960-61 and 1964-65.

Sundara, A. 1975 *Ancient Chamber Tombs of South India*, Delhi

Narasimhaya, B. 1980, *Neolithic and Megalithic Culture in Tamil Nadu*, Delhi

Indo-Aryan Rulers of Ancient Western Asia and their Documents

JAMNA DAS AKHTAR
Chandigarh

Indian scholars, by and large, have not paid adequate attention to the historic records left behind by the Indo-Aryan rulers of ancient Western Asia. These Indo-Aryans are generally considered to be the ancestors of the Vedic Aryans. In our books on ancient history, their description is generally confined to a brief reference to the Boghazkoi Tablets (which contain a text of the Treaty of Friendship between the Hitti king Supplilulium and the Mitanni king Mattiwaza), on which the four Vedic deities viz. Indra, Mitra, Varuna and the Nastyas are mentioned. Other Mitanni kings namely, Dushratta, Aatama, and Shattruhana are also briefly referred to in these books. Again a casual reference to the discovery in Boghazkoi (Turkey) of an Indo-Aryan Texton horse-training pertaining to the same period (i.e. second millennium B.C.) finds place in these books. However, these two original documents, and hundreds of other Indo-Aryan and Semitic documents unearthed in Egypt, Turkey, Iraq, Syria and Israel have altogether been ignored by Indian scholars. A close study of these documents will undoubtedly be rewarding. Lack of opportunities to study of cuneiform alphabet and the Akaddian, Hurrian, Kassite and Hitti languages. in which these documents are written, has hampered research into this phase of ancient history.

In order to avoid any controversy over the question as to whether the Hitties and the Kassities belonged to Indo-Aryan or Indo-European groups, I have confined the scope of my subject to the records left behind by the acknowledged Indo-Aryan elements in Western Asia during the first and second millennium B.C.

It has already been acknowledged that "Indo-Aryan language was spoken in S.W. Asia during the second millennium B.C." Sanskrit speaking elements were present in Mesopotamia during this period (Hauschild, 1962). Our evidence for the presence of Indo-Aryans comes from Amarna, Nuxi, Alalakh and Boghazkoi Tablets and from other miscelleneous sources. The earliest of these Indo-Aryans was Jayalatia, a Manda chief who fought against the Hitti aggression. He is described as Commander of the forces of Aleppo. The battle took place in the seventeenth century B.C. A number of western scholars are of the opinion that Indo-Aryan elements were present in Anatolia and elsewhere in Western Asia even before the seventeenth century B.C. (Kammenhuber, 1961).

We find the name of a powerful Indo-Aryan king, Kirta, who founded the royal dynasty of Mitanni about sixteenth century B.C. His successors namely, Shattruhana, Parattarna, Shaushshatar, Artatama, Shattruhana II, Dushratta and Mattiwaza are mentioned in many documents. They ruled over a vast empire and played a significant role in shaping the history of Western Asia. The Mitannis had established their capital in Washugani which was situated somewhere in the region of the head-works of Khabur River, perhaps at Tell-Fakhriyya near Ras-el-Ain. Excavation of a large mound at this place has not been properly undertaken. The relavant mound may yield royal archives of these kings.

Another Indo-Aryan dynasty founded by Artatama II had rulers like Shattruhana and Washishtta. This dynasty was overthrown in about 1245 B.C.

The name of Kirta and Shattruhana are mentioned on a seal of Shaushahatar which gives names of his dynasty's forebears. This historic seal (Bedrich Hrozny, 1953), crowded with mythological scene, was found on one of his Babylonian inscriptions at Nuzi (to-day called Yurgham Tepe). This seal is affixed on an order of the king who defines, the jurisdiction of his three women magistrates, Amminiya, Ugi and Sattawati (Spesier, 1924). While the first two ladies seem to be Semitics, Sattawatti is undoubtedly the name of an Aryan lady. This document reveals that women enjoyed high social and political status in the most ancient Aryan society. Another document reveals the name of the Hitti queen, Nikala Matti, who was probably the daughter of a Mitanni king.

The seal of Shattruhana I was found in a Babylonian inscription at Atchana, ancient Alalakh, in northern Syria. Nikemha, Semitic king of Alalakh, was a vassal of this Indo-Aryan dynasty.

Documents found at Tell-el-Amnarna, Nuzi and Alalakh reveal that in addition to Aryan's control over large parts of Syria, Iraq and Palestine, the eastern part of Silicia was also under the sway of Indo-Aryan kings. A Cannanite king, Idrimi, was one of their vassals. A Mitanni King rescued and restored him to the throne. Idrimi narrates this episode which is insribed on his own statue found in Alalakh. A large number of Mitannian seals on which pictures of Aryan deities and mythological scenes are depicted have been found in the same place. These mythological scenes can easily be interpreted in the light of ancient Egyptian Sumerian and Vedic scriptures. In some of these seals the Cult of Pillars, as axis of the universe, is depicted. The Mitannis followed this cult and the Vedic Aryans preserved. It India, famous Asokan pillars which are now claimed to have been built in the pre-Buddhist period are very significant in the light of discovery of these Mitannian seals. The nude deity depicted on some of these seals probably represents Urvashi, the Apasra, wife of the Vedic king, Puroruva. The legend is also described in the Rig Veda and the Puranas. It was probably an Aryan adoption of an ancient Samerian and Egyptain theme.

The historic Boghazkoi Tablets already referred to confirm that these Indo-Aryans worshiped Vedic deities Indra, Mitra, Varuna, and the Nastayas. It is wrong to conclude that the absence of names of other Vedic deities on these tablets proves that they were not worshipped by these Indo-Aryans. In fact there is a solid evidence that they worshipped Vayu, Svar, Soma, the Devas, Rta, Yama, Vasus, Surya and Marutas (Dument).

In one of his letters to an Egyptian king, the Aryan ruler of Mitanni, Dushratta, states that (Pefrie)" with the grace of my God Raman, I have captured and killed my rebel brother Artashuma (or Artatama)." Kama or Raman is the hero of Ramayana. In view of this reference to Raman or Rama in this historical document and existenco of other heroes of Ramayana, namely, Shatturbana (*i.e.*, Shattrughana), Dushratta (*i.e.*, Dashratha) and Washishta as historical figures in Western Asia in the second millennium B.C., the possibility of the origin of the Ramayana story in this part of Asia can not altogether be ruled out. These Indo-Aryans after their defeat at the hands of Assyrians and their own Aryan adversaries may have brought the memory of the deeds of their ancestors to India where they found asylum. The tragedy of the murder of Dushratta at the hands of one of his own sons as the result of a place *coup* in Wassuganni, was probably changed into the story of a palace conspiracy to force his abdication in Ayodhya. Mattiwaza (who is also called Kurtiwaza) was the elder son of Dushratta who like Rama of Ramayana had wandered for many years in exile until the Hitti king Supplilulima helped him to regain his throne. There is solid evidence to believe that Tushratta had more than one wife in his heram and one of these was an Egyptian. In all probability her son committed this murder. Dushratta and his predecessors were the heroes of many battles against Egyptians, Hitties, Assyrians and a number of Aryan and non-Aryan princes. It seems that the stories of these exploits were suitably adapted in the Ramayana.

In addition to more than one hundred Indo-Aryan names already published by N.D. Mironov, Roger, Calaghan, Albright and others, more Indo-Aryan names have come into light as a result of unearthing of new evidence in Western Asia. The noted scholar late Mr. Goetze claimed that Sunasura of Kizzuwatana (Cllicia) was an Indo-Aryan king. The founder of this dynasty (Goetze) is described as Parivatri. This is incorrect reading of the name. His real name is Pa-ri-var-ata, *i.e.*, Priyavarata. *Puranas* describe a similar king as founder of an ancient dynasty in India. A beautiful seal of his successor, Isu-putah-su, was discovered as a result of excavations carried out in Goyli Kule, Tarsus which proves that the Mitanni kings and the kings of Kizzuwatana cremated their dead. These kings reigned in the later half of the sixteenth century or the first of the fifteenth century B.C. Alasia (Cyprus) was governed by another Indo-Aryan dynasty. E-Su-wa-ra king of this dynasty wrote a letter to a king of Ugarit. A tablet found in the royal archives of Ugarit forms a letter written by this prince and reflects events of the late thirteenth centry B.C. on eve of the "Peoples of the Sea" invasion. Manapa Datt and Ura Datta were two other Indo-Aryan kings who ruled the "country of Setha River" in Anatolia (Steffanni).

Names of some of the Indo-Aryan princes and other are given below :-

Sanduri—King of Kundes

San—das—arme—King of Hillaka

Beg-datti, Sutresha, Aurparnis, Bagbarna, Ashabarna,

Sri-das—sh, Serila, Artia, Ennamati, Addattoi, Ari-wati, Aria, Punnia, Tur-senni, Satusha, Parusha, Kesia Partasua, Madhuwatta etc.

The list is extremely long and it is not possible to accomodate it in the paper.

The names of several places in ancient Western Asia are Aryan. Purush-Khanda was one of the provinces of the Hitti empire in Anatolia while the ancient names of Assyria and the Euphrates were Subartu and Baranun, (probably derived from Varuna) respectively. The ancient name of Lagash was Autasura.

The Mitanni rulers had matrimonial alliances with the Egyptains. Their correspondence with the Egyptain rulers is depicted in a number of cuneiform tablets found at Tell-el-Amarna (Egypt). Egyptain kings were fond of Mittanni necklaces of fine crystal stones, Lapis Lazuli, wooden furniture, chariots, horses, pottery and wine while the Mitannis expected large quantities of pure gold as present from the Egypitian rulers. Mitanni princesses who married Egyptain kings were given valuable dowries besides hundreds of slave girls (Mercer,1939). This custom of providing slave girls was followed by their successors, *i.e.*, the Vedic Aryans. Some of the laws (Gordon,1957) enforced by these kings were also followed by the Vedic Aryans in India.

Tell-el-Amarna tablets reveal the existence of a number of Indo-Aryan princess who ruled in different small states in Syria, Lebanon and Palestine (Prichard). They were either vassals of Egypt or were governors appointed for defending the Egyptian Empire in Asia. These princes belonged to the *Maryanu* class of warriors who are mentioned in various Egyptian and Alkadian documents. It is interesting to note that they are also mentioned in the Rig Veda (*Marga)*. These Indo-Aryan fighters were well-known for their valour. Several accounts of the exploits of the Egyptian rulers in Asia reveal that the invading armies took special care to make them war prisoners. These warriors and their children received education in Egypt and were later on appointed governors in Egypfian-held territories in Asia. These princes proved their valour and loyalty by repulsing raids and rebellions of the Jews. Some of these Indo-Aryan warriors acted as political and military advisers to the Egyptian kings. One of them was Pu-u-ra who was in a position to order Addiya and his garrisons out of Jerusalem (Campbell, 1964).

Addiya was the Egyptian resident governor of Palestine, with his seat at Gaza. He was an Indo-Aryan prince and had fought many a battle against the Jews (Prichard). Another Indo-Aryan prince, Shuwardatta, controlled the region south of Jerusalem. He and another Indo-Aryan prince Bir-diya defended the Egyptian territories against the onslaughts of the Jews. Widdia was governor or prince of Ashlelon. Isuya, Shubandhu, Shaiiya, Yash Datta, Biridi, Birashena, Balu-Mihir and many other Indo-Aryan princes are mentioned in Tell-el-Amarna Tablets as fighting against the enemies of Egypt. Their letters in cuneiform alphabet have already been translated in several languages.

Biryadiya (or Bira Deva) was the governor of Damascus. He claimed to be the son of Shattruhana. Shuvardatta controlled the territory of Helron. Brdashava was a powerful commander who rebelled against the Egyptian power. In one of Amarna letters, he is accused of storming the cities of Inu-ama (*i.e.*, Yanuha and Ashteroth in the region of Type). Lab' ayu was another rebel prince and he is mentioned in several reports submitted to the Egyptian king. An Indo-Aryan prince fought the Jews on the Golan front. Indrauta was another Indo-Aryan prince who is stated to have supplied fifty chariots to Shuvardatta to fight against the 'Apirus". The noted American scholar, James B. Prichard, who translated these letters, confirms that these princes were Aryans.

Indo-Aryans' contacts with the Egyptians and the Hebrews made profound impact on the social system and religious beliefs of that time. It was due to the marriage of Indo-Aryan princesses with the Egyptian kings that the religious thoughts of Egypt had undergone a revolutionary change. In place of devotion to Amun, which had controlled the previous kings, the very name of Amun, was prescribed and erased througout the country (Peterie). His place was taken by Aton, the Sun. King Amenshotep IV changed his name to Akhenation and shifted his capital to Amarna. The ruler of Jerusalem, in the fourteenth century, was a Semitic but he became a devotee of the Mitanni goddess whose worship was well-established in the Judean hills. Vedic god Maruta, was worshipped not only in Mitanni but also in Elam and Luristan (Bacon).

Indo-Aryans invented the technique of smelting iron and utilised its potentical value. "This was a mighty secret weapon comparable in its day to the Atomic Bomb" (Grant) Kikuli who wrote a treatise on horse-training was a Mitanni subject and had defeated the Hitties. The latter borrowed the war-chariot from the kingdom of Mitanni (Dembeck, 1965). The demand and popularity of these war-chariots in Egypt is repeatedly mentioned in Telle-Amarna Tablets which have already been referred to.

References

Bacon Edward (ed.) (u.d.) *Vanished Civilization,* pp. 227,

Campbell, E.F. 1964, *The Chronology of the Amarna Letters,* p. 102.

Dembeck Warmann, 1965. *Animals and Man,* p. 241.

Dument, P.E. (u.d.) Nelson 'Indo-Aryan Names from Mitanni, Nuzi and Syrian Documents' *JOBS*, Vol. 37.6.

Goetze, A. (u.d.) 'On the Chronology of the Second Millennium B.C.' *Journal of Cuneiform Studies,* Vol. XI, No. 3, p. 63.

Gordon, C.H. 1957. *Adventures in Near East,* p. 116, New Jersey.

Grant Michael. (u.d.) *Ancient History,* pp. 66–67, London.

Gurney (u.d.) *The Hitties*, p. 212.

Hauschild, R. 1962. *Uber die Friihesten Arier imm Atten Orient*, p. 26, Berlin.

Hrozny Bedrich, 1953 *Ancient History of Western Asia India and Crete,* p. 128.

Kammenhuber, 1961 *Hippologia Heathica,* pp. 15-21, Wiesbaden.

Mercer, A.B. (ed.) 1982 'Tussratta's Letters to Amenophis 11, Nos. 22, 25, 26 *The Tell el-Amarna Tablets* Vol. I, Toronto.

Petric Flindars (u.d.) *A History of Egypt,* Vol. II pp. 262-63.

Prichard (u.d.) *Ancient Near Eastern Texts* pp. 241-45.

Spesier, E. A. 1924 'A Letter of Shanshshater and the Date of the Kirkuk Tablets' *Journal of American Oriental Society,* Vol. 49, pp. 269-75.

Steffani Ruggero, 1964 'KUB XXIC33 (B0487) : Mursilis' *JOAS* Vol. 84 pp. 22-30.

The Qutb Minar: Strengthening the Foundations

R. SENGUPTA

Introduction

The battered look with fractured stones on the facade of the Qutb Minar caused concern to its custodians if all was well with the landmark of Delhi. Like the contemporaneous (12th-14th century) tower of Pisa, a companile to a cathedral, the Minar is also an adjunct to a mosque but its lean is much less to make any comparison between the two worthwhile. The tilt in the Qutb Minar is 2'-1" whereas the tower of Pisa leans 16'-6" away from the perpendicular. Nonetheless, the problem they pose is the same as strengthening the foundation.

From the following account of repairs, it will be seen that the Qutb Minar has been receiving as much attention in the recent past as it did during the medieval period. Consequent to the damages caused by a severe earthquake shock in 1803, maior structural repairs were carried out between 1805 and 1828. The cupola put up during the repairs, in replacement of the fallen one, was taken down in 1848 as its design was based on conjecture and looked incongruous on top of the minar. Bulges in the masonry of the minar and cracks appearing in the veneering stones were noted earlier with concern. About the likely causes of their development it was recorded, 'It is not improbable that the displacement of the masonry is the result of settlement that occurred while the tower was being built, due to the work being "run up" too quickly and to the excessive use of the mortar'. After the repairs carried out in 1920, the minar was again examined in the early forties and major structural repairs were executed in 1944-49. An account describes the nature of works undertaken, 'The veneer in general at the Qutb Minar and particularly the inscriptional bands had bulged out badly at places and started falling down. A few twists and bulges had also appeared on the shaft. The affected regions were carefully reset in best mortar after securing them firmly with dowels of stainless-steel encased in cement morter. Prior to this, cracks in the hearting were grouted and made watertight'. In 1960 and thereafter in 1964 the successive officers in-charge of the monument expressed their concern over the development of cracks in the stones on the outer face of the minar and suggested for its thorough examination. The foundation of the Minar was strengthened by grouting (in 1971-72) on finding its unsatisfactory condition after conducting necessary examinations (in 1964-70). The processes are narrated in this paper.

Although the construction of Qutb Minar as a Tower of Victory and a *minar* attached to the Quwwat-ul-Islam mosque was started in 1199 by Qutb-ad-Din Aibak, the Turkish commander of Muizz-ad-Din Ghori who ruled from Ghazni, it could be raised by him upto the first storey *i.e.* only 95 ft. Qutb-ad-Din's son-in-law and successor Iltutmish added three more storeys and raised the height of the Minar. In its present form including the addition and alteration effected by Firozshah Tughlaq in the portion beyond the third srorey, it is 238 ft. high about 15 ft. higher than its forerunner at Jam in Afghanistan, As was the practice with the Ghori rulers, the Minar at Jam was also erected as a tower of Victory by Ghiath-ad-Din (1157-1202).

Prior to the construction of Qutb Minar, though in Afghanistan two minars were elected at Ghazni (11th-12th century), one at Daulatabad (11th century) and one at Siah Posh (10th century) all in brickwork, it is the last one at Siah Posh with which the Qutb Minar resembles in form wits semi-circular and angular flutings arranged alternately around its outer face. The angular flutings on the plan of the first three storeys of the Qutb were produced by rotating a spuare in a circle. Origin of this system may be traced to the Greek method, used in determining the position of steps in the gallery radiating from the platform for orchestra of a theatre, as described by Vitruvius. The angular flutings seen on the fourth storey of the Qutb Minar were obtained by rotating an quilateral triangle which system, according to vitruvius, was used in Roman theatres, He says, 'The drawing of the plans may be distinguished from each other by this difference, that theatres designed from squares are meant to be used by Greeks, while Roman theatres are designed from equilateral triangles'. (Morgan. 1960).

Epigraphic records provide interesting evidences relating to the past repairs executed under the royal patrongage. The Qutb Minar was thrice struck by ligthning and repaired successively as mantioned in the inscriptions on its wall. Firozshah Tughlag restored in 1368, most of the fourth storey and made the Minar tallor than what it was. Sikandar Shah Lodi's inscription, on the entrance doorway at the ground floor, mentions his carrying out repairs In 1503 but the nature of damage and extent of repairs are not known. Delhi being situated in a seismic zone, it experiences occasional earthquake tremors. The latest in the series was in August 1803 when a shock of considerable magnitude had caused considerable damages to the minar and its crowning cupola was thrown down.

Firozshah Tughlaq had effected changes in the use of materials in the two top storeys. Red sandstone in the interior casing and marble on the exterior face were introduced. Otherwise, in the construction, the exterior face of the central shaft and the inner face of the Minar shall have ashlar facing of Delhi quartizitic stones. The veneering is made of sandstone predominately of red colour though large quantity of stones of buff colour has also been used. The hearting of the shell is made of rubble masonry held together with iron dowels and set in sand and lime mortar. The presence of brick powder in the lime mortar indicates its having been used as an additive.

The Investigations

Appearance of cracks on the veneering stones made the authorities to have a close look at the structure and carry out investigations to find out what was wrong with the minar. Analyses of specimens of mortar obtained from various places of the minar showed presence of apprecia-ble amounts of water soluble salts, mostly sulphates though chlorides have also been detected. Alumina is present in low percentage which is considered hardly sufficient to impart hydraulic properties to the lime. Repeated solution and crystalization of soluble salts present in the mortar has resulted in the weathering of the masonry. The rusting of iron dowels used in the original construction was an important cause of cracking. The deterioration of mortar and the development of cracks due to expansive forces of rusting dowels allowed ingreas of moisture leading to concentration of soluble salts. Possibly with the deterioration of mortar there has also been settlement of the masonry.

Examination of specimens of stones from the minar showed that the binding matrix in the sandstone had deteriorated. Even in the quartzite and quartzitic sandstone, the interlocking grain system, had become disturbed and the cementing material leached out. While any generalization about the deterioration was not possible, in view of the fact that the samples examined were limited in number and had been extracted mostly from the affected areas, the reports supported the hypothesis that the extent of deterioration on stone and mortar was serious enough to affect the overall quality of masonry and its performance.

A check in the verticality of the Minar was carried out through the Survey of India and a tilt of 25" on the south-west was detected. It was observed that for a base of 47 ft. diameter and 238 ft. height, the tilt was not serious. Since no previous record on the verticality of the Qutb Minar was available, it was not possible to say if the tilt noted was of recent origin. It was difficult to establish the time element, because the historical records show that the minar was built in stages and subsequently when the fourth and fifth storeys were re-built or added by Firozshah Tughlaq, the tilt apparently was adjusted to some extent as suggeted by the offset of the central shaft at the level of reconstruction.

The Minar directly rests on an ashlar masonry pedastal 6'-6" high and roughly 54 ft. square. The masonry immediately below the Minar has sunk producing an inward slope 1:4 in the south-western direction and 1:8 in the eastern direction. The differential sinking is in consonance with the direction of the tilt of the Minar. The joints in the masonry of the pedestal have been found to be open. Below the pedestal is a platform 4 ft. high which is made of rubble masonry and about 61 ft. square. A trench dug across the minar from east to west shows that the lower footing of the rubble platform rests, on the east side, on masonry set in lime concrete and on the west on a thick rubble packing in mud mortar. On the western side the trench was sunk to a depth of 27 ft. but the natural soil or bottom of the foundation pit was not reached.

The computation of the volume and weight of the Minar at each balcony-height showed that the designing of the foundation was not rational. Even assuming that the foundation had initially been designed to carry the load of the first two storeys only, as Qutb-ad-Din Aibak might have intended and the upper storeys being additions, the foundation should have been stronger.

To find out whether or not the Minar directly rests on a rock-bed, the National Geophysical Research Institute was requested to carry out geophysical work at Qutb to obtain the information. Accordingly resistivity measurements (soundings) were taken. Inspite of very limited scope of making adequate measurements, due to presence of various kinds of structures obstructing the layout of lines and destroying current flow etc., the depth of the bed-rock could be located around 150 ft. to 200 ft. In view of the fact that there are exposures of the Delhi quartzite quite close to the Minar, the depth seemed to be rather high. But these depths were not inconsistent with the available bore hole data in respect of the two wells in the neighbourhood. Although, the depth of the bedrock, below the Qutb Minar, is likely to be of the same order, one could not be entirely certain due to the rapid variations in bedrock topography. It was, therefore, suggested that a straight or slightly inclined exploratory boreholes should be drilled at the base of the Minar for more reliable information in respect of the sub-surface structure.

Two inclined core holes were drilled into the foundation. The core hole on the south-west of the Minar was driven at an angle of 45° to the base line and extended beyond the centre line of the Minar to a depth of 35 ft. from the ground level. The core recovered by drilling revealed the strata being hetrogeneous formation of quartzite stone with medium to fine sand. The matrix of sand with lime seems to be in a loose state. Due to cavities in the masonry, perhaps due to washing out of the matrix, there was loss of water. Frequent caving of the holes indicated that the matrix of sand with lime had not set or was not compact. The other core hole was also driven to the same depth, on the north-east at an angle of 10° to the base line which did not penetrate into the central portion of the foundation. Cores from this whole suggested more or less similar condition of the pedastal and platform. Below these structures rubble stones with earth filling was met. At the bottom, beyond 30 ft. yellowish earth was found.

Considering the structural stability, it was felt :

(a) the weakness of the foundation could be the cause of the tilt which though within safe limits, was liable to increase ;

(b) the differential settlement appeared to be chronologically the primary reason for the development of some of the cracks, though subsequently other factors might have also contributed towards it ; and

(c) the stress in the masonry as calculated, namely, 7 tons per square foot approximately, was within the permissible limits, but left little margin of safety. At the same time, there was no doubt that there had been local stress due to localized deterioration of materials.

In view of the existence of a larger number of pockets in the masonry of the foundation, it was decided that attempt should be made to strengthen the foundation by filling the voids both below and around the Minar proper with cement grout, keeping the grout pressure low enough to avoid any upsetting the stress equilibrium already attained. The grout would help to even out the static load of the superstructure as also any excessive stress and reactions in the sub-structure due to incremental load during earthquakes. Consolidation by grouting would also prevent any ingress of moisture or movement of soluble salt into the foundation.

THE GROUTING OPERATIONS

The grouting operations were planned into phases on and from the 54ft. square platform (fig. 1) to the minar base only to a depth of 32 ft. The first phase was further divided into three groups : to begin with the holes along the periphery of the platform and 1'-9" away from the outer edge were to be grouted to creat a curtain to prevent any morter to run out of the basal area; in the second group the holes around the Minar were to be grouted ; and in the third group the holes in the four corners would be grouted.

In the second phase the sub-structure of the foundation would be grouted through holes bored radially (fig. 2). As on the north and south there are structures which created obstructions, grouting was decided to be done from the eastern and western sides through the ashlar facing of the platform. The minimum distance between two holes at the face was to be 20" and each hole would be taken beyond the north-south centre line to a distance of 5 ft. to allow overlapping and maximum penetration of grout in the central portion.

The maximum distance between two holes was not to exceed 5ft. in the grid.

The grout should comprise of ordinary portland cement (complying with IS 269) and water-clean and free from deleterious substances. Grouting any of the holes would commence with grout with a water-cement ratio (by volume) of 4:1 progressively thickened to 1:1 and again progressively thinned till the stage of refusal. Refusal should be deemed to have been reached when the grout intake is reduced to less than 1 cft. of grout mixture in 20 minutes.

The grout holes (1.3/8" dia) would be drilled with standard non-coring rotary equipment except where core drilling was called for. A continuous circulation of grout would be ensured and permit accurate pressure control. The pressure would be: the top most 10 ft. of the hole @ 5 psi at the gauge; the second 10 ft. of the hole @ 10 psi at the gauge; and the third 10 ft. of the hole @ 15 psi at the gauge.

Drilling and grouting the holes, however, would be done in stages : for holes inclined not more than 10° to the vertical @ 10 ft. and for holes more than 10° to the vertical @ 5 ft. In packer grouting, grouting should be completed in stages from the bottom-most stage upwards in the hole, except the top-most stage which should be grouted without a packer. The stages of packer grouting would be governed by the condition of the grout holes.

Four upheaval gauges with sensitivity of 0.001" were installed at the four corners to watch if there was any disturbance caused due to the pressure grouting. There was no incident of use of excess pressure to show upheaval at any point. Although at a later stage, when grouting was almost completed and the interior spaces were packed up, grout was seen to ooze out through joints of masonry of the superstructure.

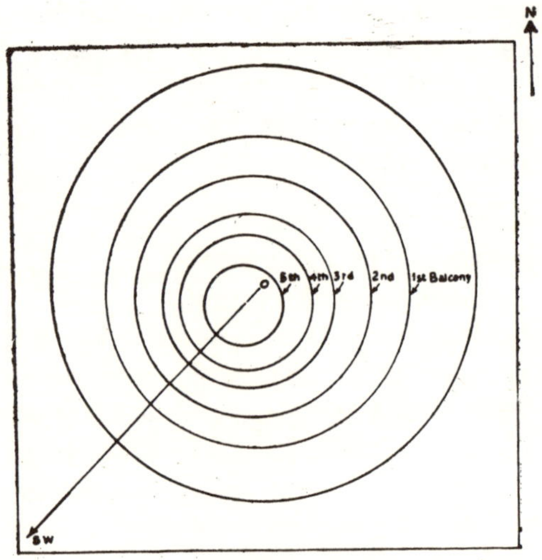

PLAN SHOWING TILTS

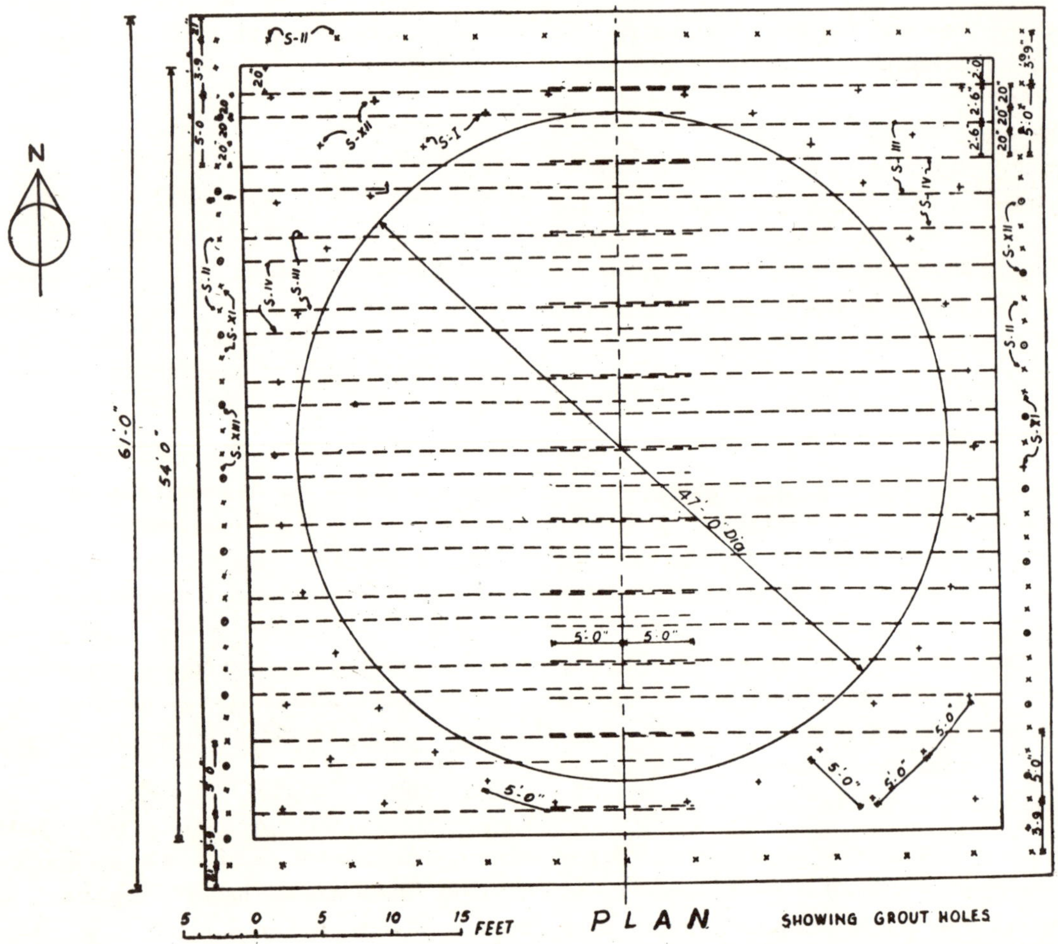

PLAN SHOWING GROUT HOLES

Fig. 1

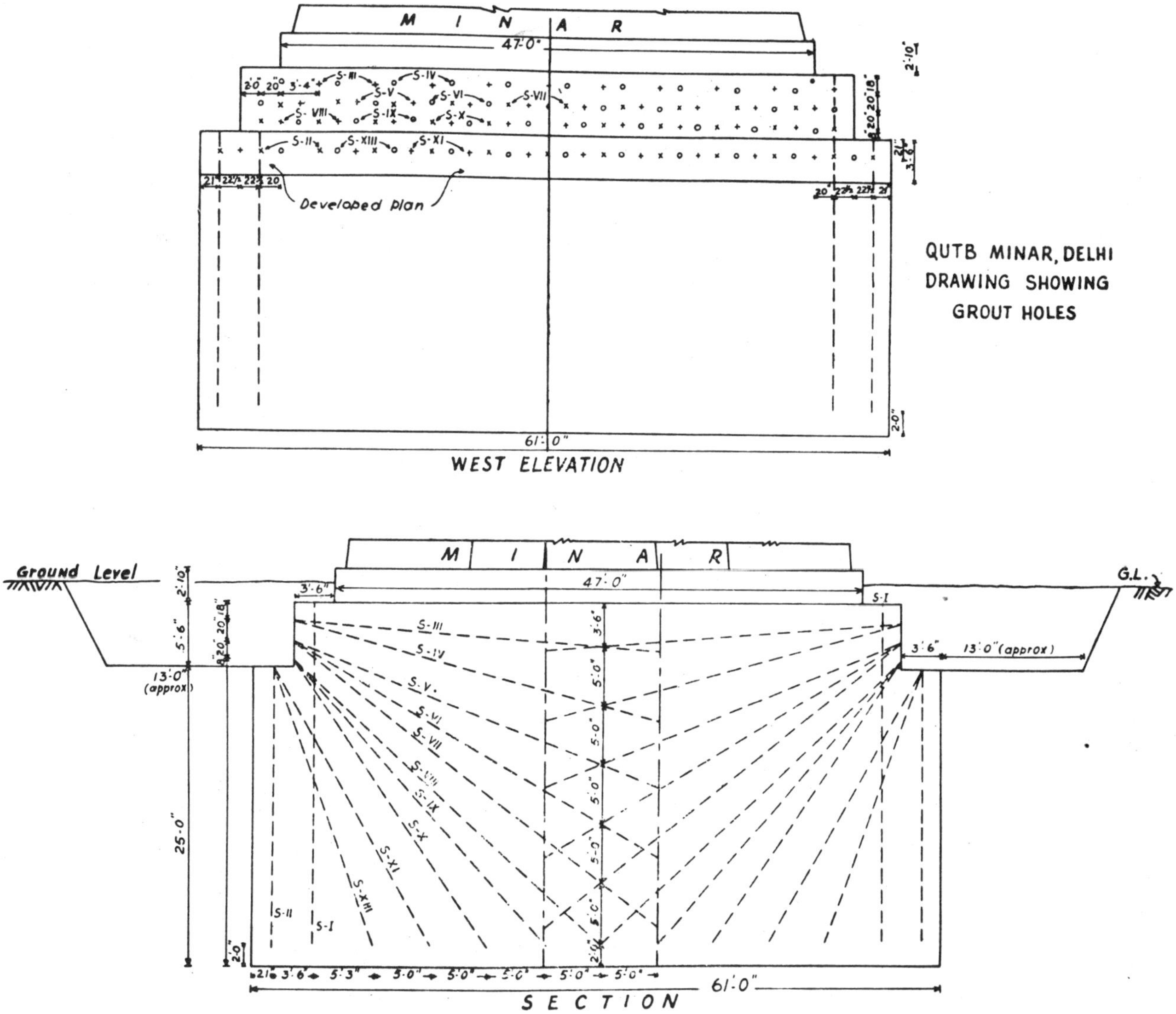

Fig. 2

During the grouting operations it was observed that in areas where the overburden was loose, casing pipes (2" dia.) had to be used.

As was planned, grouting was started from the periphery of the 54 ft. platform (S II) to create a barrier around the foundation so that grout injected inside the area might not escape out or be wasted. In this series there were in all 48 holes, 12 on each side. The maximum quantity of grout consumed in a hole was 251 bags (of 1:25 cft.) of cement in the proportions of 4:1 to 1:1 under a pressure of 5 psi; in this hole 237 bags were injected in the first stage. The minimum intake was 6½ bags of cement in 4:1 to 2:1 ratio under a pressure of 5 to 10 psi. Around the Minar in the series SI the maximum quantity used was 134½ bags of cement in 4:1 to 1:1 at 5 to 15 psi.

On the whole, consumption of the grout in the interior did not show a very different picture from what was expected on the basis of information gathered by core recovery. Test holes drilled, showed that grout did not reach the upper reaches of the 47 ft. diameter base of the structure of the Minar. Horizontal holes were, therefore, drilled from east to west and *vice-versa* to a depth of 22ft. in two stages and grouted to fill in the voids.

CONCLUSION

The information gathered regarding the foundation of the Qutb Minar has set at rest all speculations about its nature and form. Grouting, on the other hand, has been able to consolidate the loose fabric of the masonry of the foundation and to distribute the load over a wider area.

NOTES AND NEWS

THE RAMAYANA : SOME PROBLEMS RE-EXAMINED

The Rāmāyaṇa of Vālmīki is a variegated literary work incorporating interesting geographical, historical and cultural details interwoven with the main episode of Rāma. In the present form this epic is evidently an extensive composition spreading, in point of time, through several centuries. The story of Rāma (Rāmopākhyāna) seems to have gained popularity during the later Vedic period. The kernel of the story highlighted the victory of righteousnes over the evil forces. Rāma, the hero of the epic, was regarded as the embodiment of the ideals of the Vedic or Aryan culture *par excellence.* He gained victory over Rāvaṇa, who represented the non-Aryan way of life.

The Sage Vālmīki is attributed the first rendering of the popular story of Rāma into the simple *anushṭubha* verses. On the basis of the language and the literary form of the apparent early matter in the epic it may be surmised that the first versefication of the Rāmāyaṇa took place in C. 500 B.C. or near about. The lower limit of the extant epic can be assigned to C. 300 A.D. on the basis mainly of the internal evidence. Looking to the great popularity of the Rāmāyana this long stretch of time cannot be regarded as unreasonable. This also holds good in the case of the other great epic, the Mahābhārata. The main episodes of both the epics have largely been elaborated bearing profuse poetic embellishments.

It is not possible for the present author to agree with the view that the Rāmāyaṇa is a myth. Had it been a myth pure and simple, the story of Rāma could not have survived through the ages. It could not then have penetrated deep into the life of the masses of all categories throughout the country. Nor could it make any lasting impact on the life of South-East Asian countries outside India. Rāma's story can be historical in the same sense as is the story of the Pāndavas and Kauravas, of Krishna, of Mahāvīra and Gautama Buddha. We do not question the historicity of Mahāvīra, Gautama, Udayana or Kautilya. Should we doubt the existence of Rāma or Krishṇa only on the ground that no inscriptions or coins of theirs are known ? All proto-history cannot be dubbed as mythology. Otherwise, the very name 'Proto-History' would become a misnomer.

In this paper only some of the burning problems pertaining to the Rāmāyaṇa have briefly been dealt with. It may be stated here that I uphold the view, based on reliable evidence, that the time of Bhārata War was about 1400 B.C. and that Rāma flourished about 500 years before the Bhārata War.

The Rāmāyana of Vālmiki, even in its extant enlarged form, provides us with sufficient reliable evidence pertaining to the geography of the long stretch of land between Ayodhyā and Daṇḍakāraṇya of the present Bastar district. The geographical details in the Rāmāyaṇa, when studied along with those occurring in the works of Kālidāsa, Varāhamihira, Bāṇabhaṭṭa, Bhavabhuti, Rājaśekhara and others, coupled with the available archaeological evidence, lead us to the conclusion that Rāma after leaving Chitrakuta (in the Banda district of U.P.), took up the south-eastern direction to reach Daṇḍakāraṇya. In the present geographical context, Rāma on his onward journey passed through the districts of Satna, Shahdol, Ambikapur, Bilaspur, Raipur and Bastar. In the present Madhya Pradesh he must have crossed the two major rivers Sone and Mahanadi to reach the Bastar region.

Several present geographical names in the districts mentioned above furnish a clue to their association with Rāma in some form or the other.

It is interesting to note that the portrayal in stone of Rāma's story is found for the first time at Nachna in the Panna district of Madhya Pradesh. Several highly artistic panels of the Gupta period, depicting Rāma's episodes of the forest and of the construction of *Setu* (bridge) for reaching Lankā, have been discovered at Nachna. It is a probable that a temple of Rāma existed at Nachna in the Gupta period. Rāma's earliest cult-image is also likely to be traced out at Nachna, or nearabout. Another important centre, not far from Nachna, is Deogarh (district Lalitpur, U. P.). Numerous stone-slabs bearing the story of Rāma have been obtained at Deogarh. They are assigned to fifth-sixth centuries A.D. These relics no doubt indicate that Rāma's story had become quite popular in Central India during the Gupta Period.

Besides Nachna and Deogarh, depiction on stone of several episodes of the Rāmāyaṇa have been discovered at Tripurī (district Jabalpur), Khajuraho, Kharod, Shabrīnārāyan, Ratnapur, Pāli and Janjgīr. The last mentioned five sites are located in the Bilaspur district. At Sirpur in the Raipur district some scenes from the Rāmāyaṇa have been traced. From the Bhind disctrict an interesting terracotta figure representing Sīta, seated under the Aśoka tree in a pensive mood has been discovered. It may be mentioned here that unlike the portrayal of the childhood of Krishna, the sculptors of the Madhya Pradesh region were interested in depicting Rāmā's life starting after his banishment.

Numerous other sites are known where the depictions Rāma's popular story have been discovered in plastic art. Mention may be made of Bhitargaon (district Kanpur), Sravastī (district Gonda, U.P.), Pravarapur (Vidarbha), Chausa & Apsad (Bihar) Pahārpur (Bengal) and Kirādu (Rajasthan). Among the South Indian sites, where Rāmāyana scenes are well-known are Ellora, Pattadakal and Kumbhakoṇam. Almost in all the schools of Medieval Indian paintings, numerous pictorial representations of the story can be seen.

I think that Rāma's story travelled to countries like Thailand, Cambodia, Java, Sumatra and Balī through south-eastern Madhya Pradesh and Orissa. The profuse carving of scenes from the Rāmāyana in the countries mentioned above eloquently proves the popularity of Rāma's story outside India. A comparative study of the human ethnic features and also of the decorative patterns found in the plastic art of the Chhattisgarh region of the early Medieval period with the contemporary art of South-East Asia leaves no doubt as to the impact of the Chhattisgarh region on the art of those distant lands. A critical study in this field is a *desideratum*.

Rāma took the south-eastern direction in the region of Madhya Pradesh to reach Dandaka. He passed through *Dakshiṇa Kosola*, the name given to the region south of the present Satna-Rewa districts. It may be mentioned here that Rāma's mother Kausalyā belonged to this region. To distinguish from the northern Kosala of the Ikshvāku rulers, (with Ayodhya as its capital) the southern region was called *Dakshiṇ Kosala*. The route of Rāma was more or less followed by Samudragupta in the fourth century A.D. Had Rāma passed through the south-western parts of this State, some tangible traces of his route would have been found and at least some early art-relics could have been preserved in that area. By taking south-western route it was necessary for Rāma to cross the river Narmada, which is not the case when we study the Rāmāyaṇa.

As regards the names 'Daṇḍaka' and 'Laṅkā, there is a strong basis to believe that these and several other names originated from the local languages of the Śabaras who inhabited the Vindhyāvatī and the region further south in the Daṇdkāraṇya. The *āśramas* of sages like Vālmiki, Atri, Agastya and Śarabhanga, whose main objective was to propagate Āryan culture in the area of the Nishādas and the Śabaras, were located in Daṇdaka.

Rāma in his wandering seem to have reached Daṇdakāraṇya at least as far south as Rāmagir in the present Korāput district of Orissa, after passing through the (second) Chitrakuta or Chakrakotta region of the Bastar district.

From the Rāmāyaṇa of Vālmīki we learn that several powerful chiefs of the Nishādas the Śabaras, the Vānaras and the Rikshas (all human beings) become friendly with Rāma. They may have realised that they should be safer if they sided with Rāmaa gainst the Rakshasas, whose leader Rāvaṇa had become a terror to the tribal people and who had become antagonastic to Rāma.

As regards Rāvaṇa and the Lankā, the great epic leaves no doubt in mentioning that Rāvaṇa was a very powerful tribal leader of the extensive Daṇdaka area. He seems to have extended his sway in the north right upto Amarkantaka. The name Amarkantaka seems to suggest that this place was like a thorn to the *amaras (devas)* or the followers of the Aryan culture. The name of Rāvaṇas dynasty is given as *Salakaṭaṅkaṭa*. Due to several reasons, Rāvaṇa became antagonistic to the Vedic culture, which eulogised Indra and Vishṇu as supreme gods. He, on the other hands, was a great devotee of Śiva Mahādeva, the lord of the wide-spread tribal region.

From several accounts found in the epic it can be gathered that the predecessors of Rāvaṇa had to bear some sort of humilition inflicted on them by the rising Aryan forces. Rāvaṇa could not bear this. It was not possible for him to submit to any alien force. Naturally, he threw a challenge to Rāma, the Aryan Prince, who was extending his hegemony in the South.

Lankā and Siṁhala (or *Tāmraparṇi dvīpa*) are separately mentioned in several ancient works. It does not seem feasible to identify Lankā of Rāvaṇa with Simhala or Śrī Lankā. In the history of Ceylon (Śrī Lankā) no reference to Rāvaṇa or his exploits are discernible. No early relics depicting Rāma's episode or any achievements of Lankā's hero, Rāvaṇa, are traceable in plastic or pictorial form in the entire Śrī Lankā. On the basis of the source-marerial available so far it can be said that the *Lankā* of Rāvāṇa was located some-where in the borders of Bastar, Orissa and Andhra Pradesh. With the spread of the Aryan culture, several geographical names travelled from the north to south and south-east. They became current even in Siṁhala, Brahmadeśa (Burma), Indo-China and Indonesia. The name Lankā seems to have been given to the Island of Siṁhala sometime before the Gupta Period, by which time the Aryan culture had spread throughout the Indian sub-continent.

With all his mightiness Rāvaṇa was undoubtedly a human being. It seems that he had ten appellations not ten heads. In ancient art-relics Rāvaṇa is usually represented as a human and not a demon. Numerous images of Rāvaṇa in the Rāvaṇānugraha form are known in Madhya Pradesh and outside, wherein Rāvaṇa is shown in the human form with one head and two arms. The super-human attributes to Rāvaṇa were added to indicate that he was an extremely powerful enemy, who could challenge the supremacy of Rāma, his Aryan adversery. It may be pointed out here that not only Rāvaṇa but Rāma and several of his associates also came to be credited with super-natural powers.

The region of Chhattisgarh in Madhya Pradesh is intimately associated with the episode of Rāma. It is essential to make a detailed study of the geography, geology, languages and traditions along with literature and archaeological material of this and the contiguous regions. This would facilitate solution of several problems connected with the Rāmāyaṇa. Without probing into the original source-material it does not seem possible to tackle some of the knotty problems related to the great epic.

K. D. Bajpai

H-15 Padmakar Nagar
Sagar

PROF. THIEME'S ETYMOLOGY OF SKT. *así* AND ITS BEARING ON THE IRON-AGE IN INDIA

The word *así* (m.) is attested in the Sanskrit literature since the *Ṛgveda*. Its meaning, there, is 'knife' used for cutting the slaughtered animals. As 'sword', a weapon used in battles, *así* appears since the *Atharvaveda*.

What was this Rgvedic *así* 'knife' made of ?

Since the word *avas* occurs in the *Ṛgveda* and since it is usually taken to mean copper (or bronze) one inference could be that the Ṛgvedic *así* was made of copper.

But this inference would prove wrong if Prof. Thieme's suggestion (Thieme, 1958) regarding the etymology of the word *así* is found to be correct[1].

We have in Sanskrit correspondences like

hárita 'yellow' : *harít hári* 'yellow'

róhita 'red' : *rohít, róhi* 'red'

Similarly in Greek

álphito - 'barley meal' : *álphit* 'barley meal' (lit. 'the white one').

Such correspondences make the following correspondence for Sanskrit a possibiliity :

Skt. *ásita* 'black' : **asit, *asi* 'black'

This means that for Sanskrit we assume an adjective **asi* which is not attested.

In Greek we have a word *ásis* f. 'river mud'. If we assume an unattested existence of a Sanskrit adjective **asi* 'black' it is possible for us to campare

Sk. **asi* (adj.) 'black' : Gk. *ásis*-(fem.) 'river mud'.

Phonetically this correspondence becomes likely only if we assume that the two words Skt. **asi* and Gk. *ásis* are derived from IE **n̥si* which, as an adjective, would have the meaning 'black'. We have to assume that in Greek the Indo-European adjective 'black' was nominalized to mean 'river mud'.

In Latin we have the word *ēnsis* m. 'sword'. Earlier it was not possible to relate Sk. *así* (iron) sword, and Lat. *ēnsis*' (iron sword' because, although there was phonetic resemblance between the two, the meaning 'iron sword' could not be attributed to tne reconstructed IE word as iron was not known in that period[2]. But if Latin *ēnsis* 'sword', like Greek *ásis* 'river mud', is considered a nominalization of the IE adj. *n̥si* 'black', *i.e.* 'the black one the black iron sword', then the two words from Sanskrit and Latin can be looked upon as cognates. And not only these two, also Gk. *asis* 'river mud' can be considered a cognate with them as all three can now be treated as independent nominalizations of the IE adj. *n̥si* 'black'.

If the above explanation of Skt. *así* 'knife' as a later development of a nominalization 'the black one' of a potential adjective **asi* 'black' is correct then it implies that at the time (late Rgvedic period) when *así* 'knife' is attested it must have been made of iron. Otherwise the nominalization of the adjective meaning 'black' cannot be explained. This means that on *linguistic* evidence it is possible for us to say that iron was known in the late Ṛgvedic period.

All these facts about the etymology of the Skt. noun *así* have already been stated by Prof. Thieme in the review referred to above (1964). The purpose of the present paper is only to bring these facts to the notice of the Archaeologists and also to make explicit the implication of this etymology for the iron-age in India.

1 Prof. Thieme's suggestion seems to have its starting point in W. Schulze's etymological hypothesis regarding Greek *ásis* f. 'river mud' *(Kleine Schriften 116 f.)*. The latter is inaccessible to me.

2 The words for 'iron' in the languages belonging to the IE family are phonetically quite different from one another: Gk. *sídēros*, Lat. *ferrum*, old Slavic *želēzo*, old Irish *ēaru*, Skt. *Krsnāvasa*.

References

Prof. Theime 1958 Review of 'Dictionnaire etymologique du protoindo-europeen' Albert carnoy, *Language* 34 pp. 510-515

1964 'The Comparative Method for Reconstruction in Linguistics' *Language in Culture and Society* (ed.) Dell Hymes. pp. 593-594.

M. A. Mehendale

CHEMISTRY OF DECCAN CHALCOLITHIC DEPOSITS FROM DAIMABAD AND INAMGAON

Soil Chemistry is directly related to the deposition and decay of organic and inorganic debris. Every item of organic origin present in an occupation site and leaving a chemical residue is traceable by chemical means. The significance of chemical analysis of archaeological deposits has already been recognized (Cook and Heizer, 1965). It has now been established that the proportion of elements like phosphorus, nitrogen, carbon and some trace elements like zinc, copper etc., in the habitational deposits are related to the extent, intensity and duration of the occupation of a particular site. The archaeology department of the Deccan College has undertaken such chemical studies and results obtained from the Chalcolithic sites are given below.

The two sites that have been dealt with here are :

Daimabad (19°31N and 74°42'E), on the left bank of the Pravara river at a distance of 52 km. north of Ahmednagar and Inamgaon (18° 35'N and 74°35'E), on the right bank of the river Ghod at a distance of 85 km south-East of Pune. Both the sites are in Maharashtra State.

The geological foundation at both sites is the same. The Deccan Trap is represented by varieties of basalt at both places. Compact and slightly porthyrithic varieties showing well developed coloumnal joints are common. Veins of chalcedony are also seen.

Chalcolithic sites of Daimabad and Inamgaon fall under the rainfed zone of Western Ghats. Climatically they can be classed as tropical semi-arid. Average annual rainfall at Daimabad is about 60 cm., while at Inamgaon is 50 cm.

The deeply weathered mature black cotton soil are found at both places. In the interior region black soil shows shallow to medium profiles. The thorn and bush type vegetation is noted at both the sites. Besides these sites are not under cultivation. Thus these factors being common, the results of chemical analysis of the Chalcolithic deposits from these sites would be significant.

The C^{14} dates of the Inamgaon deposits are available and those of the Daimabad site are yet to be received. At Daimabad habitation begins from Savalda (*c.* 2000 B.C.) and is followed successively by late Harappan, Buff and Cream ware Malwa and Jorwe. The Inamgaon has yielded cultures of Malwa and two phases of Jorwe. Several samples obtained from vertical profile and horizontally from the cultural levels from these sites have been tabulated. (Table No. 1).

The phosphorus value at Inamgaon ranges from 1375 to 4437 ppm. in case of late Jorwe, whereas it ranges from 1937 to 4875 in case of early Jorwe. In case of Daimabad the phosphorus values of Jorwe Culture are 3452 to 3604 ppm. The phosphorus contents of all cultural levels in both sites are 4 to 5 times higher than the phosphorus content of non-cultural soils. The higher values are indications of human activities of different intensities. At Daimabad this value of Jorwe Culture is somewhat higher as compared to both phases of Jorwe at Inamgaon.

In case of Malwa Culture at Inamgaon the result shows more human activity than at Daimabad. The three lowermost cultures at Daimabad, namely Buff and Cream, Late Harappan and Savalda have fairly higher values than those of the succeeding cultures.

In view of the different values of phosphorus at Daimabad and Inamgaon in the Jorwe and Malwa Cultures, the higher values of the earlier cultures at Daimabad perhaps also show the same trend of increasing human activity at that site. It should be mentioned that Daimabad has a longer period of human occupation and that site is also larger in area than that of Inamgaon. This deducation, to a certain extent, is plausible because as far as the environmental factors are concerned there is identity between these two sites.

Table—1

DMD = Daimabad
INM = Inamgaon

Culture	Site	Trench	Layer	ph	Electrical conductivity milimhos/cm	Calcium Carbonate%	Organic Carbon %	Nitrogen%	Phosphorus in ppm.
Jorwe	DMD	DZ71	(3)	7 8	4.0	13.0	0.504	0.047	3562
Late (1000-700 B.C.)	INM	OB-1	(3)A	7.7	4.4	14.0	1.008	0.091	3187
Early (1400-1000 B.C.	INM	OB-1	(9)	7.6	10.0	4.0	0.850	0.073	3125
Malwa	DMD	CZ-61	(8)	7.8	6.0	5.0	0.777	0.042	3187
(1600-1400 B.C.	INM	OB-1	(13)	7.8	3.3	7 0	1.323	0.106	3437
Buff and Cream	DMD	CZ-61	(11)	7.9	5.0	4.0	0.714	0.050	3314
Late Harappan	DMD	CZ-61	(13)	7.9	6.0	12.0	0.861	0.060	3750
Savalda	DMD	CZ-61	(15)	7.9	6.0	12 0	1.035	0.068	3812
Non Cultural Deposit	DMD	CZ-61		7.9	3.0	2.5	0.294	0.025	687
	INM	OB-1		7.6	5 2	—	0.210	0.035	625

Reference

S. F. Cook and R. F. Heizer, 1965. *Studies on the Chemical analysis of Archaeological Sites*, California.

Deccan College,
Pune-411006

R. V. Joshi
B. C. Deotare
Smt. A.A. Kashirsagar

PREHISTORIC EXPLORATIONS IN SIKKIM

In order to ascertain the hitherto unexplored prehistoric potentialities of Sikkim, explorations were undertaken by Prehistory Branch of Archaeological Survey of India, Nagpur in October-November, 1980.

Neolithic stone implements were discovered two years back from Nepal by Shri Yaschetenko of the Institute of Archaeology of Leningrad, U.S.S.R. Neolithic implements have also been reported from Assam by a number of scholars. Since Sikkim falls between Nepal and Assam, it was expected that Neolithic Civilization may have flourished in Sikkim also.

It was decided to begin with North Sikkim. In view of the very difficult terrain, climatic conditions and near vertical location of villages which comprised of scattered huts at different altitudes, the work had to be planned very carefully. Explorations were conducted along Tista River and her tributaries. Keeping our head-quarters at Singhik near Mangan, a district town, entire Djangu area upto Dikchu on the west on Tista River on the one hand and places upto Lachen and Lachung in extreme north were covered.

The landscape of the area does not permit any formation of village units in the traditional sense of space utilization. The villages in general contain 10 to 20 houses each but are often scattered vertically. Thus, most that could be done in raising any crop is by terrace cultivation, where each terrace is only one metre broad or even less. Accumulation of cultural debris is hardly possible due to the nature of terrain, climate and typical way of constructing houses on pillars.

During our explorations a variety of well-polished Neolithic stone tools were recovered from different locations in north Sikkim. All tools except the sharpners were collected from Djangu area. The villages from where tools were recovered are Lingthen, Lingdon, Barpak, Sankalan, Lingden, Gytong, Sangdong, Gnon, Tarang, Gor-Tarand and Linkyong. Tools are generally found after the rainy season in the terraced fields.

The tools comprise of harvesters (2), knife (1), axes (7), adzes (13) and single and double perforated celts (3) Adzes are predominant. They are mostly made on schist, shale and a few pieces on basalt. Both medium and small varieties with flat or oval huts and rectangular or ovoid cross-section have found. Majority of the tools have been ground and polished all over the body while a few only at the lower half. Special mention may be made of a beautiful single eyed harvester and Honan Knife. A polisher having three concave working sides and perforation on the top was recovered from a village north of Chungthan on way to Lachen. It is interesting to note that excepting the polisher, no tool was recovered from the area north of Mangan.

A short exploration was also conducted in the district of east Sikkim around Pakhyong. Six polished celts comprising of two axes and four adzes were recovered alongwith a polisher from Pakhyong and Shamsing villages.

The adzes, perforated harvesters and Honan Knife are all typical of the south Chinese Neolithic assemblage. Harvesters with one or more perforations in rectangular or semilunar shape have been reported from Tasolu-t'ai and Hei-ku-tui, Honan Province. Single perforated celts have also been reported from the above mentioned sites and from Hua T'ing Ts' un, Kiangsu Province of China. But double perforated celt is typical of Sikkim.

Pottery is significantly absent in the sites explored in Sikkim. In such a landscape one does not expect proper earth for the manufacture of pottery. Neither could a kiln be possibly made here. The people in the northern part of Sikkim, where exploration was conducted, do not use any pottery even today. Before the coming of aluminium or brass utensils, the people used to have their vessels made of wood. They did even boil their food in these wooden vessels by plastering the necessary parts with mud. For storage of liquids hollow inter-nodes of bamboo were used.

The local population have a magical concept about these neolithic tools. These are considered a source for the betterment of material life. Local people keep them in their kitchen and worship them. Some use them for medical purposes also particularly at the time of child birth. As these tools are called 'Vjra Dunga' *i.e.* lightning stone by Lepchas, some people strike the wall and pillars of their houses with celts during lightning and thunder under a belief that by doing so, they can escape the calamity.

That these neolithic element did not enter Sikkim from north is certain. For, a vast expanse of greatly desiccated lands that separates Tibet from the tool bearing areas of north Sikkim, was found totally barren in neolithic context. In order to ascertain the route through which Neolithic Culture entered Sikkim, further work has to be conducted in other regions in adjoining Sikkim.

Archaeological Survey of India, Nagpur. A.K. SHARMA

MICROLITHS AROUND SANTINIKETAN

A lateritic gravel spread (locally called *Khowai*) marks the northern, and partly the eastern boundaries of the modern settlement of Santiniketan. The eastern section, beyond the Bolpur-Prantik stretch of the Eastern Railway, is called *Paruldanga*. The section between the residential areas of *Purvapalli* and *Shyambati* is called *Taltorer Danga*. Beyond *Shyambati* the *Khowai* can easily be traced as far west as the Ballabhpur forest, past the modern deer park, bird sanctuary and the agricultural college and rural development centre of Sriniketan. A canal of the Mayurakshi dam project cuts through the *Khowai* from the west to the east. The deer park and the bird sanctuary are located on the *Khowai* itself.

Today the *Khowai* presents an essentially denuded reddish landscape. The rains have cut deep gullies in places and the soil erosion is both extensive and heavy. Left to itself, the *Khowai*, however, could house a forest. A *Sal* forest has come up recently in the undisturbed deer park area.

The basic geographical position of the *Khowai* is worth noting. On the north it overlooks the Kopai valley and on the south it marks a kind of natural line of the Ajay valley. The modern settlements of Santiniketan and Bolpur are located on a comparatively high ground which gradually merges into the Ajay flood plain. The *Khowai* acts as a kind of ridge between the southern Ajay and the northern Kopai valleys at this point. The Kopai is hardly more than a kilometre away to the north while the Ajay should be more than 5 km. away to the south.

During their brief association with Visvabharati University in the winter of 1980–81 the third author (D.K.C.) and his wife (S.C.) made a surface collection of microliths from 4 localities in the *Khowai*. The material has been analysed with the help of the first author (D.K.B.). Although the occurrence of microliths around Santiniketan is not unknown among the archaeologists in West Bengal there is no suitable analysis of the material in published form. It may be added that in March 1981 the third author (D.K.C.) and one of his colleagues at Visvabharati, Dr Subrata Chakrabarti, undertook a small trial trench at *Paruldanga* to determine the stratigraphic context of the microliths at this locality, besides making a fresh surface collection. The results will be published in due course.

Site (or locality) 1 : Shyambati

The present collection comprises 12 specimens on a softer variety of basaltic rock. The average range of artifacts ranges between 4 and 2 cm. The basaltic material is not easily amenable to retouch but the tiny fluting marks visible on blades or blade fragments obviously show an attempt to retouch. There are 4 medium sized fan-shaped flakes (3 by 2 cm.), 3 similar flakes showing attempts to retouch (cf. nos. 2, 4), 4 slender and thick blades (cf. no. 3) and a flattened fluted core (no 1). The fluted core is about 8.2 cm. in length. It is elliptical in cross section at the platform end while the anterior end forms almost a tapered chisel edge. Fluting marks from both the surfaces converge at the anterior end to result into this feature. Incidentally, this fluted core convincingly demonstrates that the collection is a genuine one and not based on roadside stone chippings. The possibility that this collection could be based on roadside stone chippings was mentioned by Dr. Subrata Chakrabarti when this collection was shown to him.

Site (or locality) 2 : Taltorer Danga

This collection comprises 63 pieces of which the main bulk is of basaltic material similar to that found in the first collection. The rest of the raw material used are agate, quartz and fossil wood. This is a collection which is quite poor in true blade type. More than fifty percent of the collection is of various kinds of flakes. There are 27 unretouched flakes and 16 retouched flakes (cf. nos 5–7). There are 7 chips or waste flakes and the remaining 13 pieces are retouched blades (cf. nos. 8-10). Of these one specimen (no 8) seems to be burinated. The retouched flakes, as will be evident from the illustrations, demonstrate a very specific lower to middle Palaeolithic technique adopted for microlithic production. A flat based pyramidal core is taken and a number of flakes are removed from the flat base towards the narrowed apex. Finally, this core is transversely sliced off in a large number of flakes. The resultant resembles a backed knife of Bordes (nos. 36-38) in a diminutive form. That some of these flakes have finally given rise to fine backed knives or even lunates is quite evident from the smaller pieces in this collection. Most of the retouched blades are angular or thick in cross section. Only a single fragment records a true parallel sided blade (no. 9). The retouchings are mainly executed on the thicker border in the manner of a blade knife (no. 9) or often attempted to form a burinated edge on a fragment of a fluted core (no. 8).

Site (or locality) 3 : Deer Park

This is a collection of 57 artifacts of relatively large size (4 by 2.5 cm.) and is mainly of chert material. There are a few fossil wood pieces as well. There are 21 unretouched flakes, 20 blades or blade fragments and 6 pieces of core fragments, among other things. The cores are mainly flake cores with signs of blade removal. The finished tool types show some finely executed types. There is an interesting specimen of burin attempted on natural fracture (cf. no. 16) and 3 more burins on irregular blade fragments (cf.15,17). There are 5 pieces of obliquely blunted knives. The backed flakes are thinner (no.12) and seem to demonstrate a general typological evolution of backed blades from the backed flakes. There is a small but perfectly made lunate (no.14).

Site (or locality) 4 : Paruldanga

This collection comprises 34 pieces. The raw material is mainly chert, quartz, chalcedony and fossil wood. There are 4 cores from which blades have been removed by punching technique (nos. 18, 19). One of these (no. 18) seems to have been prepared for the removal of backed knife (cf. specimens in locality 2). Besides, there are 5 core fragments, 6 flakes, 3 retouched flakes and 6 core trimming blades. There are only 2 parallel sided blades with marks of fluting on their dorsal surface. The finished specimens include 5 burinated specimens (no. 20,21 and 24) and 3 backed knives (nos.22 and 23).

The localities 1 and 2 may be grouped together. The raw material is mainly basaltic in both cases. The detached blades are relatively small in size and do not include any parallel-sided blade. The retouched specimens are also not characteristic microlithic types. For instance, a true backed blade, lunate and knife are not found while thick blades

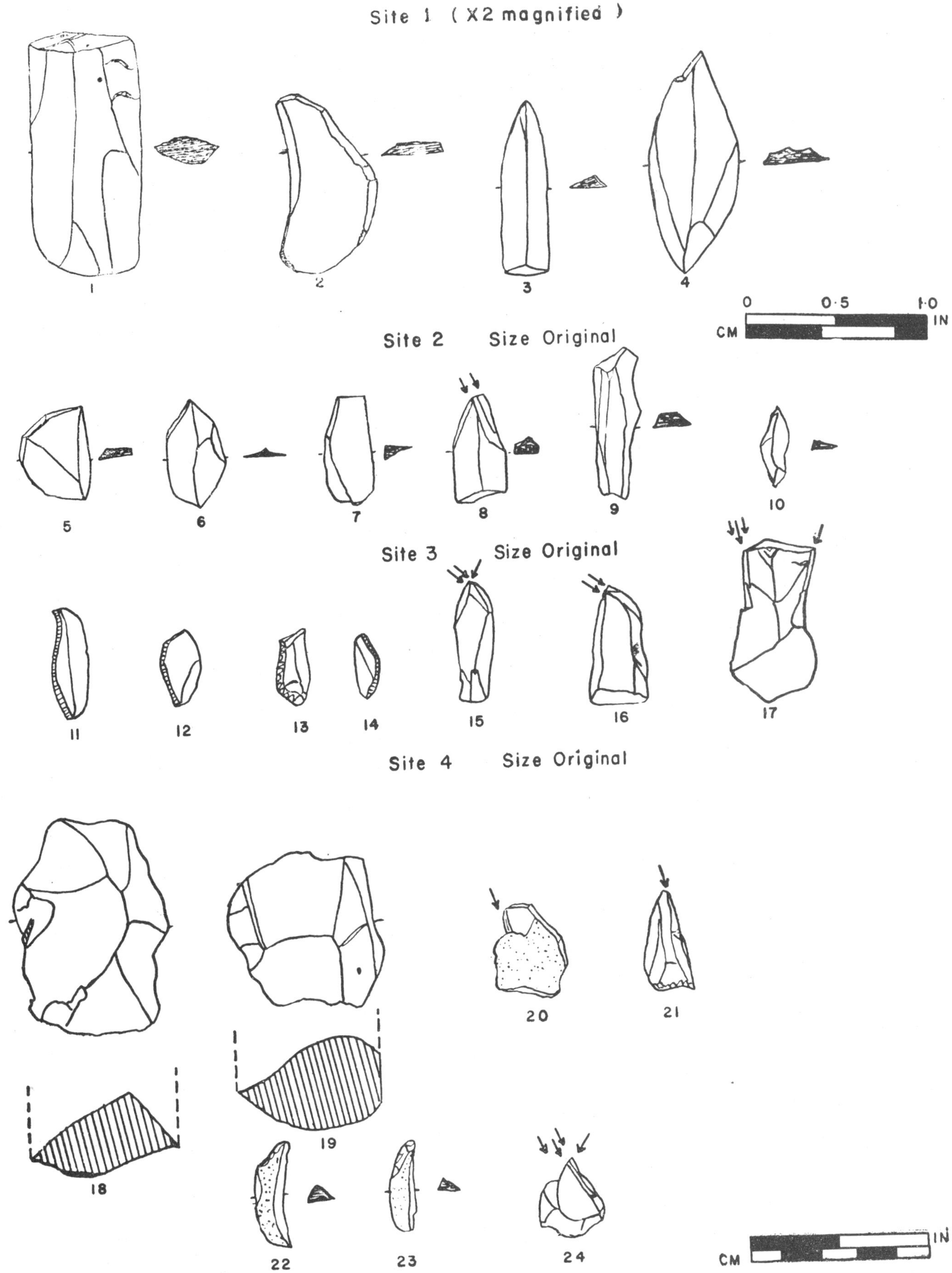
Site 1 (X2 magnified)
1
2
3
4
0 0·5 1·0
IN
CM
Site 2 Size Original
5
6
7
8
9
10
Site 3 Size Original
11
12
13
14
15
16
17
Site 4 Size Original
18
19
20
21
22
23
24
IN
CM

with burin blows or terminal retouchings occur. The size of the single blade core found is rather small and the success in blade removal from such tiny cores may be taken to indicate a fairly advanced technique of blade removal.

The material of the localities 3 and 4 is mainly fine-grained cherty material and fossil wood. There are no fluted cores in these collections; a biconical core, however, has been used for blade removal (no.19). Finished tool types are mainly obliquely blunted knives (nos.22, 23) and lunates, besides burinated pieces in good number. The burins do not demonstrate micro-burin technique and are not thus congruous with those expected in Mesolithic industries. Besides, a true Mesolithic industry should abound in parallel sided blades and fluted cores. On these considerations we feel that these collections do not represent a true mesolithic horizon. These may be contemporary with the Chalcolithic settlers in this area, In fact, the site of Mahisdal which is at the northern end of the Kopai bridge, hardly more than a kilometre away from the *Khowai*, revealed a large number of microliths both in its Chalcolithic and Iron Age levels. The Mahisdal microliths remain unpublished but a comparative study between these artifacts and those from *Khowai* would have been of great value in determining the cultural affiliation of the *Khowai* material.

D.K. Bhattacharya
(University of Delhi)
Sima Chakrabarti
Dilip K. Chakrabarti
(Deptt. of AIHC & Arch.
Visvabharati Univ.)

EXCAVATION AT MORADHWAJ—A NOTE

Moradhwaj (Lat.29° 43′ Long.78° 29′, District Bijnor, U.P.,) is about 13 km. South-West of Kotdwar, a foothill town of the Garhwal Himalayas was taken up for excavation by the Garhwal University in 1979 with a view to ascertaining the antiquity of the cultural development in this region[1]. The site in the past seems to have attracted attention of scholars like Gen. Cunningham (1924 : 351) and fuhrer (1891). Prior to them the Chinese traveller, Hieun-Tsang (A.D. 629), travelling from Mo-ti-pu-lo (or Matipura) or Madawar in Bijnor district to Po-lo-hi-mo-pu-lo (or Brahmapura) has mentioned a city on the east side of the Ganges or Gangadwara, which according to him was the city of Mo-yu-io (or Mayura) about 20li in circuit. Cunningham, therefore, thought that this Mayura ,'must be the present ruined site of Mayapura at the head of the Ganges canal". Watters (1904-1905), however, argued differently saying that Hieun-Tsang apparently did not go to Mayura and he perhaps appears to be writing, about Gangadwara only from information given to him by others. He, therefore, disagreed with the view that "Mo-yu-lo was Mayapur adding further that " Mo-yu-lo cannot be taken as a transcription of Mayapura since this town was on the west side of the Ganges where as Mo-yu-lo (Mayura) was on the east side of the river".

From almost all view-points the case of Moradhwaj for identification with Mo-yu-lo appears stronger as its geographical location fits in well with that given by Hieun-Tsang. More explicitly the place falls in the eastern direction of the Gangadwara or modern Hardwar and is roughly 30 km. straight from Hardwar.

The excavation puts the beginning of the site around fifth century B.C., continuing till the 3rd century without any cultural break. The ancient deposits of about eight hundred years displayed three occupational periods.

Period I *(c. 5th Century B.C.—2nd century B.C.)*

The earliest settlement is characterized by the use of the NBP Ware along with fine thin grey and red ware. The NBP mainly gave evidence of dish

1 Valuable assistance was received by the present co-author, and research scholars Sarvashri D.L. Rajput, S.S.Nagi, V. P. Hatwal and Vinod Nautiyal.

and bowl, but the notable point is that paint was confined to the exterior and in very rare cases it is on both sides of the pot.

The people had used burnt bricks for their houses and had also built a mud wall around their habitation. The bricks used for the construction confirmed the following size—(i) 42×20×8 cm. and (ii) 46×20×8 cm.

Period IIA *(C. 2nd century B.C,—Ist century A.D.)*

This Period is marked by the structural evidence of the Sunga Period. The people used burnt bricks in their construction and the size of the bricks confirmed to the brick size of the period at some other sites in U.P. having (i) 24×22×7 cm. and (ii) 22X15X6 cm. The excavation revealed structural remains of walls and floors made of bricks but in some cases brick-jelly was also used in the floors. The people also used burnt bricks for the constcruction of defence wall, which was built over the mud wall of the earlier Period.

Amongst the notable finds of this Period are terracotta human and animal figurines, beads cartwheels, copper bangles and iron implements.

Period IIB

This Period revealed the existence of spacious houses. The bricks of this Period confirmed to the following sizes *i.e.* (i) 24x12x6 cm. and (ii) 25x15x6 cm. In one of the excavated houses (MRD—2), the corridor width of 1.75 m. is flanked by rooms opening inside and outside. The decorated brick pieces have aso been found

The most noteworthy feature of the Period, however, was the defence wall built of burnt bricks set in mud mortar. The defence wall had an average width of 10m. to 12m. covering an area of 3 sq. km.

The pottery is represented by red ware sometimes decorated with stamped design. The important antiquities included a few terracotta figurines a stucco Buddha image. On the basis of their characteristic features these terracottas are assignable to the beginning of the first-second century A.D.

Other finds of this Period are copper bangles, iron implements, terracotta and stone beads and terracotta gamesman. A gold coin belonging to late Kushan ruler found from the top, indicates that the site was left abandoned in the late phase of the Kushan Period or more specifically around the 3rd or 4th century A.D. It was only from the eighth century onwards that the area became predominantly a Saivite centre as is indicated by the discovery of several Siva *lingas* and dilapidated stone temples.

References

Cunningham, A. 1924 *Ancient Geography of India* p. 351.

Fuhrer, A, 1891 *Monumental Antiquities and Inscription of the North-West and Oudh* p. 32.

Watters, Thomas 1904-1905 *On Yuan Chuwang's Travels in India*. pp. 322-330.

Garhwal University
Srinagar-246174.

K. P. Nautiyal
B. M. Khanduri.

PRE HISTORY OF DADRA AND NAGAR HAVELI

Many Early Stone Age tools have been discovered in the Dadra and Nagar Haveli region, this hitherto unknown geographical entity of south Gujarat. All the Stone Age sites under reference fall in the Lat. 21°3'—21°19' N and Longitude 72°—73°16' E. This is the southern most tract of Gujrat State, bounded by Maharashtra on the east and south and by Arabian Sea on the west. The prehistoric sites mentioned here can be approached by road from Vapi Rly. Station on the Bombay-Delhi main line. All these sites were explored by Shri D. B. Chitale of the Western Circle of the

Archaeological Survey of India in 1970-71[1]. But his collection of tools remained unclassified so far.

Location of Sites :

1. *Chichpada :* 6 Km. from Vapi Rly. Station towards Khanvel near the village Rahoti by road on the bank of river Damanganga. Here a confluence of rivers Samaltod and Kherdi with Damanganga takes place.

2. *Athal :* 12 Km. from Vapi Rly. Station by road near Silvassa, and the site is on the left bank of river Damanganga facing the Athal hill.

3. *Kudacha :* 25 Km. from Vapi Rly. Station by road near Rakholi village. The site is on the right bank of river Damanganga.

4. *Kherdi :* 20 Km. from Vapi Rly. Station by road beyond Khanvel. The site is on right bank of River Kherdi, a tributary of river Damanganga.

5. *Samarvarni :* 10 Km. from Vapi Rly. Station by road on Khanvel road. The site is on the right bank of river Damanganga.

6. *Amri :* 8 Km. from Vapi Rly. Station by road towards Silvassa. The site is on river Damanganga.

7. *Moti-Randha :* 20 Km. from Vapi Rly. Station by road towards Khilavani. The site is on river Damanganga.

8. *Silvassa :* Capital of Dadra and Nagarhaveli region-11 Kms. from Vapi Rly. Station by road.

9. *Lavacha :* 8 Km. from Vapi Rly. Station by road near Dadra. The site is on the right bank of river Damanganga.

Environment

Between the foot of the Sahyadri range of Western Ghats and the Arabian Sea, this is virtually a raised sea-shelf having marshy features. This tract is mainly watered by the river Damanganga which originates from Igatpuri Ghats, flows through basaltic dykes and joins the Arabian Sea near Moti Daman. Its seasonal tributaries are Kherdi, Sankaltod and Kolak.

Geomorphology of this area is simple : thick vegetation on the slopes of Western Ghats with marshy plain. The basal-volcanic basalt is covered by eroded boulder gravels and super-imposed by secondary reddish or black silts. Naturally the coastal shelf, providing safe habitat with shelter of mountain cliff on one side and needed fauna from the sea on the other, must have been best suited to Early Stone Age men some 50,000 years ago. So far, no Middle Stone Age or Late Stone Age sites have come to light in this region.

Geologically the area falls in the Deccan Traps. There is distinct erosional unconformity between the top of the traps and basal Eocene beds containing denuded detritus of trap. The soils are mainly composed of hilly talus subsequently metamorphosed into "Red" (Laterite) or 'Black' (Regur) deposits due to colloidal changes caused by varying monsoonal activity.

Observation

About 45 Early Stone Age tools have been recorded from the nine sites under study. These are surface finds mostly from banks of river Damanganga, which in its aggradation has brought these tools and has buried in its secondary gravel. It appears that the actual sites must be on the higher terraces along the upstream and the tools collected being mostly rolled and abraded by fluviatile activity supports the suggestion.

Though stratigraphically there is very little record to infer about the sequence of this Early Stone Age collection, techno-typologically following observations can be made, with the reservation that the present field work is too patchy to attempt such venture. However, tools are mostly rolled, semi-rolled and negligible numbers are fresh. There are Abbevillian choppers and hand-axes on across to late Acheulian bifaces, and cleavers, on dolerite

[1] The author is extremely grateful to Shri S.N. Raghunath of Excavations Branch, Archaeologicol Survey of India, Nagpur, who ungrudgingly helped me in classifying & describing tha tools.

and vesicular trap. The site Chichpada has yielded only 'Choppers' while the site Kherdi has yielded evolved late Acheulian bifaces, Ovate, and cleavers comparable to Early Stone Age Tools from the Krishna and Chambal Valleys. (Nagarjunakonda, etc., Verlabodu,-Sonita, Bhainsrogarh, etc.). The appended chart explains further details and frequency of the collection.

The discovery of definite Early Stone Age sites with quite a good number, and variety of tool types from early choppers to highly evolved bifaces and ovates establishes the fact that this otherwise geographically isolated region, if subjected to closer study through archaeological field work, may yield more evidence regarding habitational aspects of Early Stone Age man as this area was least disturbing to him as seen from its environmental situation. Moreover if these finds are studied in a perspective in which these are compared with the artifacts of the corresponding and out lining regions one can trace certain industrial elements or a culture contact direct or diffused from different sources.

Site & Typological Distribution of Early Stone Age Tools from Dadra & Nagar Haveli.

Tools & their condition	Bifaces (handaxes)			Cleavers			Scrapers			Ovatexa			Cores & Core Choppers			Total
	R. S.		R. F.	R. S.		R. F.	R. S.		R. F.	R. S.		R. F.	R. S.		R. F.	
Damanganga Basin.																
1. Kherdi	1	4	—	—	2	—	—	2	—	—	1	—	—	—	—	10
2. Chichpadai	1	—	—	—	—	—	—	—	—	—	—	—	2	1	1	5
3. Athole	1	1	—	—	2	—	—	1	—	—	1	—	1	--	—	6
4. Kudacha	1	2	—	—	—	—	—	—	—	—	—	—	—	—	—	4
5. Samarvani	—	1	—	—	—	—	—	—	—	—	1	—	—	—	—	2
6. Amri	—	1	—	—	—	—	—	—	—	—	—	—	—	1	—	2
7. Moti Randha	2	—	—	—	—	1	1	1	1	1	—	1	1	—	—	6
8. Lavacha	2	1	—	—	2	—	—	1	—	—	—	—	1	—	—	7
9. Silvassa	1	—	—	—	—	—	—	1	—	—	—	—	—	—	—	2

Archaeological Survey of India,
New Delhi-110003.

W. H. Siddiqui

ON PERIODS AND CULTURES IN THE SWAT VALLEY AND BEYOND

According to Gordon Childe, a culture is evidenced by various types or models, as the settlement pattern, the burial customs, the economic activities, the industries, etc., which are associated in some sites and areas because they show a common human behaviour (Childe, 1956).

It can be remarked that very often, when the archaeological evidence shows a striking difference between the pottery or the stone implements of two subsequent periods, and also in the absence of more types or models, on firm grounds, one can suppose himself to be in the presence of different cultures.

In this way one can distinguish the earliest

occupation periods in the rock-shelter of Ghālīgai, Swāt Valley (Stacul, 1969) Period I (*c.* 3000-2500 B.C.) and Period III (*c.* 1900-1700 B.C.) are marked by coarse hand-made pottery. as well as by stone implements made of pebbles, while Period II (*c.* 2500-1900 B.C.) is mostly characterized by its fine wheel-turned ware. A deep culture change again is showed by the succeeding Period IV (*c.* 1700-1400 B.C.), which is not only marked by industries, but also by some other models like the settlement pattern and the burial customs.

With reference to the most recent excavations, one can distinguish the culture of Period IV in two successive phases : (1) the earliest one which is firstly characterized by the pit-dwellings and (2) the latest one where the settlement pattern is marked by stone walled structures. Besides the earliest phase shows the prevalence of black-burnished and brown, gritty wares, while plain red and black-on-red painted wares are comparatively well represented during the latest phase. In the main, this culture shows an almost continuous evolution of life in the valley.

The culture of Period IV could be labelled as "Culture of Loebanr III", with reference to the site which produced the main evidence of this complex in the Swat Valley (Stacul 1979). Noteworthy is also, during the same Period, the "Style of Bīr-kot", with reference to the black-on-red painted pottery, most of which come to light at Bīr-kot-ghuṇdai, which includes some faunal and floral representations (Stacul, 1981).

The successive Protohistorical Periods (periods V-VII) are mainly represented by the graveyards of Loebanr I, Katelai and Butkara II, as well as by the settlement of Aligrāma. Years ago, when we surveyed some 435 graves, it was easy to recognize three typological groups of grave furnishing in chronological sequence (Stacul, 1966). The recent excavation of Aligrāma showed fundamentally this succession of periods.

During the same years, some graves similar to those of the Swāt Valley were excavated by Dani in the graveyard of Timargarha, Panjkora Valley (Dani, 1967). Dani too reported his discoveries of three successive Periods, but this sequence was fundamentally based on the assumption of different successive burial customs. This subject has already been discussed elsewhere (Stacul, 1975).

As regards the label "Gandhara Grave Culture", introduced by Dani and extended to the coeval cultural traits of the North-Western subcontinent, one may remark :

(i) After Chārsada (Wheeler, 1960), the recent excavation of the graveyard of Zarif Koruna, near Peshawar (Gulzar, 1973), and the settlement of Hatial, near Taxila, showed that some cultural traits recovered in Swāt and Dir extended over a large part of the ancient Gandhara and beyond. Consequently the reference to the Gandhara area seems well-suited.

(ii) On the contrary the label "Grave Culture" does not seem to suit properly. First because the graves, in default of other more particular features, are not sufficient for the determination of a culture. Secondly, I suppose it is premature to ascribe, to a single culture those elements which may show some cultural traits which distinguish different successive cultures. The location of the graves in the same graveyard does not prove that these belong to the same culture. Some scholars prudently used the term "complex" rather than "culture" referring to Timargarha and other connected graves.

In the Swāt Valley the graves of Loebanr I, Katelai and Butkara II, as well as the contemporary occupation phases of Aligrāma, have been reported to Period V (*c.* 15th-9th Century B.C.), Period VI (*c.* 8th-5th Century B.C.) and Period VII (4th Century B.C.). During Period V and VI the metallurgy is basically represented by copper objects only (the earliest evidence of iron occurred at Aligrama in layers of late Period VI), while iron tools and objects show a wide diffusing during Period VII.

It is quite possible that iron objects may be recovered in occupation layers or graves which belong to an earlier period. In any case it was only around the 4th Century B.C. that the spread of iron-working introduced new types of implements and consequently marked some deep changes in working methods as well as in the weapons use. This technological improvment, which breaks the so-called "Gandhara Grave Culture" records not only metallurgy but also other industries, as is evident from the new shapes of pottery which includes handled and spouted vessels.

Therefore we suggest revision of the concept of "Gandhara Grave Culture". At present we believe that it would to better to distinguish the Gandhara protohitorical periods first according to the local sequences. Later on it will be possible to relate the periods of different sites and areas. Of course a chronological period or a pottery style cannot be identified with a culture. A culture is a socio-economic unity showing some common human behaviour which corresponds to an ideology as well as some particular tools and objects. The discovery of this unity on the whole will be the main object of the archaeological research.

References

Childe, G.V. 1956. *Piecing Together The Past*. London.

Dani, A.H. 1967. Timargarh and Gandhara Grave. Culture *Ancient Pakistan*, III (special number).

Gulzar, M.K. 1973. Excavation at Zarif Kurana. *Pakistan Archaeology*, 8.

Stacul, G. 1966. Preliminary Report on the Pre-Buddhist Necropolises in Swāt (W. Pakistan). *East and West*, 16, 1-2.

Satcul, G 1969. Excavation near Ghaligai (1968) Chronological Sequence of the Protohistrical Periods in the Swāt Valley (W. Pakistan). *East and West*, 19, 1-2.

Stacul. G. 1975. The Fractional Burial Custom in Swat Valley and Some Connected Problems. *East and West* 25, 3-4.

Stacul, G. 1979. Dwelling-and Storage-Pits at Loebanr III (Swat, Pakistan), 1976 Excavation Report. *East and West*, 27, 1-4.

Stacul, G. 1981. Painted Pottery in the Swat Valley (c. 1700-1400 B.C.) *South Asian Archaeology 1979*, Berlin.

Wheeler, Sir M. 1960. *Charsada, a Metropolis of the Nort-Western Frontier*. Oxford.

G. Stacul

ABOUT THE SHORTUGHAI SEQUENCE FROM MATURE HARAPPAN TO LATE BACTRIAN : BRONZE AGE IN EASTERN BACTRIA (N E. AFGHANISTAN)

Shortughai, the frist Harappan settlement discovered North of the Hindu Kuch in 1975 has been excavated from 1976 to 1979 by a franco-afghan team.

The site is located in a small plain (ca. 30 x10 km) at the confluence of the Kokcha flowing from Badakhshan and the Amu Darya (Fig. 1). The site is small, divided into two main mounds, mound A and mound B (Fig 2). A precise stratigraphical sequence has been worked out, by various sondages and excavation units, showing a continuous evolution from the bottom to the top, with no visible gap, break or abandonment in the occupation. In a first step, combining the evidence obtained by the observation of successive layers and the transformations of the architectuarl structures (destructions, reconstructions etc...), we obtained a 6-levels sequence on mound A (Fig. 3) and a 5-levels sequence on mound B. In a second step, according to the evolution of material, mainly ceramics, using simple statistical methods, we made broader divisions, dividing the sequence into four periods : I to IV. Period I is called "Harappan"; period II "Late Harappan"; in period III Bactrian elements appear in a post-harappan context; period IV is characterized by the presence of Late Bronze Age Bactrian treits in a local context.

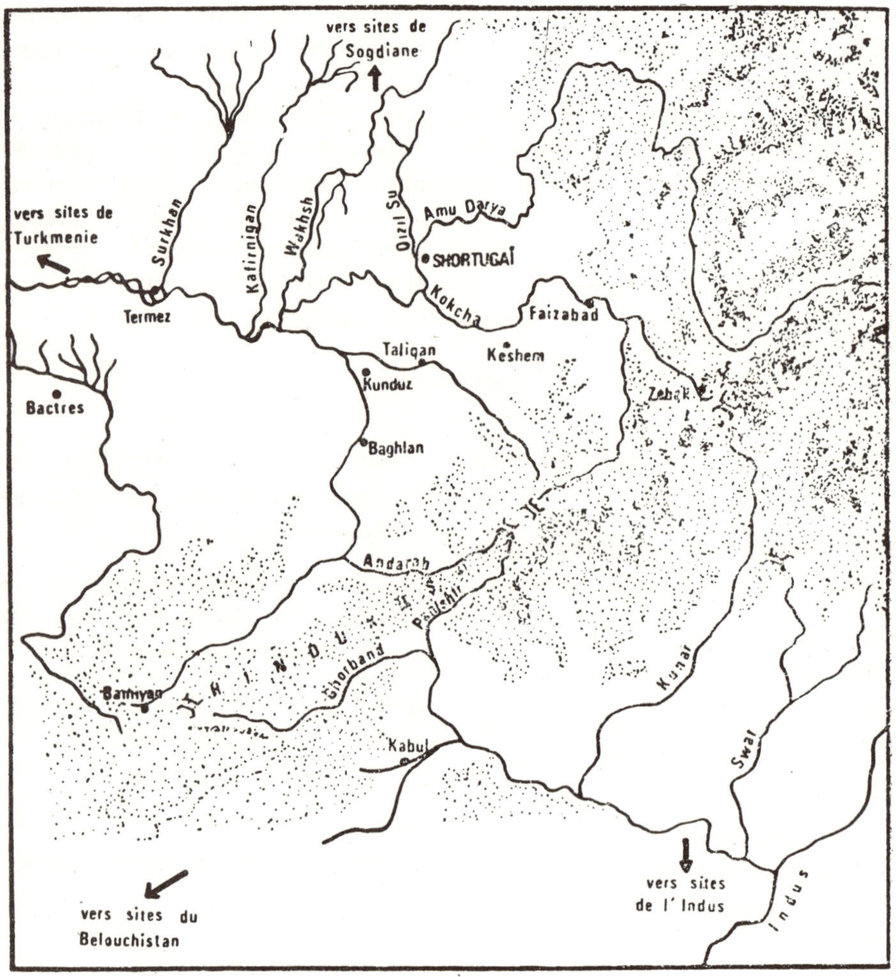

Fig. 1 : Map of Eastern Bactria

Period I : is purely Mature Harappan without any admixtion of other elements from local or other origin. No trace is visible of local neolithic or chalcolithic. The first Harappan settlement lies right on the virgin soil and only a part of mound A is occupied. The set of Mature Harappan material recovered is large : ceramic is unpainted (black on red : intersecting circles; pipal leaves, peacocks etc . Fig.26), or decorated by incisions in the Harappan manner. Various beads have been discovered including faience and steatite and etched carnelian beads, the latter probably imported. An Indus seal depicts a rhinoceros (Fig.4); shell bangles are made out of *Xancus Pyrum* from the Indian ocean (Fig.5). Interesting are the amount of lapis lazuli chunks and various fragments of clay crucibles, evidencing the workmanship of lapis and copper possibly related to trade activities. The architecture of this period is Harappan by the size of the brick (ca. x 16 x 32 cm), which are unbaked.

Period II : is more difficult to define precisely at the present stage of the study especially because a detailed sequence of the phase of the Harappan period in the Indus basin is not available to rely upon, and no general consensus appear on the meaning of the terms "Late Harappan" and "Post Harappan". Nevertheless we know that it is certainly different from the various "Post Harappan" cultures of Baluchistan and Indus basin like Jhukar or Cemetry H. Many Harappan traits still exist and we would propose to qualify this period II as a late phase of Mature Harappan. Statistically, the relative importance of Mature Harappan elements decreases and some of the ceramic shapes change. At the same time, new shapes appear that we can relate to Central Asiatic material. The architecture does not change in a significant manner but the working of lapis lazuli stops.

Period III : the Central Asiatic or more precisely Bactrian elements become preponderants. However, some Harappan traditions survive (for example: cord impressions on jars; terracotta scoops etc..). On the other hand the new Bactrian material cannot be directely related to the Dashly-Sapalli material of Western Bactria. The Shortughai III Bactrian material is local, Eastern Bactrian : the ceramic, entirely white, unpainted, include a considerble number of goblets and basins. A new and important fact is the presence of burials in the settlement : two children and one sheep. The copper industry is still flourishing. The walls of the houses are made of *pise.*

Period IV : during this period, the preceding Bactrian tradition continues but in addition, some new elements become importants. First a pebble industry recalls the local tradition, very ancient, of the Hissar culture, well known in Soviet Tadjikistan. Second, two burials and some deposits are obviously related to the Late Bronze Age of the Kafirnigan and Surkhan Darya valleys : the Bishkent and Mollali cultures. The settlement of Shortughai IV is smaller than those of the preceding periods, its architecture is badly preserved.

After the abandonnment of the settlement, a small number of steppe caramic sherds appear in the latest layer of mound B. On mound A, more than thousand years after the end of the Bronze Age settlement, a Hellenistic farm occupied the mound.

Datas for an absolute chronology :

The comparative studies give for period I, Mature Harappan, a date between 2500 and 1750; period IV, by comparison of the Bishkent and Mollali material is dated according to Soviet scholars from the very end of the 2nd millennium (ca.2000). This is long for our sequence (no more than 2.50 m of cultural deposit). According to our own dates, an early chronology seems preferable. The C14 analyses of Shortughai samples give :

-Period I-II : 1925$\pm$95 to 2445$\pm$160 B.C. (not calibrated)

-Period IV : 1585$\pm$165 to 1690$\pm$95 B.C. (not calibrated)

We can thus propose a sequence between 2200-2000 B.C. and 1800-1600 B.C.

Fig. 2 : Mound A : Section

Bibliography

Dikshit, K.N. 1979 "The Late Harappan Cultures in India", *Essays in Indian Protohistory*, (ed.) D.P. Agrawal, D.K. Chakrabarti, Delhi.

Francfort, H.P. 1981 "The Late periods of Shortughai and the problem of the Bishkent culture (Middle and Late bronze Age in Bactria)", in H. Hartel (ed.) *South Asian Archaeology 1979*, Berlin, p. 191-202.

Francfort, H.P. 1981 "The Early periods of Shortughai (Harappan) and the Western Bactrian culture of Dashly", in F.R. Allchin (ed.). *South Asian Archaeology*

H.P. Francfort, "The Harappan settlement of Shortughai (N.E. Afghanistan) and some aspects of Central Asia in the Bronze Age", in *Wheeler Memorial* (ed.) S.P. Gupta, New Delhi (in press).

Francfort, H.P., M.H. Pottier, 1978, "Sondage preliminaire sur 1'etablissement protohistorique harappeen et post-harappeen de Shortughai (Afghanistan du N.E.)" *Arts Asiatiques*, XXXIV, p. 29-79.

Gupta, S.P. 1979 *Archaeology of Soviet Central Asia and the Indian Borderlands*, vol. 2, New Delhi.

Kohli, Ph. L. 1981, *The Bronze Age Civilization of Central Asia. Recent Soviet Discoveries*, edited with an introduction by Philip L. Kohl. New York,

Masson, M.M. V.I. Sarianidi 1972, *Central Asia. Turkmenia before the Achaemenids*, London.

C.N.R.S.
Paris

H. P. Frankfort

THAPLI: A PAINTED GREY WARE SITE IN GARHWAL

Thapli (30°, 12'N, 78°, 47' E), situated on the right bank of river Alakananda in district Tehri Garhwal is 2 km. south-west of Srinagar across the river. The site has been disturbed by a massive road cutting. The total thickness of the deposit from top to bottom is 2.90 m., out of which 1.70m. has been cut in road cutting operation. To know the culture sequence of the site a trial trench (5mx2m.) was taken up on the road surface. The excavation revealed a single phase culture of the PGW along with its associated wares.

The habitational deposit consisted of three layers with a total thickness of 1.20 m., resting on river pebbles mixed with natural soil, yellow and sticky in nature.

So far as the pottery is concerned, the PGW from this site confined mainly to dish and bowl, besides a miniture painted vase which indicates towards association with the late Harappan shape as is assumed by Joshi from his evidence of this type of a grey ware vase discovered at Bhagwanpura (Joshi, 1978). The PGW from Thapli has other associated types in the black slipped, fine red, grey and coarse red wares. But the frequency of the PGW with 120 good painted sherds is 10% of the total pottery. The main shapes in the associated wares are dishes, bowls, vases an basins. It is interesting to note that some shapes like the basins and the vases are found both in the coarse red as well as in plain grey ware.

The Thapli PGW has several paintings, such as the sun symbol along with horizontal and vertical bands, dots, sigmas, concentric circles, interesecting strokes, wavy lines, spiral designs, double lines with dots, leaf, floral patterns etc. showing in most of the cases a maturity in the execution. A notable point is that both the thin and thick varieties of this ware are available with the paintings.

Among the other finds mention may be made of a terracotta bird, copper bangles, copper nail-parers and terracotta beads. A large quantity of bones indentified as that of horse (Equus caballus) and other animals have also been found. The discovery of these cultural remains in such a remote part of Himalaya is significant.

References

1. Joshi, J. P. 1978 : 'A Note on Excavation at Bhagwanpura', *Puratattva* No. 8, p. 180

K.P. Nautiyal
B.M. Khanduri
Vinod Nautiyal and
D.L. Rajput

Garhwal University,
Srinagar

THE ARECA-NUT OBJECT : IS IT A BEAD ?

A common find at most of the Indian historical sites is a perforated clay object resembling the "betel nut," *Areca catechu* Linn or *Supari*. At Ahar, it is dated by ^{14}C to 1725 B.C. (level 1-b), while at Nasik to A.D. 1875 (upper levels). This demonstrates, if nothing else, the long association of Indians with the plant.

Areca catechu is a thin palm, not native to India. The nuts range in shape from flat and disc-like to spherical. Apparently, the English authority on beads, Beck was the first to describe these objects as "pear-shaped' in his report (1930:169) on beads found in a megalithic tomb in Hyderabad State by Hunt and assumed they were beads. Theywere associated with coins from the second century B.C. to the second century A.D. A little later, Beck examined the material from Harappa sent by Vats. As they were surface finds, Beck associated them with the Gupta Period. Again, he described them as pear-shaped and called them beads (Vats, 1940 : 408).

M. G. Dikshit called attention to the likeness of these objects to Areca-nut in his report on the beads from Kolhapur (Sankaia & Dikshit, 1952: 93). He discussed the "Areca-nut beads" at some length noted, their occurence at nine other sites, and dated them from the *circa* second cenrury B.C. to the fourth century A.D.

As is commonly known, a bead is a small object with perforation for threading with others to make an ornament, a rosary or an abacus. Decorative objects which are not strung—bangles, crowns, belts—are not beads. Conversely, perforated objects not used for ornamentation are not classified as beads either. Examples of misidentification of this type are the long terracota bicones found at many sites in India. Sali (1963: 34 f) found some in a Chalcolithic site in Dhulia district, and then observed that the Bhois and Bhils of the area use these bicones as weights for their fishing nets. Parallel use has been noted among the Maria Ghonds of Bastar district (Malti Nagar, 1978).

Before continuing, we must note that there is no question of clay beads being made in India, during the period under consideration. Many of these terracotta beads were made in moulds and carry intricate designs. Others are large, heavy and plain. They might have been used for decorating animals rather than humans. (Sankalia & Dikshit 1952 : 94). Particularly imortant among the finds of decorated clay beads are those uncovered at Vaisali (Sinha & Rai, 1969 : 190), where a complete necklace of thirty-one terracotta beads and two shell pendants were uncovered. At Kolhapur a slate bead mould for a square tabular bead with an eye motif was uncovered (Sankalia & Dikshit 1952 : 132).

Not all authorities think that the Areca-shaped objects are beads. For instance 'These objects are very common on all ancient sites and have often (?) been described as spindle whorls, which, indeed, some of the larger specimens may have been.' (Wheeler, Ghosh & Deva 1941 : 96). By 1962, during Charsada, excavation Wheeler unhesitatingly called the Areca objects, and also referred to an earlier series of terracotta truncated bicones as beads.

Thapar found Areca-nut objects of clay at Iron Age and later levels at Prakash (1964-5 :

112). According to him they may have been used as beads, spindle whorls or net sinkers. One was found with an iron pin in the hole, suggesting its use either as a pendant or whorl. Ansari and Mate in their report on Dwarka (1966: 41) considered the possibility of the objects being "terracotta beads or spindle whorls" after noting Sali's discovery concerning the net sinkers. Rahmani (1969: 170 f) digging at Damkot (Pakistan) found a series of terracotta object similar to Wheeler's finds at Charsada. Rahmani thought the objects were probably spindle whorls.

Let us direct our attention for a moment to the nature of spindle whorls. The whorl ranks first among man-made machines roughly contemporaneous with the invention of the potter's wheel. Whorls are small, round weights placed atop spindle sticks to give momentum while twisting fibers into thread. They are often similar to beads; it is not uncommon to find them strung with beads in collections of museums. The earliest whorls thus far recorded are those found at Tell Soto, Iraq (Murpert *et al*, 1976: 39), dated to 5570 ± 120 B.C. They are biconical and plano-convex in shape, the two shapes found for millennia throughtout Western Asia. In general whorl can usually be distinguished from beads by several criteria. They tend to be larger, and perforations are almost always large to accomodate the stick; on beads they are a disadvantage. In section, whorls must be circular for maximum balance. Many beads are also circular in section, but they are not limited to this shape. It is in profile that whrols and beads most often diverge. Beads are usually symmetric along the length of the profile, but many whorls are not. Whether this asymmetry of whorls is of functional importance or not is not yet understood. The trend toward increasingly asymmetric profiles through time can be seen in one of the few adequate discussion of spindle whorls from Anatolian plateau, Seaton Lloyd and Mellaart (1962: 277 f). To the author's knowledge, the only broad study of spindle whorls thus far attempted is that by Liu (1978: 97 ff.).

We must also consider the possibility of these objects being net sinkers. S. B. Deo has recently (1980) communicated to the author that terracotta Areca-nut objects were currently being used for shallow water fishing. They were tied to the ends of the net. Several threads of the net were passed through the conical perforation, knotted at the top, and held in place by the small aperture. However, such use of Areca objects is not reported in the literature dealing with fishing equipment (Sarkar 1954: 284). Fishermen of Bastar district have explicitly stated that round net sinkers (Areca shape included) are not advantageous (Malti Nagar 1981). Sarkar (1954: 286) has noted the dual function of many objects among primitive peoples, and cited the custom of wearing iron net sinkers as charms against the evil eye in Bengal.

What, then, were the function of these objects? Were they beads, spindle whorls or net sinkers? The results of an examination of the Areca objects unearthed in some thirty excavated sites in India are discussed below to find the answer.

General Description

The Areca objects are generally (though not invariable) noted as being well-made and fired at high temperature so that they are durable. They are usually of terracotta, but black ones are reported from Kaundinyapura, Timbarva, and Dhatva, and stone ones from Charsada. They are always wheel-turned, that is, turned on a rotating machine (more correctly a mandrel than a wheel.) In this connection, they are often decorated with striations or a single or more deep grooves on the butt (concave) end with a sharp instrument. In shape they vary greatly ranging from the classic Areca shape to flat and concave bottomed ones with others such as onion-shape, vase (*ghaṭa*) shape or "asymmetrical beehive" shape in between. All these forms recall the different shapes of the Areca-nut itself.

Many of the Areca objects have large perforations and some have conical perforations. (Altekar and Misra 1959: 117) noted "Some of these beads are roughly made with strongly chamferred holes, which are unduly wide; indeed, the cord must have been very thick to prevent the bead wobbling upon it." The question of an unusually thick cord does not arise if the object was intended to be placed around a spindle whorl or to gather net lines.

The physical characteristics outlined above suggest that most of these objects were not beads. The large or conical holes are most telling in this connection. The mandrel-turning, achieving perfect balance recalls a prime characteristic of spindle whorls. The hard firing making the objects tough also suggests that it was meant to be used as a tool. This does not exclude the possibility that some of these objects might have been worn as beads.

History of the objects

As we have noted, the first use of these Areca objects appears to have been at Ahar, where they are found in considerable varieties from periods 1-b and 1-c (pre-1725 to 1270 B.C.) (Sankalia *et al* 1969: 167). At Rangpur one such object is reported from late Period II A (Harappan, dated *c.* 2000 to 1500 B.C.) and another one from II C (late Harappan, 1100-1000 B.C.), and then several from Period III (1000 to 800 B.C.) (Rao 1963: 140 ff). Otherwise, they never appear to be associated with Harappan materials. A few are reported from the late PGW period at Hastinapur (Lal 1955: 95).

However, it is only with the beginning of NBPW levels that Areca-nut objects are found widely. They were dated from the sixth century B.C. at Vaisali and Dhatva. They appear with NBP or in Mauryan contexts at Timbarva, Nevasa, Kaundinyapura, Navdatoli, Nasik, and reappear at Ahar.

At Charsada, Damkot, Shamalaji, Chadravalli and Brahmagiri they appear much later, usually not until the beginning of the Christian era. In the Deccan at Kolhapur, Kondahar and Yeleswarum they are introduced during Satavahana times.

Thus they seem to have been first used perhaps in Gujarat, later during Mauryan times; spreading to the North from there to the western frontier, the Deccan and south. The style was apparently exported by the Andhras in the first century A.D. or so to Burma. Excavations at Beikthano (Thaw 1968: 49) have uncovered a workshop for terracotta objects, among which were 57 unfired Areca-nut objects. Interestingly, this large-scale horizontal excavation uncovered 24 finished Areca objects, well distributed among the dwelling.

The objects remained in use for a very long time. At Kolhapur they are on the wane during the Bahmani period, but are reported from Navdatoli into the seventeenth century, from Ahar and Shamalaji until the eighteenth century, and at Nasik until the last quarter of the nineteenth century.

Two important trends are apparent from this survey.

1. Areca-nut objects often replace other terracotta perforated objects. At the earliest site we have dealing with, Ahar, at level I-a there are no Areca objects, but there were seven perforated postsherd discs. In level I b and I c the perforated discs drop to five and two respectively, and there is a corresponding increase in Areca objects. The pattern is repeated much later in the south. At Kaundinyapura twelve Areca objects, all black, appear from post-Mauryan levels, while in the preceeding period there were 27 perforated discs, which later disappear. At some sites, such as at Maski, the perforated discs were used for longer periods.

Even more strikingly, in the North and West the Areca nut objects come to replace terracotta objects which are invariably also called beads, but which resemble Western Asian spindle whorls in every detail. These bicones are found in early chalcolithic sites such as Kayatha, Chandoli, as well as at Ahar. They are reported later from Charsada, Damkot, Taxila, and Nasik. The early Charsada and Damkot specimens resemble Western Asian spindle whorls down to the white chalk-filled decorated incisions. A later stage can be seen at these two sites in which the whorls are decorated by having pinched crenellations around the central zone. At Chandravalli, the Areca nut-shape replaced an earlier ring shape which is found in the megaliths.

The point to keep in mind when considering the above is that in each case, perforated discs, asymmetric bicones or rings, the Areca shape replaces the earlier one. A new bead design may become suddenly popular over a large area. But, it does not consistently replace the other, more ancient bead shapes. However, in the case of spindle whorls this is exactly what happens : new shapes replace old ones.

2. In report after report where the Areca-nut objects are classified as beads, there are no spindle whorls. At Taxila, Marshall noted stone, bone (or ivory) whorls, but in each case remarked on their scarcity, saying that stone ones were "rare" (1951 : 502) and the bone/ivory ones "very few" in number *(Ibid* : 661). One spindle whorl was, reported from Dhatva (Mehta and Chowdhary 1957 : 15), but its design, being in the concave end can not be seen when strung as a bead, is unique. The Areca objects were listed among the beads.

On the face of it, this would appear to be highly unusual. Otherwise, whorls are known world-wide. Why are they not found in India ? Three possible answers suggest themselves : One, that whorls were always made of perishable materials in India. Two, that the Indians did not spin. Three, that what have hitherto been identified as Areca-nut beads are, in fact, Areca-nut spindle whorls.

Wooden whorls would be subject to undesirable warping. That Indians spun cloth and have been doing so since a very long time is well known. The spinning wheel (the *charkha*) is a medieval introduction (G. Lal, 1980). Where does that leave us ? At least one scholar tracing the history of textiles in India has concluded that spindle whorls are found at every archaeological site and were used for spinning thread. He could only have been referring to the Areca-nut object (G. Lal 1980).

The question whether spindle whorls were also worn as beads by the people who made them is not discussed here. Thus far, no satisfactory archaeological or anthropological evidence has surfaced to answer this question in the Indian context or elsewhere.

Conclusion

These terracotta Areca-nut objects may have had more than one use. Crude ones may have been used as net weights, while fine ones with small perforations might have been worn as beads. Others, appearently, served as spindle whorls. Perhaps some of very finely made ones were used especially to spin the scared thread.

The evidence suggesting that most of these objects might be spindle whorls consists of following: One, the large holes on most of them make ill-suited for beads. Two the, final wheel (mandrel) turning of the majority of them make them finely balanced and especially suited for spindle worls. Three, their asymmetrical profiles would typologically place them much closer to whorls than beads. Four, the objects replace older clay objects at many sites; anyone familiar with Western Asian material would have no difficulty in agreeing that the Areca objects are replacing spindle worls at Charsada, Damkot, etc.

If the Areca-nut objects are not spindle whorls, then what are they?

References

Altekar, A.S. and V. Misra 1959 *Report on Kumrahar Excavations 1951 - 1955* K.P. Jayaswal Research Inst., Patna,

Ansari, Z.D. and M.S. Mate 1966 *Excavations at Dwarka*, Deccan College, Poona.

Ansari, Z.D. and M.K. Dhavalikar 1975 *Excavations at Kayatha* Deccan College, Poona.

Beck, Horace C. 1930 'Notes on Sundry Asiatic Beads' *Man* 30. 134.

———1940 "Report on Selected Beads from Harappa" Ch. XV in M.S. Vats, *Excavation at Harappa* (rept. Bhartiya Pub. House, Varanarsi, 1974).

Deo, S.B. 1980 Personal communication.

Deo, S.B, and Z.D. Ansari 1965 *Chalcolithic Chandoli*, Deccan College, Poona.

Dikshit, M.G. 1968 *Kaundinyapura*, Dir. Archives & Archaeology, Marahrathra State, Bombay.

Khan, Abdul W. 1963 *A Monograph on Yeleswarum Excavations*, Govt. of Andhra Pradesh, Hydrabad.

Lal, B.B. 1955 'Excavations at Hastinapura and Other Explorations in the Upper Ganga and Sutlej Basins' *Ancient India* 10 & 11.

Lal, Gauri and P.T.I. Staff Reporter 1980 'Controversial Charkha' *Indian Express*, Bombay, 23 November.

Liu, Robert K. 1978 'Spindle Whorls : Part I Some Comments and Speculations' *Bead Journal*, (Los Angeles) 3 : 3/4.

Seton Lloyd, and J. Mellaart *Beycesultan Vol. I* British Inst. of Archaeology at Ankara, London, (1962).

Marshall, John 1951 *Taxila*, Cambridge U. Press, Cambridge U.K.

Merpert, N., R. Munchaev, and N. Bader 1976 ',The Investigation of Soviet Expedition in Iraq 1973' *Sumer* XXXII : 1 & 2.

Mehta, R.N. 1955 *Excavations at Timbarva*, M.S.U. Baroda.

Mehta, R.N. and S.N. Chowdhary 1975 *Excavation at Dhatva*, M.S.U. Baroda.

Metha, R.N. and A.J. Patel 1967 *Excavation at Shamalaji*, M.S.U. Baroda.

Nagar, Malti 1978 and 1981 Personal communication.

Rahmani, Abdur 1969 'Excavation at Damkot', *Ancient Pakistan* IV,

Rai, Sita Ram 1965 *Karian Excavation*, K.P. Jayaswal Research Inst., Patna.

Sali, S.A. 1963 'Probable Use of Certain Chalcolithic Terra cotta Beads,' *Bul. Deccan College Research Inst.* 23.

Sankalia, H.D. and S.B. Deo 1955 *Report on the Excavations at Nasik and Jorwe*, Deccan College, Poona.

Sankalia, H.D., S.B. Deo an Z.D. Ansari 1969 *Ahar* Deccan College, Poona.

Sankalia, H.D., S.B, Deo. Z.D. Ansari and S. Ehrhardt 1960 *From History to Prehistory at Nevasa*, Deccan College, Poona.

Sankalia, H.D. and M.G. Dikshit 1952 *Excavation at Brahmapuri (kolhapur), 1945-46*, Deccan College, Poona.

Sankalia, H.D., B. Subbarao and S.B. Deo 1958 *The Excavations at Maheswar and Navdatoli 1952-53*, Deccan College, Poona.

Sarkar, H. 1954 "Artifacts of Fishing and Navigation from the Indus Valley' *Man in India* 34: 4.

Sinha, B.P. and L.A. Narain *Patliputra Excavation 1955-56*, Directorate of Archaeology & Museums, Bihar, Patna.

Sinha, B,P. and Sita Ray Ram 1969 *Vaisali Excavations*, Directorate of Archaeology & Museums, Bihar, Patna.

Thapar B.K. 1957 "Maski 1954 : A Chalcolithic Site of the Southern Deccan', *Ancient India* 13.

——1965 'Prakash 1955 : A Chalcolithic Site in the Tapti Valley,' *Ancient India* 20 & 21.

Thaw, Aung 1968 *Report on the Excavations at Beikthano*, Min. of Union Culture, Rangoon.

The Wealth of India 1948 Raw Materials, Vol 1, Delhi.

Wheeler R.E.M. 1948 'Brahmagiri and Chandravalli 1946 : Megalithic and Other Cultures in Mysore State' *Ancient India* 4.

——1962 *Charsada* Oxford U. Press, London.

Wheeler R.E.M, A. Ghosh, and Krishna Deva 1941 "Arikamedu : An Indo-Roman Trading-station on the East Coast of India" *Ancient India* 2.

Deccan College, Pune **Peter Francis**

TERRACOTTA DISCS

Terracotta discs, a common item generally reported from the protohistoric and historic sites, have not received the attention they deserve. They are casually described in the excavation reports, along with other minor items. An attempt therefore, is made here to show their significance.

Terracotta discs mostly are in fine fabric and are found in red, grey and black colours with varying thickness. Some of them have been treated with fine lustrous slip. While majority of the discs bear impressed or incised notches around the circumference, many have specific symbols or motifs on their sides as well. In some cases their edges have also been decorated. It is interesting to note that the discs can be graded into more than a dozen groups according to their diameters.

At Atranjikhera their diameters range from 2.25cm to 5.25cm. with almost a uniform increase of 0.25 cm. from one group to another in ascending order in period III (the PGW phase). It may be added here that periods I and II of Atranjikhera have not yielded any wellknown modelled disc so far. How ever, the tradition of using terracotta disc continued in the following period of our cultural history represented by the well-known industry of the NBP ware. At Atranjikhera a new size having 5.5 cm. diameter was also introduced during this period which remained confined to the lower phase of the NBP ware period only and did not continue further. It is noteworthy that though the diameters of the discs varied from 2.25 cm. to 5.5 cm. only three groups having diameters of 3 cm, 3.25 cm and 3.5 cm. respectively were popular. However, the smallest size in the series, having 2.25 cm. diameter appears most uncommon and the discs having diameters between 4.75 cm. and 5.5 cm. were also not in much better position,

On the basis of the decorations around the circumference, the discs may be divided into three types :

Type-1 : Discs having impressed or incised notches on the circumference.

Type-2 : Discs having crescent like notches (some times looking like 'U' or 'V') on the circumference.

Type-3 : Discs having plain circumference.

Among the three, Type-1 perhaps was very popular throughout the PGW and the NBP periods. In period III of Atranjikhera, they account roughly for 92% of the total number.

The notches on them have been executed either sparcely or closely. However. they are broadly divisible into two categories : (i) short and (ii) elongated, each having simple and curved varieties.

Similarly, the notches found on the discs of type-2. also have two categories :

(i) Linked crescents or 'U' like notches and

(ii) Unlinked crescents or 'U' like notches.

It may be mentioned here that at Atranjikhera while the discs showed an upward trend in their popularity throughout period III (the PGW phase), it was just the reverse in the following period of the NBP were (period IV). However, the highest number of discs were recovered from the earliest sub-phase of period IV, during the time of overlap of the PGW and the NBP ware industries.

Generally, these discs are supposed to be gaming counters (Lal, 1954-55 : 87-88). But the decorative symbols (see the plate) representing Sun, Moon (crescent), stars, fire altar, chariot and motif depicting two eye like designs intersecting each other, arrows etc. may suggest that these were for some religious purpose. Most of the above designs [1] appear to represent the familiar deities of the Vedic Aryans. Even arrows and chariots, the invariable items of the Aryans life, had religious sanctity. The numbers of pecked marks or circles on them may be indicative of some suspicious numbers denoting the heavenly bodies *etc.*, including eleven *Rudras*. These discs with delicate symbols on them apparently do not favour the idea of their being used as gaming counters lest the symbols might be rubbed off in constant handling.

Could then they be used as votive or ritualistic objects? It may be mentioned here that the tradition of disc making still continues in Bengal and they are made both in terracotta and metals particularly at the time of Durga-Puja celebrations.

It is quite possible that the idea of punch-marked coins was derived from the long tradition of the discs having marks on them. Atleast the symbols of sun and crescent generally found on them either are identical or tally to a great extent with those depicted on the coins. The gradation of diameters might have given the concept for the size and weight of the punch-marked coins. The hypothesis however, is too tentative and merely suggestive.

References

Lal, B.B. 1954-55 'Excavations at Hastinapur and other explorations in the Sutlej basin 1950-52' *Ancient India* nos. 10-11. pp. 87-88.

Narain A.K. and Roy, T.N. 1968 *The Excavations at Prahaladpur*, Varanasi.

Sinha, K.K. 1959 *Excavations at Sravasti*, Varanasi.

Aligarh. R. C. Gaur

IVORY AND BONE PLAQUETTES — A NOTE

The ivory or bone plaquettes in a restricted chronological bracket *i.e. circa* 600-200 B.C. have been recovered from Taxila (Marshall, 1951 pp. 654-655, pl. 199-12), Ropar (Sharma 1953, p. 124, fig. 4-11), Mathura (Joshi, Pers. Comm.), Sonkh (Hartel 1976, p. 87, fig. 24), Hulas (*IAR* 1979-80), Ujjain (*IAR* 1956-57, fig. 11, pl. XXXIII A-7), Nagda (*IAR* 1955-56 p. 14, fig. 4, pl. XXIV B), Navdatoli and Prabhas Patan (*IAR* 1956-57. p. 17, pl. XVIII B-5). (fig. 1-2). It has also been reported from Atranjikhera (Gaur, Pers. Comm.) These plaquettes shaped in conventional human form have been prepared out of some kind of flat bone or ivory pieces and are as a rule, decked with incised circlets and horizontal and oblique lines all over the body. Most of the specimens bear a hole on the top probably to tie a string for using them as amulets. A detailed study of these plaquettes recovered from above sites revealed that they differ in shape from one region to the other.

Among the sites located in north-western region in India only stratum IV *(*fig. 1, 6) of Taxila (*circa* fifth century B.C.) and Period III (fig, 1, 5) of Ropar (*circa* 600-200 B.C.) have yielded such bone plaquettes. The specimens resemble profile of two bottles placed mouth to mouth. The head has a straight horizontal line on the top and three

[1] Among the illustrated discs of Hastinapur (Lal, 1954-55) disc no. 6, pl. XLVI belonging to the PGW Period (Period II) deserves our attention. The photograph shows incised mark on it which is not distinct and has been ignored by the excavator, nos 2 & 3 of the same plate are also of interest for their sun and floral motifs. Disc no. 10 (pl. XXI) from *Prahaladpur* (Narain and Roy, 1968) is noteworthy for its *swastika* mark. The discs of *Sravasti* (Sinha, 1959) fall broadly in two groups (i) the plain one in which the decoration is around the circumference and (ii) the others in which both the sides show symbolic decorations mainly representing Sun and *Swastika*. Some interesting discs have also been found by M.C. Joshi, at Mathura and by K.N. Dikshit at Allahpur (Distt. Meerut) during the course of excavations. I am grateful to these excavators far showing their unpublished material.

incised circlets each enclosing a dot, arranged in inverted triangular fashion, possibly representing eyes and mouth. The lower part of the plaquettes also bears incised circlets arranged within and outside of the inverted traingle. Both the plaquettes are provided with circular hole possible for using them as amulets.

Mathura, Sonkh and Hulas are the sites in upper Ganga-Yamuna *doab* which yielded similar objects respectively from Period II (from the closing decades of the fourth century B.C. to *circa* 200 B.C.), Level 34 (beginning of third century B.C.) and Period III. Due to fragmentary nature of specimens obtained from Mathura and Sonkh not much idea can be had about their shape but the specimen from Hulas (fig. 1,1) which is almost complete indicates that the plaquette used in this region was not similar to north-western examples and instead has an almost triangular head with a deep incised horizontal line on the top and three circlets enclosing dots arranged in traingular position, short stretched arms and gradually expanding lower body. The chest arms and the body are decked with incised horizontal and oblique lines and circlets each enclosing a singular dot. This specimen having a hole on the head is made of tortoise shell (Dikshit, 1980).

The human-shaped plaquette recovered from Period I of Ujjain (fig. 1, 7) does not help much in carrying out the regional comparison because of its fragmentary nature. The headless specimen obtained from period III of Nagda (fig. 1. 3) located in central India, suggests that the plaquette was again different from those of north-western and upper Ganga-Yamuna *doab.* The legs of this specimen are stretched away besides, more prominent treatment provided to the fingers by carving short incised horizontal strokes at the ends of the feet and arms.

The site Prabhas Patan (fig. 1, 4) situated in western India has yielded a single plaquette from period III. The specimen appears to be more nearer to Hulas plaquette as it has a triangular head, stretched arms with stylized representation of fingers and pentagonal lower body decorated with usual circlets and horizontal and oblique strokes.

The foregoing account clearly indicates that there was a practice prevalent in the north-western upper Ganga-Yamuna *doab* central and western India of using such ivory or bone plaquettes, as revealed from the late levels of the Northern Black Polished Ware except Ujjain, where it had been found in the levels earlier to NBP horizon (Period II) although on stylistic grounds it is not different than other known examples.

Some scholars have associated these plaquettes with the primitive mother-goddess on account

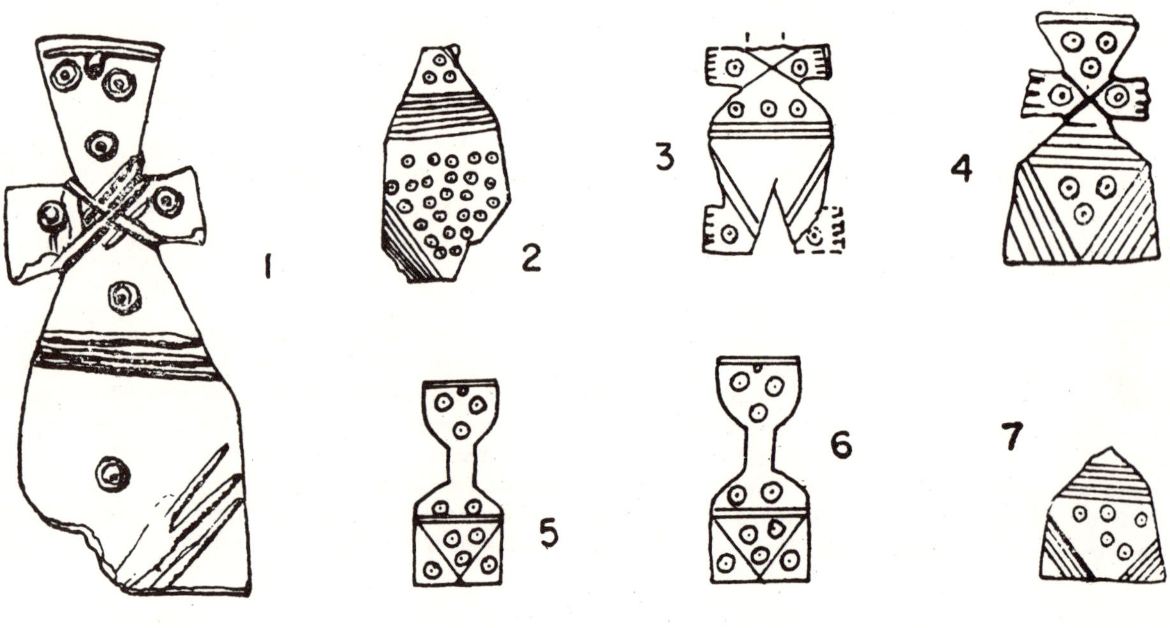

of traingular decoration on their body (Joshi, 1978). Besides above the incised circlets enclosing a dot on these plaquettes easily recalls similar type of decoration executed on Mauryan mother-goddess figurines of Ganga-Yamuna *doab*. It is most likely these may have been used for magico-religious purposes as amulets. Almost similar type of objects prepared out of *Tulsi* stem are still used as amulets by orthodox Brahmins of north Bihar.

References

Dikshit, K.N. 1980 'Excavations at Hulas and further explorations in Upper Ganga-Yamuna doab, *Man & Environment* Vol. V.

Hartel, H. 1976 'Some Results of the Excavations at Sonkh', *German Scholars on India* Vol. II (New Delhi).

Joshi, M. C. 1978 'Ritualistic objects in Ancient India', article contributed for *Dictionary of Indian Archaeology*, (ed.) A. Ghosh (in press).

Marshall, John 1951 *Taxila* Vol. II & III (Cambridge).

Sharma, Y. D. 'Exploration of Historical Sites', *Ancient India No. 9* (Delhi).

Indian Archaeology — A Review 1955-56.

Indian Archaeology — A Review 1956-57.

Indian Archaeology — A Review 1979-80 (inpress).

Archaeological Survey of India
New Delhi-110001

A. K. Sinha

STUDIES IN ANCIENT BUILDING MATERIALS : A NOTE ON BHITARI PLASTER

Plastering is one of the most ancient techniques known to man. Plaster is defined as a material used for coating walls and mortar may be defined as a plastic building material, generally made by mixing lime with sand and water.

Plaster samples from Bhitari[1] famous for Skandagupta inscription, is a historical site excavated by K.K. Sinha, have been taken for analyses.

Description of samples :

Site	:	Bhitari (Ghazipur)
Location	:	Trench-4
		Stratum-3
		Depth-1.5. m.
Colour	:	Reddish brown

Organic matter absent in samples. Presence of minute white spots.

The similarity of compositions of samples suggested its same location. It was a lime plaster. SiO_2 reduced the sand carrying capacity of lime but did not change the hardness or strength (Lucas, 1962). If too much sand is used the mortar will be short and if too little, it will be sticky. The reddish brown colour of sample, is mainly due to Fe_2O_3 (Ferric Oxide) which affects plasticity and sands carrying capacity but higher percentage actually increase the strength and hardness. Small amount of Al_2O_3 (Aluminum Oxide) improves the lime (Jasterzebiski, 1959).

Chemical Composition

Percentage	1	2	3	4	5
SiO_2	73.50	72.02	73.4	73.24	74.2
Fe_2O_3]		6.00	6.45	3.4	4.5
Al_2O_3]	8.64	0.50	0.65	3.6	2.6
$CaCo_3$	13.80	13.74	13.65	13.34	13.42
MgO	2.59	1.71	1.85	1.86	1.76
K_2O]	1.08	1.81	1.75	1.58	1.46
Ka_2O]					

[1] Dr. H,C. Bhardwaj is gratefully acknowledged for the valuable guidance.

Sand was mixed with lime to prevent excessive shrinkage on drying. The hardening of lime plaster is caused by following reaction :

$$Ca(OH)_2 + CO_2 = CaCO_3 + H_2O$$

The process occur very slowly. MgO content of sample was perhaps due to dolomitic lime stone $[CaMg(C)O_3]_2$ and shows very low shrinkage and better plasticity.

Analysis of samples from the Harappan sites revealed the fact that the use of both gypsum and lime was well known to the Indus people. Gairola analysed and studied the lime washes and plaster on Bhubaneshwar and Konark temples and pointed out that they do not contain gypsum (hydrated $CaSO_4$), but are composed of lime and sand in different proportions. Paramsivan (1937) analysed Nayak and Chola plasters. His result shows that a pure and rich lime, containing up to 65.59% CaO was used for finish plaster, and it was found associated with small quantities of gypsum which is detrimental. Plasters of Kaushambi (Satya Prakash and Rawat, 1965) have been analysed by Rawat, who found that approximately one part of sand was mixed with one part of slaked lime. Analysis of mortars show that a number of mortar samples consisted simply mud and it appears that the sand in mortars was added slightly in higher proportions than the plasters.

Thus it can be concluded that leaving Indus people, who use both gypsum and lime as their building materials, others analysis of plaster samples from Bhubaneshwar, Konark, Nayak, Chola, Kaushambi and Bhitari established the fact that lime plaster was in vouge throughout the ancient period.

References

Jasterzebiski, D. 1959. *Nature and Properties of Engineering Materials*, (Japan) p. 484,

Lucas, A. and J.R. Harris, 1962. *Ancient Egyptian Materials and Industries* London, p. 79,

Paramsivan, S. 1937. *Technical Studies in the field of Fine Arts*, 5 pp. 228-31.

Prakash Satya and N.S. Rawat, 1965. *Chemical Study of Some Indian Archaeological Antiques* pp. 14-19, Lucknow.

Banaras Hindu University
Varanasi

R. N. Singh
K. K. Jain

SOME INDETERMINATE TERRACOTTA OBJECTS—A STUDY

Some interesting terracotta objects were recovered from the Harappan levels of Bara, Sanghol, Bhagwanpura, Bargaon and Hulas. An attempt has been made to study the various aspects of these objects including their stratigraphical position, manufacturing technique and their possible use, besides a comparative analysis.

The objects recovered from Bara [fig, 1(3)] is entirely hand-modelled and is about 10 cm. square at the base tapering towards inside with bifercated ends (Sharma, 1976) measuring about 17.5 cm. The base of the object is marked with three finger-tip depressions arranged in a row on front as well as back. The object, red in colour, is of coarse fabric and ill fired. An almost similar object was unearthed from the late-Harrappan level of Bargaon [fig. 1 (2)] (Dikshit, 1980). The basal part of the object has been found broken. This specimen too is broader at the base and narrower at the terminals. Bhagwanpura too has yielded almost an identical find. The excavations at Hulas also yielded identical specimens. The basal part of one object [fig 1 (1)] is broken, whereas another one was found almost completely intact. The basal part of the objects are as usual broader and the bifurcated ends narrower. One of the objects (1980-81), which was slightly thickened at the base was recovered from a pit alongwith Harappan pottery. The pit lined with mud bricks (48x26x7 cm.) from two sides has been observed to be in a bad state of pre-

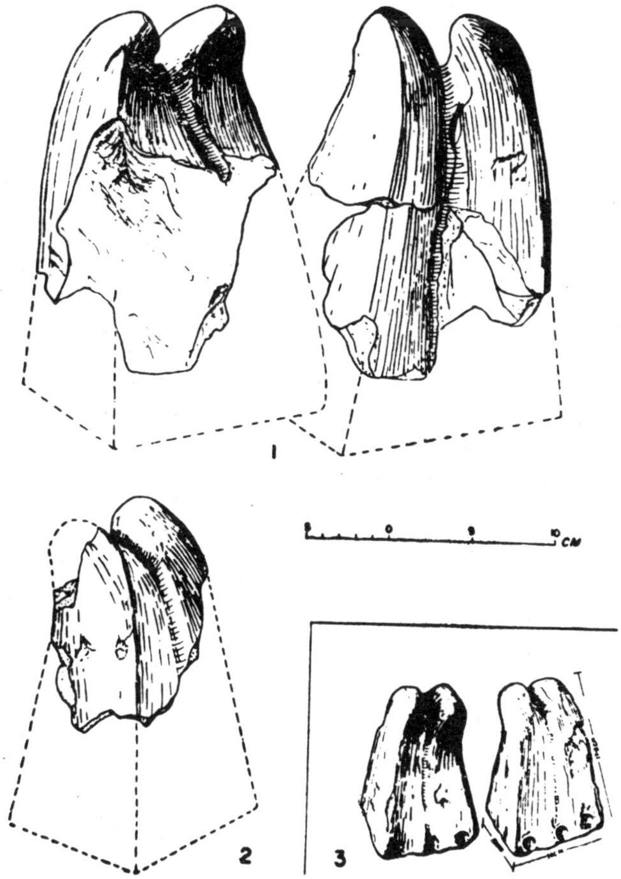

Fig. 1. Indeterminate objects

servation. These objects are comparatively bigger in size and are of coarse fabric besides being ill-fired (Dikshit, 1981). A similar type of object has been found at Sanghol too but in the absence of any published data, it is not possible to furnish the details of the object (Sharma, 1976).

The objects recovered from various sites are in principle similar to each other in manufacturing technique though some difference can be noticed in size and stylization when closely observed, as the bifurcated ends of few of them are more tapering than others. The basal portion of some of the objects specially specimens from Hulas is more broader.

Excepting Bhagwanpura and Hulas, we do not have any idea of the exact context in which these objects were recovered. At Bhagwanpura it was found from the working level of one of the oval-shaped structures of the second structural phase of Period IB. It is interesting to note that the working level of the structure has yielded burnt earth, pottery, uncharred bones and terracotta animal figurine. At Hulas also, one of the objects were encountered from a pit, along with Harappan dish and bone pieces. On the basis of the present available meagre data it seems that these objects were possibly used for some ritualistic purpose, although Sharma relates them with *Naga* cult.

References

Dikshit, K.N. 1981 The excavations at Hulas and further exploration of the Upper Ganga-Yamuna doab; *Man and Environment*, Vol. V, pp. 70-76.

Joshi, J.P. 1978 A note on excavation at Bhagwanpura, *Puratattva No. 8* pp. 178-180

Joshi, J.P. & Madhu Bala 1978 Life during the period of overlap of late Harappan and P.G.W. Cultures. *Journal of the Indian Society of Oriental Art* (*N.S.*), Vol. IX, pp. 20-29.

Sharma, Y.D. 1976 Transformation of the Harappan Culture in Punjab; *Archaeological Congress and Seminar*, 1972 pp. 5-15

S.Jamal Hasan
Archaeological Survey of India,
New Delhi-110011

A NOTE ON AGUNCHA, DISTRICT BHILWARA, RAJASTHAN

Aguncha (Lat. 25° 45' N, Long. 74° 46' E), on the bank of river Mansi, a tributary of Banas, is situated about 10 km. south of Gulabpura in Hurda tehsil of district Bhilwara. The local legend ascribes this place to be the capital of epic-king Dwanda. The place was also known as Tāmbāvātī (now an important centre of Zinc ore mining), which according to tradition was the seat of Mauryans. And interestingly enough, peacocks are abundant in this area.

The ancient mound measures approximately 1500x800 metres and is about 10 metres in height. During the course of exploration ringwells and traces of parallel brick walls, 5.30 metre in width and 1.60 metre in height located at a distance of 5.40 metre from each other, were observed. The size of bricks used in the walls are 57 x 27 x 9 cm., 54 x 27 x 8 cm. and 45 x 28 x 9 cm.

The pottery of the site consisted of red ware' black-burnished and black-slipped ware, the types being bowls, dishes, vases, jars and carinated *handies*. Other finds include terracotta mother goddess, dog and bull figurines, beads and sling balls, shell and ivory bangles and 55 copper punched-marked and cast coins. Other important antiquities were stonesculptures of Vayū, Ekamukha *Śiva-linga*, four-armed Vishnu, *yonipaṭṭa* with three *kichakas*, female standing figures, Karttikeya, lintel of the sanctum doorway of a Vishnu temple., Mahisha suramardini and the feet portion of a standing Tirthankara figure on a lion throne.

During the course of exploration the exposed Section on the road from Aguncha to Bhilwara along with brick wall was also scraped. On the basis of this the cultural deposits can be divided into three periods from the early historical to the Gupta Period.

Period I which is pre-Maurya and Maurya is marked by the occurrence of plain red ware, black and red ware, black-slipped ware, Painted Grey Ware and Northern Black Polished Ware. The representative types in plain red ware were vases, jars, bowls, dishes, a lip of a basin while the representative type in black and red were and black slipped ware is only the bowl. The main types in the NBP ware included dishes and bowls in silvery and golden hues. The other material found was iron slag, terracotta weight discs, beads, burnt bricks, two punched-marked coins, terracotta Mother Goddess, male figure including a nude and animal figurines.

Period II, assigned to Sunga and Kushan Period is characterized by a brick structure, measuring 5.30 metre in width and 1.60 metre in height.

The antiquities assignable to this period are a stone plaque of Vishṇu, terracotta beads, a double-convex wheel, head of an elephant, a camel, torso of a standing male figure, bust of female, bust of an ascetic, ear stud and animal figurines.

Period III, which is Gupta is characterized by the presence of double course of brick floor. Other finds included terracotta beads and terracotta head of a Saiva ascetic.

Archaeological Survey of India, Vadodara-390009

B.L. Nagarch
P.K. Trivedi

A SUGGESTED CLASSIFICATION OF NORTHERN BLACK POLISHED WARE

In 1946, an upto-date list of the distribution of Northern Black Polished Ware was published, by Wheeler and Krishna Dev (1946). On the basis of limited sherds of NBPW found from Ahichchhatra and Taxila they had given the first definition of the NBP. After the excavations of Hastinapur, a more precise and detailed definition of this pottery was attempted by Lal and Thapar (Lal, 1954-55).

This definition of NBP having usually thin section, grey core and distinctive glossy lustre was accented by most of the fied workers. A careful study of the above definitions shows that it does not cover all the types of NBP.

At Rajghat, the NBP is the major Ware of the early and late phases of NBP, i.e. of Sub-Periods IB and IC. It accounts for nearly fifty percent, of the total pottery recovered from these deposits (Narain and Roy, 1977). The NBP recovered from Prahladpur, Ayodhya and Takiaper, the other NBP sites excavated by us, besides Rajghat shows two very clear and broad strains in it:

1. Monochrome NBP or NBP having one shade of colour.
2. Bichrome NBP or NBP having two shades of colour.

Monochrome NBP

The surface colour of about ninety percent of the sherds in this group is jet-black or brownish black or bluish black. The remaining ten percent are in steel blue, pinkish, silvery, golden, brown, chocolate, violet or deep red. All these colour variations may not be intentional (Keslo and Thorley, 1943). We have attempted in this paper to classify the monochrome NBP into five fabrics.

Fabric A :

NBP coming under this head is hard, dense having a fine fabric with thin sections. The sherds have a glossy suface with highly lustrous sheen and it is difficult to scratch their surface with a nail or knife. These pieces, when struck, give a sharp metallic sound. There is a complete harmony between the type of the slip, firing and the clay in this fabric. Being a prized commodity, this pottery has been referred as 'De-Luxe' ware of the time. Instances of its repair by copper wire or pin-revetting are also reported from sites like Ropar, Bairat, Besnagar, Ujjain, Broach, Sonepur and Kumrahar. It was in limited supply due to less potting or high cost of production. However, it is found in fairly large quantity on sites of the eastern U.P. and Bihar. This fabric had its root in the early phase of NBP which was its formative period too. Its occurrence in the late phase of NBP, admittedly in a small numbers, may indicate its survival as a treasured fabric. It is mostly, this fabric of NBP which has been defined, dealt at length and technically examined by various scholars. The flanged and corrugated bowls are the only shapes so far reported in this fabric. Dishes are not found in this fabric.

Fabric B :

These are not hard and compact like those of Fabric A. The sherds are comparatively thick and can be scratched with a knife more easily than those of Fabric A. A limited number in them bear prominent burnishing marks and they do not show the same lustre as is retained by the top-graded NBP. These are less glossy and smooth. It is difficult to distinguish these sherds from the Black-Slipped Ware. In typology, however, there is clear distinction between the two. The straight sided,carinated and sub-ovaloid bowls which are very common shapes of the black slipped ware are totally absent in this type of NPB. Dishes are found in large number. The bowls are akin to those found in Fabric A. No large sized vessel like vases or storage jars has been reported. It appears that this fabric was also sparingly shaped and technologically represents a stage in between Black-Slipped Ware and the top-graded NBP (Fabric A).

Even though there is a fair amount of variety in these two fabric mainly in the colour, these are linked by some common features :

(i) The nature of clay used is well-levigated and does not show any sign of tempering material.

(ii) The core is always grey. Below a thin slip of shinning black or any other colour, a grey surface (both outer and inner) is seen. This shows that all the pots in these two fabrics were fired under reducing condition.

(iii) The paste is fine and the pots were invariably potted on a fast wheel.

Fabric C :

In this fabric, the core of the sherds are red but

also tends to be greyish in some cases. Below the shinning black or brown slip there is always a red, buff or orange-yellow matt surface. The peeling of the slip, the red matt suface and greyish-red core suggest that the pots may have been fired in both oxidizing and reducing conditions. But this point needs to be checked by technical analysis.

Fabric D :

In this group, the sherds are usually black and red but other modification of colours are also found. These are invariably thin in section and have a lustrous finish similar to those of Fabric A and B. The shapes are restricted to bowls and dishes but the colour combination of black and red appears to have been produced by process of inverted firing. But these are definitely different from the black and red ware, we find alongwith NBP in the early phase of NBP. This associated black-and-red ware is poor in texture and firing. The core in this case is highly porous, thick and gritty. The shapes are also different, Thus Fabric C may justifiably be construed as the sub-variation of NBP in which the colour combination was produced by inverted firing.

Fabric E :

This is the coarser variety of NBP. It is more prolific in the late phase of NBP. The sherds, thicker in section and having darkened unoxidized smoky core are relatively low-fired. The surface colour of the pot ranges from dull black to dull grey. The example of true shinning slip being rare. The surface dressing is either a self-slip or a wash. Most of the pots were without any slip treatment. The fabric as a whole is coarse and debased. Occurrence of small sized bowls and dishes, vases, basins and carinated *handis* in this fabric is noteworthy.

Bichrome NBP

Their chief characterstic of this type of NBP is that they exhibit the combination of colours, employed on one vessel. The surface colour in the monochrome group of NBP is always one although there is wide range of colour variations. In this variety a design in one colour is set off against the other, so that, there may not be any overlap between the two colours. It is in these sherds that we have some designs which appears to have been copied from the painted designs of the PGW. The common pattern of producing thick and thin horizontal bands, vertical strokes, vertical strokes coming out from a horizontal rim band, transverse band or stroke and simple circular bands or arches common in the Painted Grey Ware are also found in the bichrome variety of NBP of Kaushambi, Rajghat, Sravasti, Prahaldpur in Uttar Pradesh and Bahal in Khandesh, (Roy, 1969), In this fabric we also get some sherds in which the horizontal division of the two grades of colour is very clear. The upper portion of the pot has better quality of lustre and colour while the lower portion has less superior finish and different colour. Such sherds have also been reported from Sravasti. But the technique of producing these painted specimens of NBP totally differs from that of the PGW. In the PGW the unfired pots are painted with a colour-dipped brush. This results in the production of a seperate layer of painted design superimposed over the plain grey surface. So on PGW, the designs are pigment colour-oriented. But in case of painted NBP it is slip-colour oriented in which one colour is set off against the other. Although a few designs have been copied from the PGW, but the technique of painting totally differs. It is somewhat similar to the one found on Athenian vases, In this connection Mis Richter's (1951) observation on Athenian pottery is worth to mention. She says that accidental and intentional red glaze on Athenian pottery is due to double painting and double firing. At first only that portion of the pot was painted which were to come out black. The pot was then subjected to oxidizing and reducing stages of firing. The firing was then stopped and the pots were allowed to cool down, then that part of the pot which was to come out as red was painted. This was again fired under oxodizing condition. The area which was painted later came out as black. It is doubtful whether these NBP pots were also prepared in similar manner, but the procedure was known to our potters. The most common specimens in this group are the sherds in which a design in black is set off against the red or a design in red against the black. In both the above cases, there was no overlap between the red and black areas. The other combination of colours are dark steel blue set off against red, grey against light red, black against dark-brown, black against brown, and black against ash-grey. The shapes are similar to these which commonly occur in other fabrics.

References

Lal, B.B. 1954-1955 'Excavations at Hastinapur and other explarations in the Upper Ganga and Sutlej Basins, *Ancient India*. No 10 & 11, pp. 50-52.

Narain, A.K. and T.N. Roy, 1977 'Excavations at Rajghat, Part II, pp. 25.

Keslo and Thorley, 1943, 'The Potters Technique at Tell Beit Mirsin, *The Manual of the American School of Oriental Institute*, p. 90.

Roy, T.N., 1969 A comparative Study of the Paintings from the NBP and PGW levels, paper read at the Annual Conference of Indian Archaeological Society, Patna.

Banaras Hindu University
Varanasi
T.N. Roy

COMPOUNDABLE PROSODIC SIGNS IN THE INDUS SCRIPT

Introduction

I. The script is an Indian invention, made on Indian soil, and with phonetics of an Indian and no borrowed language. The European epigraphers developed concepts to classify distinct types of graphic symbols and classified whole systems into pictographic, ideographic, syllabic and alphabetic according to attributes of external forms and formulated broad scale comparative strategies, which continue to be used by decipherers of Indus texts resulting unfortunately in bias, distortion and complete failure. Different writing systems need different criteria and the Indus script is one of these which requires hitherto undeveloped criteria to reveal the basic principles that impart a scientific structure to this script as a whole. Methodological problems of a different nature, hitherto unknown or unapplied, are needed to determine the kinds of conceptional skills that were actually used by Indus scribes to produce and read written messages.

II. The Indus writing system was devised and used for the sole purpose of producing a lexicon (as is transparent in the hundreds of solo, two-three-four or five-lettered texts, torn out of their contexts), in my opinion, of obsolete and un-intelligible Vedic Sanskrit words (proofs given elsewhere), and not as a vehicle for secular speech and mundane purposes. This hypothesis made me start with research on the use of numerous short and long vertical strokes used in the texts, and helped me to discover the underlying principles according to which the Indus numeral notational system operates (Gupta, 1982) and the kind of the message the texts convey for use of posterity, or the concepts the children of Indus divines and seers must learn to become literate.

2. Classes of Signs.

I. The signs (394) in the Indus Sign List (Koskennieni and Parpola, 1979) can be broadly classified into seven classes as in Fig. I. A large number of these signs (118 out of 394 or 30% in the Finnish List) are composed of isolable sign elements. Some of these consist of one or more elements or 'compoundable signs', Such signs do not stand or found solo, or as discrete graphic components that can be dissected further, It must be clearly understood that we are here not concerned with compound or conjunct consonants that can be deserted further. It must be clearly understood that we are here not concerned with compound or conjunct consonants which are about 100 in the above sign list. Moiner Williams (1962) has noted 382 such forms of 2, 3, 4, or 5 letters.

II. The Indus Sign List has a very large proliferation of arcane symbols and signs. Scholars of

Fig.I. Broad classes of Indus Signs (394 + Allomorphs)

Sr No.	Class	Examples	Approx No.
I	Alphabetic, Syllabic	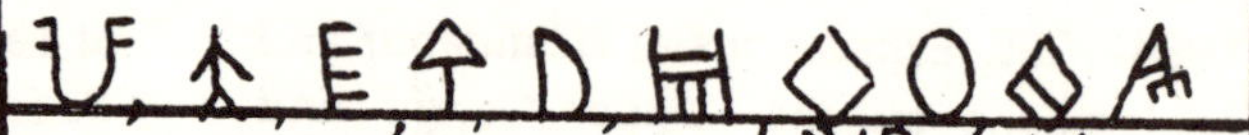	180
2	Compound Consonants		84
3	Vowel prosidies		24
4	Numerals, ideograms	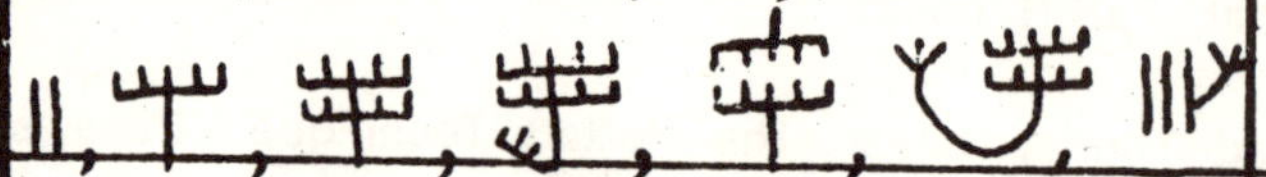	32
5	Onomatopes (avian)		8
6	Compoundable prosodies	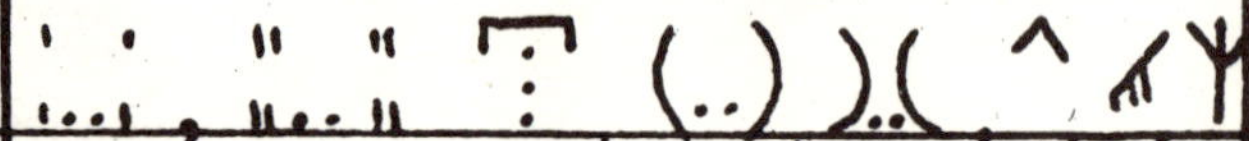	118
7	Miscellaneous		12 MNG

a research turn of mind will find intutive appreciation of the nuances of the Indus language and the message of the seal texts when they become adequately familiar with this script.

III. The Indus texts presuppose a long history of linguistic effort as has been demonstrated by me, on archaeological grounds, elsewhere (Gupta u. d.)

IV. The sleights of signs end symbols and grammatical pecularities have to be deligently searched, classified and formed into laws to provide pertinent meaning.

V. The original symbol or sign shapes are sacred and not the *'Normalised Signary'* of Mahadavan (1977) the Soviets and the Finns. They are the basic facts of a study which must on no aocount be tempered with. There should be no temptation to 'edit' them. To temper with them will be like faking the sounds and an unpardonable sin. All elements are essential, even though they (Wallis Budge, u. d.) may run into hundreds (Egyptian hieroglyphs are over 1200). We may, however, allow reasonable allowance for scribal inaccuracies and constraints due to the very small size of seals, etc., in space and time. All these must be put into categories of human sound types. Speech sounds in this script are purely phonetic and hence not liable to personal idiosyncratic behaviour, even though they are eneumbered with diacritics or peculiar prosodic elements as will be shown later. The Indus signs, as in Fig, 1 are from numerous assorted founts and appear very distressing. To have a computer typographically equipped to deal with over 600 signs (Parpola's 394, Mahadevan's 419 and Vats 450) is a huge task. These elements however when put togather should produce out of them a system of the target language. Their large number shows that they have been established on purely phonetic grounds. The Indus scribe also introduced an hitherto unrecognised set of 'compoundable signs', described and shown in Fig. 2.

3. Prosody

I. Beach (Firth, 1948) appears to have been

Fig.2. Compoundable Prosodic signs.

Sr No	Class or type of Prosodic sign	Sign	Examples of radical signs enclosed	No. of signs involved
I	Circumgraphs			118
	-Bracket,straight,on either side	|...|		4
	-Bracket,slanting	/...\		3
	-Bracket,double	||...||		1
	-Bracket,double lines below			1
	-Bracket ½ on right			1
	- Bracket ½ on left			6
	-Bracket on top,single			9
	-Bracket,double on top			1
	-Brackeţon top & left			1
	-Bracket,broken,single			18
	-Bracket ,double			5
	- Double line below			2
	-Bracket,broken+ single on top			1
	-Parenthesis,bow type	...)		1
	- ... ,convex	)...)		4
	- ... concavo-convex			1
	- ... proper	(...)		5
	- ... in reverse	)...(		2
	- ...oval			1
2	Semaphore type			6
3	Supra-segmental,angular			11
4	Onomatopes (avianforms)			8
5	Ladles,dumb-bells			5
6	Pterographs(smallwings)			8
7	Pine needles,wave forms			5
8	Tridents,triangles			8
9	Miscellaneous			
10	Text.No.7071. Jar Sign			MNG

the first (if not the first) to employ the term 'prosodies' to denote what had been previously called 'sound attributes'. The London School of Linguistics, headed by J.R. Firth, has proposed a different kind of approach of phonological analysis called the 'Prosodic Approach' (Firth, u.d.). In developing phonological analysis on prosodical lines there is no suggestion that phonemic analysis is wrong, invalid, or untrue.

II. "Phonetics and phonology have their ultimate roots in India. Very little of ancient Hindu theory has been adequately stated in European languages. The method of writing used for writing Sanskrit is syllabic, and the Devanagari syllabary used for it is to this day model of phonetic and phonological excellence. The word analysis is syllabic and clearly expressive of the word structure. Within that structure the pronunciation, even the phonetics of the consonants, can be fully discussed and represented in writing with the help of prosodic signs for a consonant closing a syllable (Firth, u.d.). The diacritics point out the vowels and the consonants in detail and some may function as prosodic marker, some as separate vowel signs or separate sounds in Roman sense. Diacritics in Indus script are of two main types, phonematic and prosodic. The prosodic diacritics include Vriddhi, rhotacization, retroflexion, thematic letters of roots, various kinds of suffixes, endings in personal and demonstrative pronouns and numerals, etc. Examples of prosodic devices are found in plenty in Indus texts and that is the reason why I have preferred this approach in my interpretions of the phenomena of the texts.

III. The study of these Indus prosodic elements or structures has bearing on all phonological studies. Their study will be found to have epoch making function, if proved valid, in the history of Indus linguistics and will be a big step forward in the understanding of the complexities of the orthography and the ABLAUT and other phenomena studied from Grimm to Brugmann in the last century. This approach will make the highly complex problem of Indus language clearer. The phonological character of the words of the texts has to be expressed as a plurality of systems of inter-related phonematic and prosodic categories. A systematic study of the prosodies alone, in my opinion, will help and is helping me to understand the complexities of the orthography and the phonological systems : Proto-Indo-European versus Indo-Aryan and Aryan, or Indo-European versus Sanskrit and Dravidian versus Sanskritic. Much of the work is laborious, yet it calls for a great deal of ingenuity of a very high order.

IV. Prosody is defined (Webster's dictionary) as that part of grammar which treats of quantity, accent and the laws of versification. In Indus script, certain other peculiar features (elements) have not attracted the attention of any previous decipherer. These I consider some of the most important 'KEY SIGNS', hitherto understood features for detailed scientific analysis. These prosodies are found written above or below, at the end of a sign, or enclose a sign, or even in the middle of sign (may be seen in Fig. 2.). Such prosodic formulae are difficult to read as their domain is explicit in their symbolisation. The elements of diphthongs are also prosodic features of a syllable.

V. The special prosodies seen in Indus orthography, in my studies, of the sign list, fall into nine main classes (Fig. 2).

VI. The prosodic structure of ONOMATOPES however, the most difficult subject to study, and this has been to a certain extent explained and examined elsewhere. Are the AVIAN signs to be considered as 'speech, signs' proper and what may be termed as 'phonemes' and significant elements of speech or 'ideograms', or a method of phonetic transcription ? I have not yet made any detailed research on this aspect.

4. The object of the Study of Prosodic Features as revealed in the Indus Texts.

I, The objects are :

i, to prepare a 'phoneme inventory' of the Indus language,

ii. to study the 'combinatory lattitudes' of each phoneme,

iii. to study 'conventional Vowel/Consonant dichotomy',

iv. to study the relative frequency of various 'syllable-initial and syllable-final' consonant and vowel combinations, thus furnishing a basis for 'Euphonic (Sandhi) Laws of Sanskrit', or method of 'syllabication', or 'inflectional endings' (SUP and TIN terminations), etc,.

v. to study the prosodic structure of onomatopes.

There can be other modes of analysis. I have, however, found this method as the most economical and comprehensive; right valid and true; easily applicable and helpful, We are interested in learning the technique, used by the Indus scribe, for reducing the Indus language to writing in a form of orthography unparalleled in the history of paleography of antiquity.

II. The identification of the prosodic elements is thus a prelude to prosodic analysis. the results of which will be dealt with in another article in the series. No sign or symbol, as far as possible, has been regarded as allophonic or phonemically irrelevant in phonemic analysis.

III. The Indus texts present a large number of affixes, which have been already identified. The suffixes, in my opinion are nominal and verbal endings. The Indus lexicon seems to have verbs in various tenses. moods, person ond number. There are prefixes and infixes, to be detailed later.

IV. If the forms of target language are known (in my case, I have proposed, on sound linguistic basis, Sanskrit as the language), the other remaining forms can be derived according to certain rules (*e.g.*: Yāska's Nighaṇṭu, varies treatises on applied phonetics or the Pratisākhyās, Pāṇini's Asṭādhyāyi, etc...). This is a laborious task as the orthography is likely to impose great restrictions on their interpretations. A prosodic approach appears to be the only way out (unlike the imaginative, spurious and subjective approach of the present day decipherers) to solve this tangle. The prosodies can make it possible to set up forms whose basic CV (consonant and vowel) structure can be found.

V. In the prosodic elements of the Indus orthography, I have made an attempt to sort out into phonological classes categories and systems (as is done in treatises on anatomy : the blood-vascular, nervous, digestive, bony, etc., systems) a large number of signs or characters with their distinguishing diacritica, whereever they occur.

VI. The study of the proposed prosodic structure will, in itself, be a study of syntagmatic relations, and a few, if any body will deny or object to this approach which I have made.

VII. In the Soviet and Finnish theory and S. R. Rao's assumptions the feed back from observation to theory is very weak, artificial, superficial and spurious. They consider that the large amount of prosodic data, numeral notational signs, onomatopes, etc, are useless, because this material imposes great strain on their ingenuity. They handle texts in which prosodic signs are the least or vowel and numeral signs are missing or they do not know which are vowel signs and what is the function of numeral notations. They have not taken into account the statistical properties of various signs as initials or finals. They have failed to consider that certain Indus signs occur only in specific phonetic contexts (e.g. the jar' sign occurs in all three positions in a single text No. 7071 (Fig. 2). The sign is considered by the Finns as the genitive case marker. If so, how on earth can three genitive case markers occur in a single text of 8 signs ?).

VIII. The aim of prosodic analysis takes into account not only of paradigmatic relations and contrasts (the Indus texts abound in these) but also of the equally important syntagmatic relations and functions.

5. **Prosodic Analysis**.

I. In my analysis of these features I have made use of two types of elements :

i. Phonematic Units, which are those aspects of phonic material which can be referred to as minimal segments having a serial order in relation to each other in structures. Such units constitute the C and V units of a phonological structure.

ii. Prosodies. At times a greater part of the phonic material is referable to prosodies which are, in my opinion, and by definition, of more than one segment in scope or domain or relevance and belong to structures. Thus there are many kinds of prosodies.

iii. The meaning and function of these 32 prosodies, in my study as classified by me in Fig. 2, has not yet been established. This entails selection of all readable and unduplicated texts where phonetic elements are associated with these prosodic signs, arranging them in an endocentric fashion and learn their positional behaviour and then to find if they fall in certain patterns and systems. This may help in identification of the parts of speech (verbs, substantives, adjective, adverbs, particles, etc.) to which a word with this kind of prosody is associated, or other grammatical phenomena. The result of this analysis will be presented in another article in the series.

II. One component, *i. e.* 'the compoundable sign', itself is not found solo or a separate element in the list of signs, but becomes meaningful only when accompanied with the other radical component. Such elements have been grouped in nine classes in Fig. 2.

6. Function of These Prosodic Signs.

I. It has been shown in Fig. 2. that these signs are dependent elements. They have to embrace or be associated with a radical sign to become meaningful, or disclose their purpose or meaning or function. Any number of uncertain guesses can be made, but only those will be acceptable which can provide incontrovertible evidence in the maximum number of inscriptions.

II. This can be done by a detailed, long term study as laid down in para four above. The value of systematic prosodic analysis in linguistic pedagogy needs no emphasis. Positional criteria in classifying them as initial, medial, intervocalic or final are useful. In the prosodic system of Indus orthography one must sort out into phonological and phonematic classes and categorise this large number of characters which will make a real-contribution to linguistic knowledge of Indus texts. A paradigmatic study, later on, of ranges of possible sound substitutes will lay the ground for detailed phonematic study and a syntagmatic study of the word complex whereever found. Peter Lodefoged (u. d.) has very aptly pointed out that, "A phonetic description can be considered adequate only if it has the same meaning for all who use it". An interpretation of it which has a personal impressionistic explanation has no value in decipherment.

III. In our approach we hope to discover the involved phonological and grammatical systems in this manner. Those who are well aquainted with the prosodic features (many have been mentioned in Panini's grammar) of the sanskrit language will derive great benefit from the results of this analysis and possible confirmation that many grammarians anterior to Pāṇini had devoted a great deal of thought to this subject, The prosodic features discovered in these texts will be compared side by side with the features laid down in the aphorisms at a later stage, especially so when the combinatory capacity of lattitudes of these prosodies has been worked out.

Conclusion

I. I have advanced elsewhere new theories against the current views on the nature of the script and its language, the iconographic motifs. the avian signs, the method and purpose of use, and the message of these seals based on modern methods of linguistic research (Gupta, 1980).

II. I have been more sympathetic to prosodic aspects than any of my predecessors because these have been neglected in the past and have been detected by me only in the course of my dissection of the Indus corpus of texts.

III. I have made tentative suggestions of my own with proofs which the linguists are welcome to test, to criticise and comment on. Many will disagree with many of the views that I now hold. I should like them to look upon this as a tribute to the genius of the Indus linguist and the scribe. I hope they will be tolerant of its shortcomings and give constructive suggestions.

References

Firth, J.R. 1948 Sounds and Prosodies, *Tran. Phil. Soc.*, pp. 127-132.

u.d. Phonetics in Linguistics, A *Book of Readings* (eds.) W.E. Jones and J. Laver, pp. 50-51

Gupta, M.N. 1981 A New light on Indus (Harappa, Mohenjo-daro (Script Language and Message. Lecture delivered at the University of Kentucky, Lexington, Sept. U.S.A.

1982 Digitary Notation In The Indus Script (Being presented at the third International Conference on South Asian Languages and Linguistics, Mysore).

u.d. Age of Writing in the Indus Valley. An Archaeology Supported Evaluation (unpublished).

Kimmo Koskenniemi and Asko Parpola, 1 79 *Corpus of Texts in the Indus Script*, Helsinki.

Lodgefoged, Peter u.d. Phonetics in Linguistics, *A Book of Readings (eds.)* W. E. Jones and J. Lever.

Mahadevan, Iravatham 1979. The Indus *script, Texts, Concordane and Tables.*

Wallis, Budge, E. A. u.d. An *Egyptian Hieroglyphic Dictionary.*

Williams, Monier, 1962 *A Practical Grammar of the Sanskrit Language.*

B-2 Parul Apartments
Ahmedabad-380009

M.N. Gupta

DRAWING IN ARCHAEOLOGY : SUGGESTIONS

Introduction

The use of drawings in archaeology is manifold, such as drawing of pottery, antiquities and other works in the field. Drawings are made to scale. Scale is important for making comparative studies of objects from their drawing. Isometric or perspective views alone may not fully serve the purpose, although these can be shown in addition to orthographic projections for further convenience of the user as in, A. Ghosh and K.C. Panigrahi, 1946, *Ancient India*, No. 1, Fig. 3, 44.

I would now put forth my ideas on how in drawing pottery sectional elevation of a pot is required to be shown : elevation is to be drawn on the right half and section on the left half, both halves being divided by a centre line in the middle or vice versa. Complication comes in when there is a Painted, incised or applique design on the pot which is to be shown in the drawing. If the design can be traced on a vertical plane in its full definition, then it can be accomodated in elevation only if not, it can be represented on the horizontal plane for which a plan of the artifact has to be incorporated.

Plan, elevation and section of an object have to be orthographically projected and should coordinate with each other, otherwise the drawing is incorrect In most of the cases, the designs on the body of the pots have not been mechanically projected from plans but these have been skectched on a random basis (Wheeler, 1946, 'Harappa, 1946 : The Defences and Cemetery R-37', *Ancient India*, No. 3, Fig. 22, XLIa, XLIc and XLId and Fig. 23, XIV, 1947, 'Brahmgiri and Chandravalli', *Ancient India*, No. 4, Fig. 6, 27j, Fig. 9. 41b, Fig. 10, 45d, Fig. 27, T130, 131, 133, 134, 135, 136, 138 and 14c.

Plan is necessary when a design from the body of the pot is to be correctly projected to the

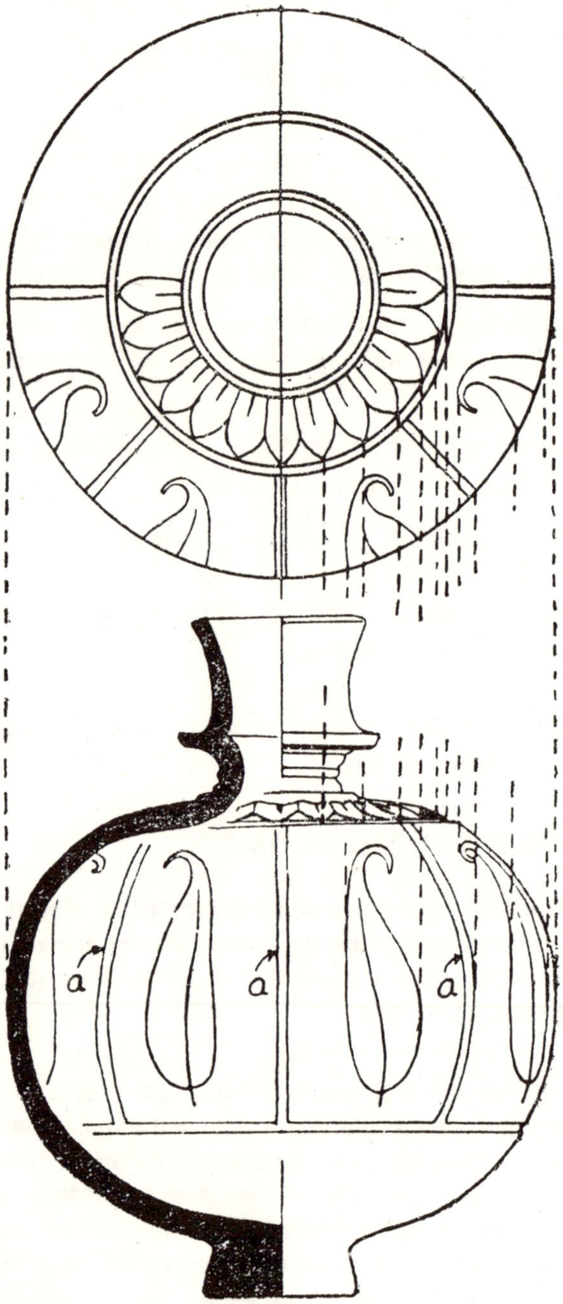

(Fig. 1)

elevation which may, however, be avoided inking. An ideal method of drawing is suggested as under:

Plan and elevation of a pot are drawn in Fig. 1. The characteristic bends and boundaries of the design are marked on the plan. Marked points are projected from plan to the elevation. Correct prespective of the design is thus traced on the elevation with the help of these projections.

In case of smaller sherds the design alongwith the sherd is to be marked on the plan and then projected to the elevation. The design becomes distorted, if it is placed on the right or left of the centre line. To minimize the distortion, the sherd may be placed in the centre and not on the sides, as in Wheeler, 1962, *Charsada*, London.

To develop the design on a plain surface is another method for the sake of design only, in which case the shape of the pot has no relevance. If it is required to show as to how the design is composed on the body of the pot, it must be projected to the elevation or plan. It has to be emphasized that visual distortion of some sort is necessary if the drawing has correctly to be done. A vertical straight line in the centre will become curved while the pot is turned, (see Fig. 1).

Antiquity drawings

The drawing of antiquities involves some of the basic concepts of Fine Art. Elevation and plan after being drawn mechanically to the scale, are to be given a touch of light and shade to highlight the characteristic features of an artifact. An antiquity has to be tackled in a particular manner to achieve this end. As to the number of views required for an object to be drawn, no definite rule can be laid down ; it is dependant upon the form and character of the artifact and must be decided by the best judgement of the draftsman. The positions of plan, elevation and section are so placed on the paper that minimum space is covered without making it too congested.

Field drawings

All the evidences at the site are recorded on plans, sections and other detailed drawings in such a way that these are readily available to the scholars in proper form. The records should be prepared keeping in view all the aspects which may lead to difficuities when these are placed on the table away from the site. Off and on it has been found that the records are not adequate enough to guide the excavator in finalizing his report. It may so happen that the report is written after a considerable gap of time which makes it necessary that the records should be complete and adequate.

All aspects and views of an object or structure or other archaeological feature should, as far as possible, be drawn by one and the same person. Where this is not possible, correlation of different drawing of an object should be done on the field before removing them to the records. Drawing plants in isolated pockets, as is generally the practice ; it is like fathoming a sea without knowing its depth. What is required is an overall idea of the site with the penetrating eye of a surveyor.

The section drawing of the site tells the story of the site objectively and gives the chronological background. It is the back bone of the excavator. Therefore, every excavator should take great care to see that it is prepared accurately.

A smaller scale rather than a larger one is ideal for preparing field drawings, so that these are manoeuvrable while placed on the table. The general plan, for example; can be taken up at such a convenient scale so that it may serve the purpose of a key plan as well. Attempts have to be made to prepare the plan of the site as a single unit. Detailed drawings of important evidences, however, can be recorded separately. Section drawing should also be drawn on the same scale.

References

Ghosh, A. and K.C. Panigrahi, 1946, 'Pottery of Ahichchatra', *Ancient India*, No. 1, pp. 37-59.

Wheeler, R.E.M. 1946, 'Harappa, 1946: The Defences and Cemetary, R-37', *Ancient India*, No. 3.

Wheeler, R.E.M. 1947, 'Brahmgiri and Chandravalli', *Ancient India*, No. 4.

, 1962, *Charsada*, London.

Archaeological Survey of India, New Delhi, 110011. **S.S. Saar**

THE BLACK LUSTROUS WARE OF HIMACHAL PRADESH

In 1979, I got an opportunity to visit the annual Dari Fair near Dharamsala in District Kangra of Himachal Pradesh where I was attracted by some black lustrous pots displayed in a potter's shop because of their near resemblance with the Northern Black Polished Ware. On enquiry, the potter, Shri Saran Das of village Sarah, narrated the technique of manufacturing this black lustrous ware which as below—

The potters of the villages near Dharmsala bring the earth from Teeka Baidi, sand from the streams (not from the river), sandy earth from Sarah, clay for the slip from Teeka Gharoh (Peetlu), whitish earth for coating from Teeka Sadu and black pigment from Talwara and Mukerian in the Punjab.

The potters pound the earth, sieve and knead it into dough. This dough is placed in a pit and covered with a lid. In the pit, the clay releases moisture and the longer the clay is allowed to remain there easier it becomes to mould it on the potter's wheel because it acquires plasticity. To achieve good result, sometimes the clay is allowed to remain in the pit even for fifteen days. When the dough is taken out from the pit, a little water is added to bring it to the right consistency for use on the wheel.

The potter's wheel, a solid disc, is made of wood, sand, clay and stone. In the clay used for making the wheel, goat's hair, coconut fibre, etc. are mixed. This wheel is placed in a shady place for about three months to dry up. The wheel thus made lasts for thirty years or even more. Such a wheel was shown to me in Bundi village.

The prepared clay is put on the wheel and turned into the desired shapes. In this way jars, big and small bowls with lid, *lotas* hāndī, dish, *chilam*, etc., are made. These are kept for drying in the sun for a day in summer and for two or three days in winter, depending on the day's temperature.

The locally available earth known as *banni matti* is made fine and then a coat of this thin paste is applied on the pots. In order to give lustrous finish to the pots, a piece of muslin cloth is folded and is made a little greasy by an application of a little mustard oil. The unbaked pot is warmed in the sun for some time and then rubbed and polished with the slightly greasy piece of cloth till one can see one's reflection on its surface. In this process of burnishing, the worker sometimes gets his or her hands blistered.

Thereafter the pottery is fired in the following manner. For firing the pots are placed in an inverted position and in a closed earthen jar or iron barrel which is sealed so as to make it airtight. Pieces of the heart-wood of the pine tree *(Pinus roxburghu)*. These wooden pieces along with the pots are placed which are known a *jaggan* in Kangri, are resinous in charactor and, therefore, produce a lot of tarry smoke when fired directly or indirectly.

The sealed iron are placed in the open-air kiln. For producing the desired temperature, forty to fifty big basketfuls of dried up cattle dung cakes are needed. When the pots are taken out from the cooled kiln, their outer surface is black and lustrous. There and the Northern Black Polished Ware.

In these black lustrous pots, curd, pickles, jam butter, ghee, etc. are kept.

From the above, it is evident that the slip, burnishing with a slightly greasy piece of muslin cloth, and firing in a sealed barrel with pieces of heartwood of resiniferous pine are together resposible for the lustre of the pottery.

State Museum
Simla-171004.

A. N. Khanna

THE PROBLEM OF ANCIENT INDIAN CHRONOLOGY

The problem of ancient Indian chronology has bedevilled scholars since the middle of the nineteenth century when, thanks to the study of Sanskrit by western scholars, attempts began to be made on scientific and historical lines to determine the chronology of ancient Indian literature and history. In 1859 the great Sanskrit savant Max Muller recognizing the fact that the composition of the entire Vedic literature was complete before the birth of Buddha in about 600 B.C., fixed 1200 B.C. as the date for the beginning of Vedic poetry by arbitrarily assigning 200 years to each of the different literary epochs in the origin of the Vedic literature. It must, however, be remembered that Max Muller regarded this date only as a *terminus ad quem* and expressly stated "that we can not hope fo fix a *terminus a quo*. Whether the Vedic hymns were composed 1000 or 1500 or 2000 or 3000 years B.C., no power on earth will ever determine". Yet surprisingly enough it became a habit with Indologists to say that Max Muller had proved that Vedic literature began to be composed in 1200 B.C. Even after, the advancement of Sanskrit studies it was, therefore, only timidly that a few scholars like Tailak, Jacobi, A.C. Das, Sten Konow and Macdonell proposed new dates on the basis of astronomy, geology, archaeology and linguistics. Their assertions, however, met with opposition since the data in no case admitted of incontrovertible interpretation.

Disciplines like astronomy, geology, linguistics and archaeology having failed to deliver goods M. Winternitz wisely turned to the evidence arising out of the history of Indian literature and religion and gave very sound reasons for dating the beginning of the Vedic age in 2000 or 2500 B.C. No scholar has so far been able to controvert the arguments advance by him. Yet it has to be admitted that the evidence on the basis of which Winternitz tried to determine the date of the beginning of Vedic literature did not by its very nature permit him to arrive at even a tentatively fixed date and he had to be content with giving a range of 500 years for the beginning of the Vedic age.

Of late some noted archaeologists like B.B. Lal and H.D. Sankalia, completely ignoring the arguments of Winternitz, seem to be inclined to put the composition of the Rgveda at a date even later than that proposed by Max Muller by co-relating the Vedic Aryans with the 'painted grey ware' and by asserting that there was no possibility of city life developing in the Ganga Valley before the 6th century B.C. as without iron technology which they date to commence in the sixth century B.C. the jungles could not be cleared. They further maintain that writting was unknown in India before the 3rd century B.C. The untenability of these contentions has been fully demonstrated by K.C. Varma in his learned article entitled "The Kaliyuga Era" published in the Diamond Jubilee Volume of ABORI. The problem of the date of the beginning of Indo-Aryan civilization has thus remained as much a subject of dispute as it was when Max Muller tried to grapple with it.

Under these circumstances the question which perpetually haunts every lover of Indian history and civilization is this; Is it all possible to arrive at an approximate date of the beginning of Indo-Aryan civilization? In other words is it possible to supplement and confirm the literary evidence of Winternitz by some more concrete and tangible evidence ?

The only tangible evidence which can enable us to arrive at an opproximately fixed date for the beginning of Indo-Aryan civilzation is that of Purāṇic genealogies. Unfortunately despite the fact that a lot of work has been done in the realm of Purāṇic studies, sceyticism still persists. This scepticism has token the form of a hapit, precisely as faith in the date proposed by Max Muller for Veda has taken the form of a habit. It is therefore necessary to analyse the evidence of Purānic genealogies.

The Purāṇas give the genealogies of kings that ruled in India from the beginning of Indo-Aryan conquest to the beginning of the Gupta period. Now it has to be admitted that so far as the history of the various kings mentioned in these genealogies is concerned, the tendency of the Purāṇic account is that the more ancient the king the more liable to errors is his account and the more his achievements have been exaggerated and mythologized. This was the reason why in the infancy of Purāṇic studies scholars had come to the conclusion that the Purāṇic accounts are worthless as source of history. A patient study of the Puranas has, however, made it clear that though the Puranic accounts of ancient kings may be and actually are in a great measure untrustworthy it does not necessarily follow that the names of kings themselves, their order of succession and their number are also to be regarded as fictititious and untrustworthy. The trustworthiness of these things can be tested in many ways.

Fortunately the Purāṇic genealogies from the time of the founder of Buddhism onward can be tested by the evidence supplied by the Buddhist and Jain literature, dramas and inscriptions. This test shows that although the Purāṇas have given, detailed lists of kings of no less than ten dynasties viz. those rulling over Avantī, Magadha, Kosala and Vatsa in the time of Buddha and those of Śiśunāgas, Nandas, Mauryas, Śungas, Kaṇvas and Andhras that succeeded them, barring a couple of mistakes, the names occurring in these lists as well as their arrangement are entirely trustworthy. The only two mistakes are; (i) the inclusion of Bimbisāra and his successors in the dynasty of Śiunāga (ii) the insertion of the names of Śākya, Suddhodana, Siddhārtha and Rāhula in the list of Kosala kings as predecessors of Prasanajit. Let us examine these mistakes.

The genesis of the first mistake is as follows : After giving the account of the Bārhadratha dynasty of Magadha, the ancient Purāṇas, Vāyu, Brahmāṇḍa and Matsya, proceed to give an account of the two most important dynasties of India that ruled contemporaneously and struggled for the suzerainty of India viz. the Pradyotas of Avantī and the Bimbisāras of Magadha. They first deal with the Pradyotas whom they difinitely associate with Avantī, and while giving the cause of their fall they have to mention Śiśunāga and Kākavarṇa of Magadha who destroyed them. They then deal with the dynasty of Bimbisāra whose grand-father Kṣemadharman was the first king of this dynasty. After the fall of the dynasty of Bimbisāra they have naturally to mention the Siśunāgas again who succeed the Bimbisāras as well as the Pradyotas. Now the Vāyu manuscript says this about them :

Etāni triṇi varṣāṇi dviṣaṣṭyabhyadhikāni tu
Siśunāgā bhaviṣyanti rājānaḥ kṣatrabandhavaḥ.

"Śiśunāgas, the vile kṣatriyas, will be kings for these 65 years". It is clear that the word 'these' here refers to the figures 40 and 26 already mentioned as the reign periods of these kings[1] when they are spoken of as the destroyers of the Pradyotas. What later happened was that by misreading 'etāni' as 'śatāni' in this verse some editor came to the conclusion that the dynasty of Bimbisāra began with Śiśunāgas and consisted of ten kings who ruled for more than three hundred years. He therefore added the line "*Ityete bhavitāro vai Śaiśunāga nṛpā daśa*".[2] If we delete this line and restore 'Etāni 'in place of 'Śatāni' the account becomes faultless. This mistake is thus not really serious and is the result of the lacking of two dynasties mentioned one after the other due to the misunderstanding of a late editor. The second mistake consisting of the insertion of the names of Śākya, Śuddhodana, Siddhārtha and Rāhula in the list of Kosala kings is no doubt serious, but a solitary mistake cannot detract from the value of the otherwise correct ten dynastic lists.

The Purāṇic genealogies from the time of Buddha onward having thus been proved to be almost faultless, the presumption is that the earlier genealogies too are not mere figments of imagination. Mere presumption, however, cannot produce conviction. We have, therefore, to examine them from three points viz., as regards the authenticity of the names themselves, as regards the authenticity of their arrangement and as regards the authenticity of their number.

So far as the names of kings in the earlier genealogies are concerned there are two clear proofs of their authenticity. In the first place a large number of these names occur in the Vedic literature which is quite independent of the Purāṇas. Secondly even those names which do not occur in the Vedic literature are so archaic that they could not have been coined by the authors of the present Purāṅas in whose time the style of names had completely changed. The numerous variations prove that often the authors of the Purāṇas even failed to write them correctly.

The arrangement of names is a very important matter for even if the names are genuine the genealogies will still be worthless if the arrangement of these names is borne out by evidence of the Ṛgveda and other works of Vedic literature. In the first place whenever kings are mentioned by their patronymies such as Yayāti Nāhuṣa, Marutta Avikṣita, Māndhāta, Yauvanāśva, Bharata Dauhṣanti, Trasadasyu Paurukutsi, Dhṛtarāṣṭra Vaīcitravīrya etc., the Purāṇic lists are corroborated. In the case of the Tṛtsu dynasty the names of eight generations from Bhṛmyaśva to Somaka occur in the same order in the Ṛgveda and other Vedic works as in the Purāṇas. The correctness of the arrangement can also be judged in another way. It is noteworthy that only those kings whose names occur in the early parts of the Purāṇic genealogies are found mentioned in the Ṛgveda outside the tenth book, while those kings whose names occur in the later parts of these genealogies are mentioned only in the tenth book of the Ṛgveda or the later Vedic literature, but never in the early part of the Ṛgveda consisting of books I to IX. The most important two early dynasties according to the Purāṇas were those founded by Ikṣvāku and Sudyumna respectively. In the former some of the fomous early kings were Māndhātṛ, Purukatsa, Trasadasyu and Tryaruṇa who are all mentioned in the Ṛgveda. In the latter the earliest kings were Purūravas, Āyu, Nahuṣa and

[1]The difference of 1 year is easily understandable, since figures like 39½ and 25½ are naturally rounded off as 40 and 26.

[2] It is possible that the second line of the verse beginning with "Etani" was originally "*Sisunagau tato bhavyau rajanau ksatra-bandhavau*" and was changed when this additional line was introduced.

Yayāti who are all mentioned in the Rgveda. Yayāti had five sons named Yadu, Turvaśa, Druhya, Anu and Pūru who are all mentioned in the Rigveda. The most famous of these was Pūru whose early descendants, Bharata, Vidatha and Ajamīdha are all mentioned in the Rigveda. Among the successors of Ajamīdha, the most powerful were the Tṛtsu monarchs, seven, of whom are mentioned by name in the Rigveda. But the names of kings who according to the Purāṇas ruled after that occur anly in the later Vedic literature including the tenth book of the Rigveda, but never in the bulk of Rigveda. Further it is to be noted that in accordance with the Purāṇas according to which the Vedic canon comprising the four Samhitās was closed before the Bhārata war we find that no king of the Purānic genealogical lists later than Dhrtarāstra, Vaicitravīrya is mentioned in the Vedic Samhitās. The Brāhmanas and Upaniṣads do mention the names of some kings who ruled after the Bhārata war such as Janamejaya Pārikṣita of Kuru, Ugrasena, Janaka of Videha, Pravāhaṇa Jaivali of Pancāla and Ajātaśatru of Kāśī, but they too do not mention a single king of the post-Buddha period which again proves the trustworthiness of the arrangement of names in the Purāṇic genealogies. The last but not the least important thing which proves the correctness of the arrangement of names in the Purāṇic genealogies is that of synchronisms. There are numerous synchronisms recorded in the Vedic, Purāṇic and epic literatures which are in consonance with the arrangement of names in the dynastic lists of the Purāṇas (Bhargava). These facts clearly establish the correctness of the arrangement of names in the Purāṇic genealogies.

We now come to the third point viz. the authenticity of the number of names in the lists. If the names are all correct and the arrangement is also faultless the implication is that the number of kings is also correct. But luckily another source belonging to the fourth century B.C. is available to prove the antiquity of the number of kings in the Purāṇic lists. I am reffering to Megasthenes, the Greek ambassador at the court of Chandragupta Maurya. The Greeks, as is known, had the peculiar habit of identifying the heroes and gods of other nations with their own heroes and gods. They identified the Indian hero, Kṛṣṇa, with their own hero Herakles. Similarly identifying the first Indo-Aryan king Manu with the Greek God Dāonysus, Megasthenes made the statement that "from the time of Dāonysus (Manu) to Sandrakottos (Chandragupta Maurya) the Indians counted 153 kings (McCrindle). The actual number of Kings who ruled during this period according to the Purāṇas comes to 135. This slight difference is really immaterial and we may well regard the statement of Magasthenes as an additional proof of the correctness of number of kings in the dynastic lists of the Purāṇas.

If the Purāṇic genealogies are substantially correct they can render valuable help in solving the problem of Indian chronology. The approximate date of the foundation of Maurya dynasty is about 320 B.C and it is fortunately no longer a subject of dispute. The number of kings who ruled in Magadha after the Bhārata war and before the accession of Chandragupta Maurya was 34 according to the Purāṇas. Since it appears to have been a period of peace and prosperity comparable to the Gupta Period of post-Christian era, we would not be unjustified in assigning an average length of 20 years to each reign. The total period of 34 reigns would thus be 680 years. Adding 680 to 320 B.C. we get 1000 B.C. as the date of the Bhārata war.

From the time of Manu Vaivasvata, the first Aryan king, to the Bhārata war there ruled 100 generations of kings according to the Purāṇas. Scholars are chary of assigning even the not very high average length of 20 years to each generation for such a long period. We may therefore reduce the length of each region to 15 years which is really a very low average. On the basis of this average the reigns of a hundred generation of kings would be of the duration of 1500 years. Adding 1500 to 1000 we get 2500 B.C. as the latest possible date of the beginning of Indo-Aryan Civilization and the commencement of the composition of Vedic literature. This date is in aggrement with the date proposed by Winternitz on the basis of the evidence arising out of the history of Indian literature and religion. I would be grateful if, instead of just scoffing at the evidence supplied by Purāṇic genealogies, some scholar gives concrete proofs of the untenability of my arguments in support of it.

References

Bhargava, P. L. *India in the Vedic Age* (2nd ed.) Chap. VII.

Maccrindle *Ancient India : The Indica of Arrian*. Chap. IX.

Jaipur **Dr. P. L. Bhargava**

THE HARAPPANS AND THE ARYANS

Of late archaeologists have come to recognize increasingly the importance of literature in the reconstruction of the past. Vedic literature is rightly receiving a closer attention in this context and the authors of Vedic culture—the Aryans—may be said to be knock in gat-even forcing—the doors of the archaeologists to mean 'business' and not to be given a 'holiday'. (Wheeler, 1959).

Identification of the authors of the Harappan culture and pinpointing a material culture which could also be considered as Aryan, has engaged the minds of historians and archaeologists for quite some time, and wide divergence of opinion exists on the subject. Harappan culture 'has been ascribed variously 'Dravidians, Brāhuis, Sumerians, Panis, Asuras, Vrātyas, Vāhīkas, Dāsas, Nāgas, Aryans' etc.' (Pusalkar). At the same time, authors of the Harappan Culture, Cemetery H, Jhukar Culture, Copper Hoards, black-and-red ware, and Painted Grey Ware etc, and sometimes even two of these culture together (taken as representing two waves). In short the progenitors of all the main cultures of northern India of the third-second millennia, have variously been considered identical with the Aryans. On one point, however, there seems to be unanimity among scholars, viz, that the Hindu culture, as known today, is a blending of the Harappan and the Vedic traits. A logical corollary would be that there were close contacts between the two cultures-Harappan and Vedic.

A comparative study of Vedic literature and Harappan remains suggests that the Aryans, whosover they were, came in contact with the Harappans. The following may be taken as significant pointers in this direction[1].

Rigveda and the Fortified Harappan Cities :

In the Rigveda, Indra is addressed as *'Purandara'* and *'Purehā'* and *'Purām bhettā'*, *i.e.* destroyer of fortified cities, or is praised as one who destroyed the *'Puras'* of the enemies. Since the fortified cities of the protohistoric period discovered so far belong to the Harappans (except a few which also have some Harappan affinities *i.e.* Harapppa, Mohenjo-daro, Kalibangan, Sutkajendor, Alimurad) inferred that the *Puras* attacked by the Aryans (Wheeler, 1953) were Harappan cities.

Rigvedic Allusion to Bunds

It has been suggested that the myth of Indra killing a demon to free the pent up waters may signify the destruction of the river bunds constructed by the Harappans.

Aryan Invasion & Harappan Skeletal Remains

In the last phase of Mohenjo-daro some thirty-five skeletal remains lying in various postures, apparently without proper burial, and a few bearing cutmarks from some weapon suggest that men, women and even children were cornered and massacred. This would indicate, as suggested by some, that the Harappans at this site met their end at the hands of some invaders—in all probability the Aryans.

Rigvedic Sisnadevas and Harappan Phalli

The Rigveda contains references to the śiśna-

[1] The evidence put forth below has been discussed by different scholars in differenf contexts,

devas. They have been mentioned alongwith the *rākshasas*, and Indra is specifically invoked not to let them approach their sacrificial fires (Yajñas). The same deity is also stated to have slain *śiśna-devas* (*RV* X. 99.3). *śiśnadevah* may be taken to refer to phallus-worshippers (Banerji). Even Sāyana, who interprets the word differently, while commenting on *RV*, X. 27.9, finds in it an allusion to the *rākshasas*, which word refers disparagingly to the non-Aryans, who in this case may be identified with the Harappans, as numerous phalli of various shapes and sizes have been unearthed at Harappan sites. It may thus be inferred that the Aryans who did not worship phallus hated the Harappans who did so.

Rigvedic Muradevas and Harappan Images

In the *Rigveda* Indra (*RV*, VII. 104.24) and Agni (X. 87.2 ; X. 87.4) have been invoked to kill the *mūradevas*. Sāyana explains this term as referring to *rākshasas* who were destructive, and some scholars take them to be non-Aryan settlers. Das suggests that *mūra* may mean 'senseless' and *mūradavas* might refer to those who worshipped images (Das). Scholars like Max mullar and Macdonell are of opinion that the Aryans (Banerji) were not image worshippers. So *mūradevas*, may denote the non-Aryan folk, who worshipped images. Since some of the images in terracotta, stone and other material, found in the excavations at Harappan sites seem to be cult objects, the *mūra-devas* may be indentified with the Harappans.

Rigvedic Pani and Harappan Traders :

Passages in the Rigveda referring to the Panis suggest that they were (i) greedy and miserly merchants (ii) were hated as demons, (iii) did not perform sacrifices and that (iv) the Aryans prayed to Aśvins for their destruction. When the Aryans, according to a hymn in the Rigveda. raided the settlement of the Panis, the latter retailiated by attacking the Aryans. Such references may be taken to denote that the Panis, despised by the Aryans were non-Aryans, and engaged in trade and commerce (chanda). They may be identified with the traders and merchant-folk (Marshall, 1931) among the Harappans, some of who, undoubtedly, traded with countries outside India as is clear from the Harappan objects to Mesopotamia sites and *vice versa*. Excavations at Lothal have brought to light a Harappan dockyard which too bears witness to the maritime activities of the Harappans.

The Rigvedic Dāsas and Asuras and the Harappans :

The *Dāsas* were distinct from the Aryans ethnically as well as culturally. They were flat-nosed, black-skinned (in contradition to white hued Aryans they did not perform śacrifices, followed curious customs (*vratas*) and spoke an unintelligible or insolent (*mridhra*) speech. The *Asuras* too, find mention in the Rigveda but, unlike the *Dāsas* they are not referred to as black complexioned but a brown and sometimes praised by the Aryans and even compared with the Vedic gods. The Harappans, as known from anthropological studies of their skeletal remains, did not belong to one ethnic group. (Marshall, 1931). The *Dāsas* and *Asuras* might have been two of the components of the heterogenous Harappan population.

Vedic Literature and Certain Harappan Statues :

Certain stone statuettes from Mohenjo-daro, of which only some busts are in a fair state of preservation, are characterised by a stiff erect posture of the head, the neck and the chest, and half-shut eyes looking fixedly at the tip of nose'. This is typically a *yogic* posture and in the words of Chanda' is not met with in the figure-sculptures, whether prehistoric, or historic, of any people outside India, but is very conspicuous in the Image worshipped by all Indian sects including the Jainas and the Buddhists............'. Chānda also points out that generally such images do not go to a period earlier than the beginning of the Christian era, though Upanishadic literature, the *Bhagavadgitā* and Pali Buddhist early *Suttas*, datable to a few centuries before Christ, do speak of *dhyāna-yoga*. Chanda is of the view that the *dhyāna-yoga*, as outlined in the pali canon, includes primitive elements going back to a still earlier stage than the one represented in the *Upanishada* and early Buddhism. The religion of the Rigvedic Aryans, according to some eminent scholars, have no place either for image worship or *yogic* practices and, therefore, the Harappan status cannot be said to belong th the Aryans. Vedic literature refers to 'Yatis' and the *Atharvaveda* and some other later Vedic-works, to the *'Vrātyas'*. The references cited by Chanda indicate that these were non-Aryan priest magicians who, on the one hand, were praised and respected by the Aryans because of their *yogic* feats and were disliked and even destroyed because of their being non-Aryans on the other (which incidently reminds us of the treatment of Alexander the Greek to Indian *yogis* in the beginning of the last quarter of the 4th century B.C.). According to Chanda, the Harappan statues represent the images of *Yatis* and *Vrātyas* of the Vedic literature. Karmarkar adduces evidence from the *Māhabhārata* and the *Purānas* to show that the *Vrātya*-cult mentioned in the *Atharvaveds* is non-Aryan. The Aryans started the institution of *Chāturvarṇya* and subsequently accepted the *Vrātyas* into their fold after converting them by the *Vrātyastoma* rite.

Rigvedic Hariyupiya and the city of Harappa

The city of Harappa itself seems to be referred to in the *Rigveda* (VI. 27.5) as *Hariyūpiyā*. Raychaudhuri observes that is the name *Hariyūpiyā* (which is the designation of a river or a city according to Vedic commentaters and is as sociated with the Vrichivats, who broke the sacrificial vessels and who were defeated by the Srjnjayas led by a prince who is styled as a Pārthava-a name reminiscent of Iran can be connected with Harappa, then we have a reference to a battle between the victorious Aryans, riding horses, and the Harappans significantly there is want of evidence regarding the presence of horse-an animal which had an important place (Marshall, 1971) in the Aryan society—in the early Harappan levels; and iron, which was known to the Aryans from the time of the Atharvaveda, if not earlier, has not yet been found in the Harappan context, (Banerji 1965).

The points discussed above and some other consideraiions almost rule out the possibility of identifying the Harappans (Marshall, 1931) with the Aryans, and the impact of the cumulative evidence seems strongly to favour the view the Aryans in their victorious march into India encountered the Harappans whom they ultimately vanquished.

However, the fact that horse (Marshall, 1931) is known in the levels at Mohenjo-daro and mature levels at Lothal, (Sharma, 1961) and that there is evidence of the presene of brick enclosures for fire worship at the last-mentioned site and at Kalibangan and of rice at Lothal suggest contacts between the early Aryans and the Harappans in the mature phase of their culture.

Harappan cities of Mohenjo-daro and Harappa were already in a decadent stage before their final fall as is clear from the marked degeneration in civic standards during the later phases of Mohenjo-daro (Wheeler, 1959) at the time of Aryan invasion. Several factors, both natural and man-made, may have been responsible for the decadence. Recurrent floods in the area ravaged the cities, indiscriminate flling of trees and over grazing deprived the land of its moisture, faulty methods of irrigation denuded the top soil, and over-cultivation reduced the fertility of the land. Over population which lowered the living standards of the people coupled with a slackening of administration also, seems to have led to the decay and decline of this culture. To cap it all, the Aryans invaded the fortified cities of Harappa and Mohenjo-daro. In the *Rigveda* frequent prayers to Indra for destorying the walled cities show, on the one hand, the desire of these Aryans to conquer them and on the other, imply the tough resistance they were offered in the initial phases of their raids. Ultimately, the Aryans succeded in vanquishing their enemies and many Harappans were slaughtered. Skeletal remains lying in various postures without being given a proper burial and found in the last phase of Mohenjo-daro belong to that phase of Aryan conquest.

Early Aryans do not seem to have brought potters with them. As make-do, they perhaps used vessels of wood and leather which, because of their fragile nature, are lost to us. Later they seem to have pressed to potters of the conquered people into their service, and the latter fashioned the type they were accustomed to manufacture. The art of writing which seems to have been confined mainly to city merchants and their assistants, gradually fell out of use with the decline in trade. It is significant that Alamgirpur and many other Harappan village sites have not yielded a single seal. The Aryans do not seem to have been accustomed to city life and for this as well as for other reasons were averse to permanently occupy the decaying Harappan cities. The refugees Harappan migrated to other places; their culture further degenerated and underwent modification due to geographical and climatic factors and, in some cases, also due to the impact of local cultures. This is clear from large number of late Harappan sites, discovered in recent decades.

Several hordes of the Aryans may have followed in succession after the initial invaders had emerged victorious and also brought with them some potters and other craftsmen. On this assumption, the Jhukar Ware, the Malwa Ware, and the Painted Grey Ware would belong to different settlements of the Aryans[1]. Meanwhile the fierce antagonism of the earlier time of the two–the Harappans and the Aryans died out and their followed a period of synthesis between the two culture-patterns. The conquerors were greatly influenced by the culture of the conquered, and as a result of the give-and-take, a new culture was evolved which became the fountain spring of the subsequent Indian Culture[2].

References

Wheeler, R.E.M. 1959 *Early India and Pakistan*, p. 126.

Pusalker, A.D. (u.d.) History and Culture of the Indian People, Vol. I, *Vedic Age* (ed.) R.C. Majumdar, p. 193

Wheeler, R.E.M. 1953 *Indus Civilization* pp. 90-91

Banerji, J.N. (u.d.) *Development of Hindu Iconography*, pp. 42.

Das, A.C. (u.d.) *Rigvedic Culture*, p. 145.

Chanda, R.P. (u.d.) 'Indus Valley in the Rigvedic Period' *Memoir of Archaeological Survey of India* 31, pp. 4.

Marshall, John, 1931, *Mohenjo-daro and the Indus Civilization*, pp. 84; 107-108; 111.

Banerji, N.R, 1965 *The Iron Age in India* pp. 158.

Sharma, Y.D. 1961 *Archaeological Remains Monuments and Museums* Part I p. 31.

Lucknow **K.K. Thaplyal**

1 Since the P.G. Ware is datable to a period later than the end of the Harappan Civilization as evidence by a hiatus between the Harappan and PGW levels at Rupar and Alamgirpur), D.D. Kosambi (as quoted by Buddha Prakash *Rigveda and the Indus Valley Civilization*, p. 173) suggests that the PGW should be associated with the Puru branch of the Aryans, and not with the Aryans in general,

2 The above is a probably reconstruction of the course of events relating to the Harappans and the Aryans, with the evidence at hand. However, a final pronouncement awaits further exploration in this direction.

BOOK REVIEWS

Balram Srivastava : *Iconography of Sakti*, Varanasi : Chaukhamba Orientalia, 1978; pp. X+174. Price : Rs 80

The book under reference is based on *Sakti-nidhi*, a great chapter of an early Sanskrit text *Sritatt vanidhi*, a first work on Brahmanical and Tantric gods and goddesses. Besides the actual text, rendered in devanagari, the author takes full support from the Puranas, Tantras, Agamas, and other cognate literature to discuss various aspects of the iconography of Sakti.

Divided into five chapters, the book deals first with the mother goddes cult in general on a global plane, from Stone Age down to the present. It is followed by a study of Sakta beliefs in relation with the ideals of mother goddess. The third chapter deals with the various forms of Durga, the *adisakti*. The fourth chapter is devoted to the iconography of *Mahisasura-mardini* and *saptamatrikas*. The last chapter deals with the consorts of Brahma, Vishnu and Siva. A good number of photographs and line drawings help the reader in following the text.

It is a book prepared after a great deal of labour. It clearly shows the in-depth study of a text about which we had enough knowledge but had not properly utilized for the iconographic study of this kind. The examples collected by the author to bring home his points shows the wide expanse of his knowledge of Indian art. But to my mind the first chapter is rather redundant. Why should every study on one aspect or the other of mother goddess start with Stone Age Europe ? In fact, it appears that even on the nude female figures on the Mauryan and Sunga Periods the author has nothing of his own to add. To my mind, now-a-days when printing and publishing has become so costly, it is better to start with the subject straight away ; moreover, it is a great research work and not a Ph.D. thesis.

But, when the author starts dealing with mediaeval sculptures and literature he is in full command of the source material. Every student of iconography will benefit from the book.

S.P. Gupta

Iravatham Mahadevan : *The Indus Script, Texts, Concordance and Tables*. New Delhi : The Director General, Archaeological Survey of India, 1977; pp. viii & 829. Price : Rs. 250

A team of three renowned Indologists (Asko Parpola-scholar of sanskrit and classical philology, Simo Parpola-scholar of assyriology, Seppo Koskennieemi-Computer Programmer), under the sponsorship of the University of Helsinki, working at the Scandinavian Institute of Asian Studies, produced the first Concordance to the Indus Inscriptions which was published by the Finnish Academy of Science and Letters in 1973.

Not satisfied with this (for reasons not known) a very generous fellowship was awarded to Shri Mahadevan, an I.A.S. officer, to excel the Finnish effort, in the race for competing with foreigners for what they had done an Indian should also do. Work over a period of seven years has resulted in the production of a beautifully bound volume priced at Rs. 250/- (beyond the buying capacity of a research worker in India) for "advancing research in the field of decipherment of the Indus Script".

Dr. Gurov (a specialist in Dravidian Linguistics and Culture) paid a high tribute to Shri Mahadevan's work (Times of India, July 31,), and called it as the "springboard for the research of others".

The following Review is made to assess in detail the true worth of this work and substantiate the above claim of the author.

It is a document that has all borrowed but not one new idea to justify expenditure of a couple of lakhs of rupees, from the public exchequer.

All accepted tenets of copying epigraphic material have been set aside and conjectural restoration of dozens of illegible, indistinct and broken signs has been made. The heart of such mutilated texts has been disfigured beyond recognition. Since I do not have access to 634 (or one-fifth of total) hitherto unpublished texts, the actual number of tempered texts is difficult to assess. The "true text" of most seals, etc., has not been produced in 'toto', with the result that their "correct reading" will be an impossibility as the "grammatical forms" have been distorted giving rise to grotesque results, by such injudicious attempts. By contrast the copying of Brāhmi. Pāli and Prākrit epigraphic material was scrupulously true which enabled their decipherers to make these texts understandable. It is all the more necessary to have a true copy of Indus inscriptions as they are very brief and contain one, two or three words, divorced from their proper context and not complete sentences. Thus the listed purposes of the book are not fulfilled and a research scientist, to his great annoyance, has to fall back on the published photos of the seals, etc., to get the original text.

In these and countless other ways the canvas so presented, containing useless repetitions of countless texts has marred the true purpose of a Concordance as detailed below. The perennial charm of Bloomfields *Vedic Concordance* is an example to be emulated if any body wants to prepare a concordance.

The academic stasis in research in this subject is likely to continue as the book provides little or no useful material not available in the four hitherto published Excavation Reports.

Normalised Signary.

The tempered "normalised signary" has corupted hundreds of texts beyond recognition. The Indus scribe did not waste his labours on producing a large repertoire of signs for no reason. He, like a trabadour, knew grammer. syntax and vocabulary of the language of the texts before he engraved the miracle of his speech using more than 650 signs. How can a liguistic research scientist using an alerted and abbreviated signary (419 or 63.8% of old signs) be expected to unlock the meaning and purpose of the now printed texts? The task required commissioning a specialised group of scholars of accredited stsnding, temperament and training to produce a really useful book and not a second Concordance four years after the publication of Finnish Concordance to the Indus inscriptions in 1973.

The 'Sign List of the Indus Script' (p. 32-35) does not represent the total of signs and has completely disregarded and ignored the order of signs and the presence of many signs in the earlier published 'sign lists' of world authorities like Langdon, Gadd and Smith, Marshall, Vats and Hunter; as also the 'new signs' found in Mackay's FEM and copper tablets by Shri B. M. Pandey, which has added to the confusion of a research scientist.

The author has accepted A. H. Dani's concept of 'Normalised Signary' to arrive at the 'Normal Form of the most frequent type'. The Concordance method of the Finnish Group (1973) has been adopted which includes only a few recorded variants: But the present author, in his unwise judgement, has recorded only 419 signs as his 'Normalised Signary'. He has listed 641 'Sign Variants' (Intro. para II. 4 and Appendix I. p. 785-792) for 179 signs which means that :—

i. Out of a total of 641 signs, used in the original texts of the seals, only 462 (641-179) are considered by him as useful representative, if substituted for signs on the texts of the seals.

ii. Again out of these 462 signs he has used only 417, a further loss 45 (462-417).

iii. He has thus taken no notice of 179+45= 224 signs in the original texts. This big list of so called 'redundant signs', in the text material, he ascribes to: different hands of the scribes, the mode of writing, material used, regional variations, evolution in course of time (for which he has provided no proof, as there are no signs of hieretic, cursive or demotic writing. "The characters retained their original form right from the day of their first invention—Langdon").

His criteria for selection of a 'Normal Sign' are :

i. If variant sign looks similar.

ii. Have same positional and functional characteristics (This cannot be decided till the script has been deciphered).

iii. Variations are too gradual or too numerous to denote meaningful differentiation (Intro. p. 15. para II.4). Here again he has defaulted as he has not grasped the meaning of gradual difference in the shape or form of the characters and their large number running into 641 signs).

iv. Variations betwoen rhomboid and oval forms. (This is his biggest error and a slur on the Indus scribe).

He has thus used one example of occurrence for each recorded variant group and produced a sign list of 419 signs (417 on p. 32-35 and two on p. 25, which occur solo and not in any text).

His morphological classification of signs (Intro. p. 16. para II.5.) into 9 classes, is again mostly borrowed from Dani (Indian Paleography, 1963) minus the exactness of the classification of Egyptian Hieroglyphs which have 25 classes and a count of 1445 symbols (cf. E.A. Wallis Budge. 1960. The Egyptian Hieroglyphic Dictionary). All this has resulted in a big distortion, mutilation, redactorial mess of the texts of the seals and an inapt at correction and modification of the pristine beauty and meaning of the texts and a fraud on research workers, who will still have to depend on the published Excavation Reports for the original text on the seal. The system of preparing the 'Normalised Sign' list is irrational, unscientific and baffiling to a linguistic analyst in finding a total 'stock' of signs and the texts using a particular original Indus sign. Both the texts and those repeated un-necessarily in the Concordance (with the normal signs of the author) have been mutilated by an act of ommission and commission, and make the wise Indus scribe an object of ridicule before the world, without the realisation that *he was a designer par excellence.* The author has shown his shown his incompetence to understand the graphic structure of this script and incapability as a linguistic analyst. If the same method of selection and a 'Normalised Signary' had ever been used by Egyptologists the Egyptian Hieroglyphs could never have been deciphered and their meaning and significance properly grasped. The author seems never to have consulted this dlctionary and faithfully followed a scientific method. It is high time that the Archaeological Survey of India publish an up-to-date list of signs in consulation with a Panel of Linguistic Analysis.

II. Incisions on Pottery Graffiti

Webster's Dictionary (1960) defines *Grafitto* as a rude writing or sketching on ancient buildings and tombs. Out of 2906 legible or partly legible inscriptions on Indus objects, there are 119 (or 4.1%)graffiti on pot-sherds which have been included in this book (Intro. p. 7. para 6.2.). The texts on 59 out of 85 pot-sherds (Harappan. Vol. II. Pl. No. CII-CIV) are shown as Text No. 4801-4884 and these are discussed below :

—9 texts with asterisk marks are considered by him as doubtful reading. (59–9 leaves 50).

—17 show numeral signs from 1-10, easy to identify and which any illiterate potter could mark on his green ware (50=17-33).

—9 have raised relief markings or are embossed (33-9=24).

—24 have sketchy markings (often incomplete) which have been reconstructed by him with wild imagination, which is unwarr-anted, inaccurate and an unscientific attempt as the characters on the sherds are mutilated and mis-shapen, and also because :

i. there is abrasion of edges and sides and makes identification of original signs difficult even with a powerful hand lens.

ii. As such the signs on these 24 sherds, barring a few, are of no value in comparison to a neatly engraved text on a seal.

iii. The direction of writing on most cannot be ascertained with scientific accuracy. Still, in Table VII, He has recorded, on 128 pot-sherds, the direction of writing from all sites as follows :—right to left-74, left to right-10, top to bottom-1. Others include single line signs, symmetrical lines and doubtful cases 43. (What can a research worker find useful in this sort of reading ?)

iv. 8 pot-sherds show text in raised relief as if impressed by a stamp seal on green ware H.P. Pl. CII-CIV, viz. Nos. 4, 8, 23, 24, 46, 53, 73, and 76, which too have been reconstructed in total disregard of the signs already printed over some of them.

v. The scribbling on the pot-sherds does not indicate any proficiency in lettering as the potters were illiterate.

vi. These sketchy signs are neither potter's special marks or used for ornamentation.

vii. Not one original or reconstructed graffiti text is meaningful or repeated on texts on proper seals in the HP volume.

viii. The illiterate Indus potter must have seen a few Indus seals or happened to find them from old deserted rubbish heaps on resett-lement and tried his hand at imitation by scratching them on his green ware. The crudity of imitation is visible on these pots which shows no artistic ability or merit. He has rarely tried to draw the picture of any animal figure as this was beyond his capa-city. We know now how worthless these graffiti are as a source of learning the method of writing or the direction of writing.

ix. The inclusion of all material from these graffiti has vitiated the text, concordance and the tables.

III. Concordance

A concordance is a very useful tool for a re-searech scientist who does not have the basic original material which the author could collect as seen from the list of References in Appendix IV.

The concordance portion occupies 572 pages (163-714). Bloomfield's Vedic Concordance, *a magnum opus*, in comparison, uses 1078 pages only, for material drawn from 119 sources. It is an alphábetical Index to every line or *Pāda* of every stanza of the published Vedic literature, containing many thousands of Vedic verses. The author's concordance deals with a petty 2906 small texts only, which could easily be written in 50 pages (as have done). The reason for using 572 pages is not far to seek. He has coied Hunter's method of 8 endo-centric concentration for each sign and also the Finnish method with certain modifications in a text. This has resulted in swelling the size of the concordance without providing the most essential information as under :

i. Total stock of completelely and unduplicat-ed texts out of 2906, as most of these texts have either the initial, the medial, the ter-minal signs which are not legible. The table below gives details extracted from the Text Chapter (39-160) as an illustrative example.

Table. Illegible Texts, because signs in various positions are illegible

Site	Total Texts	INI	MED	FIN	INI+FIN	Total Loss	Balance	Loss %
MD	1541	129	9	133	21	292	1250	19
HP	985	120	5	103	20	248	737	25
CD	66	6	0	3	0	9	57	14
LL	165	35	0	25	7	67	94	49
KB	99	10	1	12	4	27	72	27
OS	34	4	0	0	1	5	29	18
WS	17	1	0	1	2	4	13	24
	2906	305	15	277	55	652	2252	22

Note :- 652 illegible texts do not include texts with asterisk (*) mark or doubtful reading.

ii. A very large number of texts out of 2906 are found to be repeated or duplicated once twice or thrice, upto 38 times as will be seen from the table below. This sample includes repeated texts from the same site or from other sites as well. The count of repeated texts in the table below was done from pages 163-300 only as an illustrative example.

Table. Repeated or Duplicated texts and times repeated

Times repeated	No. of Texts. repeated	Times repeated	No. of Texts repeated
Two times	78	Eight times	1
Three ,,	28	Nine ,,	2
Four ,,	15	Ten ,,	2
Five ,,	9	Eleven ,,	1
Six ,,	4	Fifteen ,,	1
Seven ,,	4	Thirty eight ,,	1
			146

These 146 texts were repeated as follows : MD-263 times, HP-228, CD-2, LL-14, KB-13 = 520 times.

Hence :-

i. 374 (520-146) texts in the corpus of 2906 texts are redundant.

ii. 1878 (2252-374) now represent the total texts on this partial sample count.

iii. If a simiiar count is done from the total concordance chapter (p. 163-714), the TRUE number of repeated texts will be known the TRUE number of legible texts which and also will be known only are useful to a decipherer. (The concordance prepared by me contains about 1450 such texts which forms the corpus of my research material).

Uses of A Concordance in its proper Meaning and its preparation.

a. Primary use. A concordance should be a comprehensive alphabetic index (and arbitrarily fixed in this script) of all texts found scattered over diverse places, sites, books, journals published or unpublished, and faithfully copied from the original, which alone are useful to a research worker.

The variants, not wholly identical, which occur only a single time, or appear in a wholly identical form in two or more texts, if properly arranged in an alphabetical index require on comment. Again texts whic are not wholly identical, but are alike in their beginnings, will also fall into the same class, or nearly the same place in a direct alphabetical arrangement. The places of occurrence of a given text of this kind may be advantageously grouped together with a statement of the various readings of the different texts. If the form of the text in question differs at the beginning, then obviously again they will occupy places in the alphabetic arrangement more or less widely apart and it will be necessary to connect them by some system of cross references. Thus a concordance, should in reality. afford an easy method to ascertain

(a) where a given text occurs if it occurs once.

(b) whether it occurs else where, either with or without variants and in what sites,

(c) If it occurs with variants, what these variants are.

(b) Secondary use.

i. It should advance our knowledge of the method of derivation of texts from the use of one, two, or more "cluster of signs", used in initial, or terminal positions. (this is a very peculiar phenomena in the Indus texts).

ii. It should be a helpful FINDING INDEX of similar or identical texts on various types of objects with various devices.

iii. A tool for future editors of such volumes, when some more texts are discovered in the future and the revision of some which are in wrong places.

(iv) As a repertory of the most archaic Indus script and language for future study ef INDUSOLOGISTS.

c. Other uses.

i. To determine the relation between texts and field symbols, if any. (Interesting project).

ii. Other interesting questions which will suggest themselves to different scholars according to their bent of mind. For example, the concordance shows that one sign occurs 1395 times (971 times as final and once only as initial though I do not believe that such a phenomena is ever found in any language. It is seen here because the texts are read from right to left which I do not agree to for reasons of my own which I have detailed in an article being sent tor publication).

d. Scope of Concordance.

i. A concordance should prove useful in restoring text signs marked by an asterisk (*). and also lost, damaged or illegible passages marked by the (///). This will add to the total of TRUE TEXTS (about 1500 only) which appears as a ridiculously low number written over a period of 750-1000 years, with singular effort, deligence and art.

ii. Graffito texts are of no value and should better be discarded once for all.

iii. A large number of texts have a "cluster of signs" nearly or wholly alike in their 'beginnings' or' endings'. These could be grouped in a separate place. These will reveal the relations among the signs and words formed from them. (I have prepared a list of such "clusters" with 2, 3, 4, 5 or more signs).

IV. Pairwise Combinations (Table II. p. 724-745).

The FINNISH method of computer drawn concordance to the pairwise occurrences of the Indus signs inspired Shri. Mahadevan to repeat a similar exercise which is futile and has resulted in disastrous and meaningless results.

While the Finnish method has very wisely represented the same phenomena in the Text portion itself by showing "Key-combinations", quoting for every combination all the texts where it occurs and associated relevant data, Mahadevan has used:

i. extra 22 pages uselesly (724-745), and has,

ii. given the frequency of each combination without quoting the text or inscription where it occurs and hence worthless as a tool of research. These combinations are very often drawn from distorted, mutilatated and incorrect and fancifully restored texts (p. 39-160), which are unreliable.

iii. The frequency figures are of no scientific value as shown below :—

—Total pairwise combinations shown = 2758.

—1691 combinations occur only once. How on earth this adds to scientific knowledge, ?

*A combination"  occurs 291 times

 " 184 "

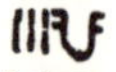 " 126 "

 " 124 "

Taking  combination, in which  is a normalised sign' (sign No. 176) with 9 variants (Appendix I. p. 178). It is sheer absurdity that 184 represents all the original pairwise combinations on the Indus seals wiih nine variants. For the same reasons the whole table II is a mis-representation and distortion of the true position and true combination. Such a table is never seen in a book on Linguistics and never attempted by any linguistic analyst in the past. This table is an example of the incompetence of the author to work on this most intricate script.

V. Distribution of Signs by Sites. (p. 23. para 15.4 and **Table III)**

Whether a sign is found in a text in M.D., HP. CD, LL, KB, OS or WA site depends upon the number of seals found in each one of these places. The larger the number of seals from one site the larger is the chance for a particular sign to be found there. Similar remarks apply to tables IV, V and VIII.

Table VI. VII and IX.

The less is said about these three meaningless tables the better it is.

Table I

This has some meaning. I have, however, my own views regarding the initial and final positions of the signs. A frequency of 971 for the final position of the most frequently found sign  on the text of the seals is a phenomena not to be found in the random collection of words of any language and statistically analysed. This can, however, happen only when this sign occupies the Initial position. (The engraving has to be done from right to left so that the reading is from left to right.

All these eight tables are like the tables in a Doctoral Thesis to impress on the examiner the hard labour put in by the candidate and to gain praise, sympathy and aplomb of the examiners for his success.

General Remarks

No "Normalised Signary" of the Indus script can 'faithfully" reproduce, as asserted by the author, the "neat monumental form" of the original signs. There may be some genuine variants, but by and large, the "normalised signs" are no "faithful" replacements. These will not be acceptable to any epigraphist. The sign variants of the following 31

"Normalised Signs" (p. 785-792) can never be accepted.

—Sign No. 19/1, 38/2, 48/3, 56/2, 59/1, 119/3, 121/1, 136/2, 167/2, 169/4, 171/3, 176/5, 178/2, 173/2, 182/3, 186/3, 193/5, 204/3, 205/4, 214/2, 244/9, 245/10, 252/3, 253/3, 254/4, 267/2, 305/2, 348/4, 387/1, 402/3, 332/1. (The denominator shows the loss of original signs (70 in number) in the texts in this sample count.)

Many lost signs have been restorted conjecturally.

These observations may be found unsavoury at the first reading, they will become palatable and digestible if serious thinking is done about the whole subject which is of great national importance. No modern book on linguistics mentions even once the word "pairwise combination" (cf. Robert A. Hall, *Jr. Introductory Linguistics* 1960).

M. N. GUPTA

P. K. Agrawal : *Early Indian Bronzes* Varanasi Prithvi Prakashan, 1977; pp. xii+160 Price : Rs 200.

The *Early Indian Bronzes* is possibly much more and diverse than the matter of fact implied in the title. In Indian art studies the term 'bronzes' is usually applied to icons made of different alloys with copper as the main ingredient, it does not include pots and pans, tools and weapons, beads and pendants, coins and toys. But the reviewer welcomes this archaeological approach in art history, particularly for the period dealt with here since the number of icons belonging to this period is small.

The book is divided into eight chapters, six of which deal with the bronzes starting from the Harappa, passing through the Vedic, Pre-Mauryan-Mauryan, Sunga, Kushan and ending in Satavahana periods; one deals with the influence of the mediterranean styles and the other with the literary evidence on casting the metal images. The book, therefore, deals exclusively with pre-Gupta bronzes.

The book is virtually a catalogue with complete documentation of the subject. It is thoughtfully illustrated with as many as 278 photographs and 154 line drawings. But it is not merely a hand-list of objects, the author, like his father, the Late V. S. Agrawala, has gone deep into various problems of origin and development of concepts, styles and models, types and technology involved in the objects. It is, of course, a different matter whether one agrees with the author on his views on Daimabad bronzes, origin of *Srivatsa* symbol, etc., since scholarly opinions always differ on such issues. However, every researcher in the history of bronze art and craft of early India will find it most useful. It is indeed a very valuable contribution and should be considered almost a reference book where all old and newly acquired objects find place. By and large the illustrations are neat and crisp. The text is also clean and clear.

S. P. GUPTA

S.P. Gupta : *The Roots of Indian Art* : Delhi B.R. Publishing Corporation, 1981, pp. XXIV & 378 including 6 Colour photographs 385 Black-and-White, 171 Figures and a dozen maps. Price Rs. 500

The Roots of Indian Art by one of the eminent archaeologists of India, Dr. S.P. Gupta, of the National Museum, New Delhi, is possibly the most comprehensive book ever written on the Early Indian art and architecture since although the chronological bracket includes only the third and second centuries B.C., *i.e.*, the period of the Mauryas and the early Sungas, the text covers some 400 pages illustrated by as many as 562 illustrations.

The monograph is divided into six major chapters—the Pillars, Ringstones, Sculptures and Art Motifs, Terracottas, Rock-cut Caves, and Architecture. Each chapter is further divided into three major parts—Introduction, detailing important publications on the topic; Documentation, nearly exhaustive cataloguing of the objects; and Discussion which makes indepth study of the subject. A fairly long Backdrop raises some fresh but basic question, such as the Origin of Mauryan art, Second Urbanization: its impact on Indian art; Factors of change in art, King's Will and Social Mobility, Oral Tradition, etc. The Polemics deals with various problems such as the Men behind the Mauryan Art, Pataliputra—Sarnath School of Art, Asokan Pillars and Indradhvajas, origin of Nagapushoa, Triratna and Trisula motifs, Bulandibagh terracottas and Greek clay figurines, etc. It takes care of various theories which place the origin of Mauryan art and architecture in one country or the other in West Asia. Here the author is at his best. The whole discussion is penetrating. Indeed, the format is very wide. Still, it does not repeat what Niharranjan Ray, John Irwin, John Marshall and V.S. Agrawal have said except where the writer has reasons to differ from the views of these writers.

Dr. Gupta draws heavily on the excavated material, particularly on that material which comes from the recent digs conducted scientifically (and here he differs from John Irwin who tries to derive his data from the old reports, often ill digested). He takes into account the historical processes through which history moved in West Asia, including Greece and Egypt. He rephotographed not only rock-cut caves, but also ringstones and valuable fragments in the godown of the Sarnath Museum to elicit new information. He discovers the existence of a so far little understood school of Indian art, The Pataliputra—Sarnath School.'

It is bound to become the most controversial book on Indian art history, for it has shaken many of our age-old beliefs by raising fresh questions and offerings alternate suggestions. It must be conceded that it is a model of intellectual enquiry through critical examination of the entire gamut of Mauryan and Late Mauryan art objects. No one should miss it. However, such an extraordinary book possibly needed a better publisher. The paper, both for the text and the plates, is poor, even two coloured, while the printing of the plates, both colour and black-and-white, is just average. Still, for the Indian students, who rarely see the West Asian material in visual form in books on Mauryan art, it is a boon.

B. P. Sinha

Shereen Ratnagar, *Encounters, the Westerly Trade of the Harappa Civilization,* **Delhi 1981 : Oxford University Press**

The focus of Dr. Ratnagar's work is not on the Harappan civilization but on the entire area between Mesopotamia and the Indus. The Harappan civilization, according to her, is only one of the several Bronze Age cultures between the Euphrates and Gujarat. This civilization. according to her again, is not a part of the mainstream of Indian history. She is not interested in the in-depth analysis of artefacts but in formulating an over-view. Her methods to formulate this over-view-are: the consideration of "local environment and the economic potential of each region for external exchanges", the identification of "important places mentioned in the Cuneiform texts (mainly Dilmun, Magan and Meluhha)", the kind of goods which were carried between people in the Bronze Age", the notion of trade and" the role of the long distance trade in the Harappan economy in particular and the Harappan urban development in general", and finally, an examination of "the possibility of a casual connection between the origins of sustained long-distance trade on the one hand and the emergence of stratified urban society in northwest India on the other". She argues that "in the mature Harappa period the main thrust of external connexions was no longer northwestwards towards Turkmenia but directly westwards".

Dr. Ratnagar's reference points are Mesopotamia and the Gulf. It was the sea trade which was more significant. The eclipse of this sea-trade can partly explain the collapse of the Harappan urban system. Shahr-i-Sokhta was not ideally located for long-distance contacts and Tepe Yahya did not "enter into long-distance exchanges on any wider scale, say as a consumer of merchandise from distant lands, or as an overland entrepot between India and Sumer". Shah-Dad owed its importance only to its position on the internal routes of Iran. "In the ED II period there was a crisis in Mesopotamia due to the non-availability" of lapis lazuli and when this crisis occurred the Indus people "stepped in as suppliers of lapis lazuli to Sumer" and got "inducted into a wide-reaching network of exchange". It is this induction into a wide-reaching network of exchange that induced social dtfferentiation and urbanisation in the Indus valley. In fact, in Dr Ratnagar's analysis the Indus civilization, both in its origin and decline, was dependent on Mesopotamia's need of raw materials and exotic goods.

The theory speaks for itself. In a new form this is a resuscitation of Wheeler's and Gordon's hypothesis that the Indus civilization was by and large a a Mesopotamain colony. We even refuse to refute it point by point by showing how tendentious the author has been in her treatment of archaeological data. We on our part have enjoyed the stray bits of wisdom (cf the Kulli people were "simple pastoralists, constantly on the move", as the profusion of clay bull and female figurines in the Kulli levels seems to indicate).

On a more serious note, if attempts to go beyond artefacts, strata and dates result in this kind of book in Indian archaeology we do not want to go beyond artefacts, strata and dates. A clever way of writing, an impressive bibliography (a little more than 10% of which is filled by the writings of native Indian scholars), a good publisher and invocation to some regulation academic deities have not prevented the book being what it is : a remarkably tendentious statement of an important archaeological problem.

Dilip K. Chakrabarti
Delhi University
Delhi

A; B.B. Lal & K.N. Dikshit : a view of tank A.

B; B.B. Lal & K.N. Dikshit : a view of tank A and tank B with interconnecting channel.

B.B. Lal & K.N. Dikshit : a view of tank B, showing the ramp which leads down to the bed of the tank.

A; M.L.K. Murty : with the cow moving close, the birds enter the tubular net trap.

B; M.L.K. Murty : method of laying the multiple noose trap.

A; M.L.K. Murty : Tubular net trap with the rectangular netted frames on 1 either side as barricades (2, 3) and the trapper on the right taking corer behind the cow.

B; Jamna Das Akhtar : an Indo-Aryan prince on an ancient Egyptian monument.

A; Jamna Das Akhtar : a seal.

B; Jamna Das Akhtar : Bogazkoi tablet on which the Vedic deities Indra, Varuna, Mitra and the Nastyas are mentioned.

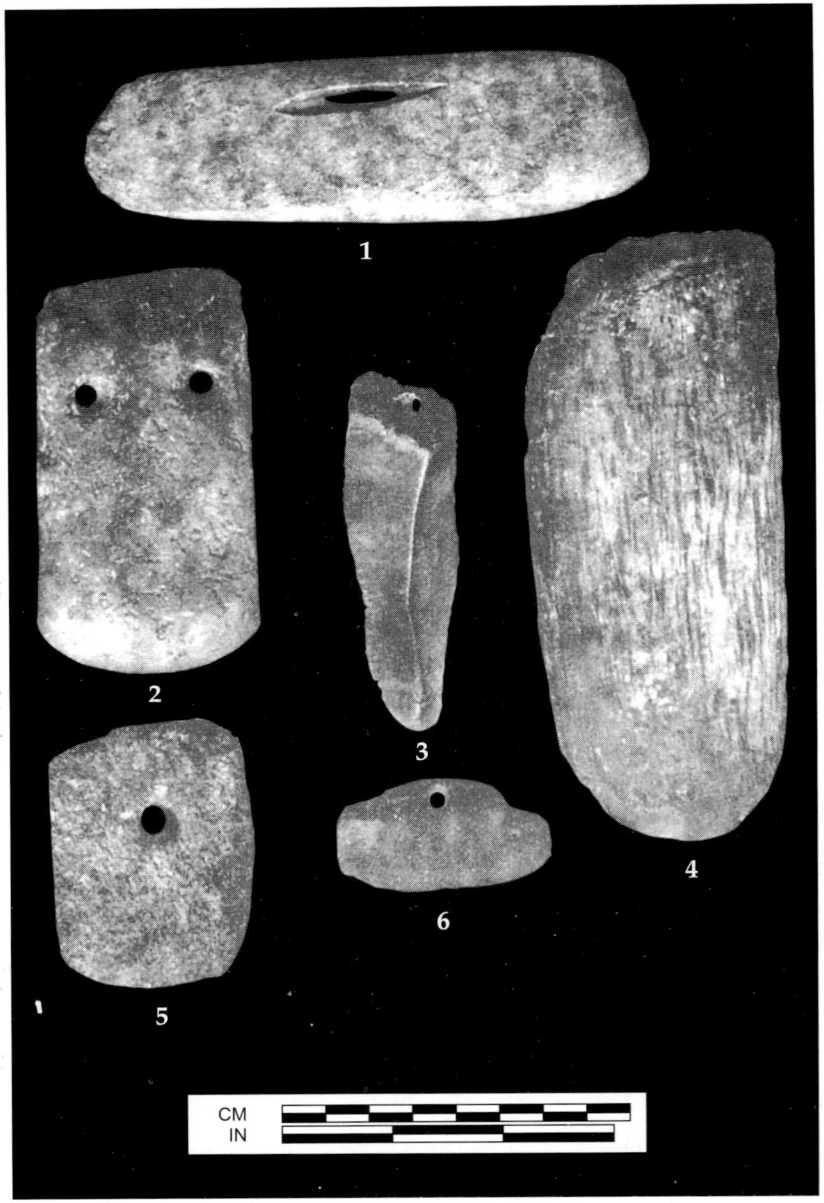

A; A.K. Sharma : Neolithic stone tools, north Sikkim, 1 & 6 Harvesters from Lingden, 2 & 5 perforated celts Barpak and Sangdon, 3 polisher from Manshitang, 4 Honan Knife from Barpak.

B; A.K. Sharma : Neolithic adges, north Sikkim, 1 Linkyong, 2 Gytong, 3 Terang, 4 Sangdong, 5-6 Lingdong, 7 Lingthen, 8 Sankalang.

A; A.K. Sharma : Neolithic axex, 1. Barpak, 2. Gor-terang, 3. Lingdong, 4. Linkyong, 5. Gnon.

B; K.P. Nautiyal & B.M. Khanduri : Human and animal terracotta figurines (Sunga and Kushan).

C; K.P. Nautiyal & B.M. Khanduri : terracotta figure of Buddha (Period II B)

A; K.P. Nautiyal & B.M. Khanduri : terracotta figure of Krishna slaying the demon Keshi (Period II B)

B; H.P. Frankfort : Shortughai, Harappan pottery.

C; H.P. Frankfort : Shortughai Harappan seal showing a rhinoceros.

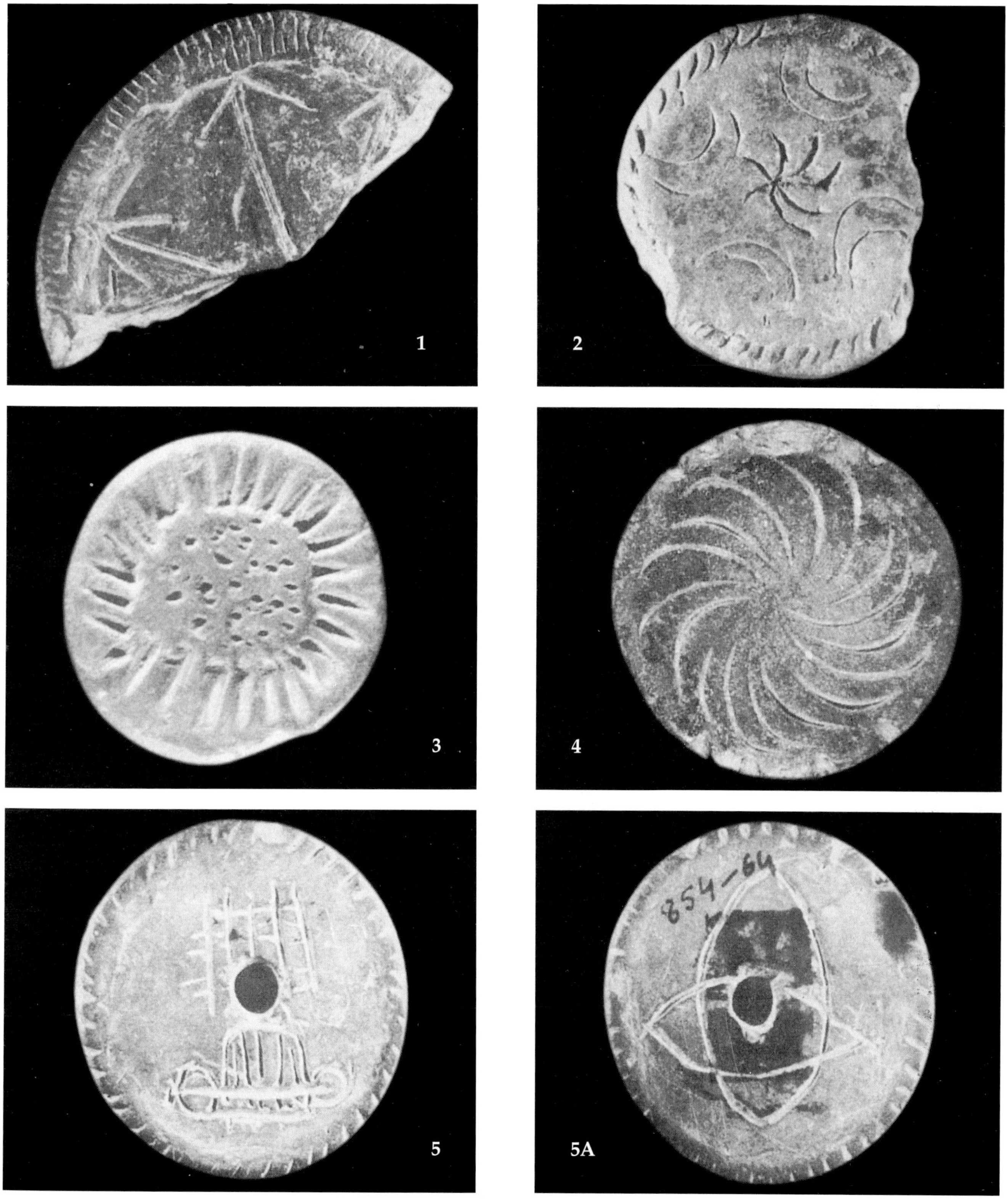

R.C. Gaur : Terracotta discs